WITHDRAWN

PROMISE AND FULFILMENT

PROFESSOR S. H. HOOKE

PROMISE
AND FULFILMENT

Essays Presented to

Professor S. H. HOOKE

IN CELEBRATION OF HIS NINETIETH BIRTHDAY

21st January 1964

BY MEMBERS OF THE SOCIETY FOR
OLD TESTAMENT STUDY AND OTHERS

EDITED BY F. F. BRUCE

EDINBURGH: T. & T. CLARK, 38 GEORGE STREET

© The Society for Old Testament Study 1963.

PRINTED IN GREAT BRITAIN BY
MORRISON AND GIBB LIMITED
FOR
T. & T. CLARK, EDINBURGH

FIRST PRINTED 1963

CONTENTS

DEDICATION

Professor S. H. HOOKE,

M.A. (Oxon.), B.D. (London), D.D. (Glasgow),
D.Th. (Uppsala), F.S.A., Emeritus Professor
of Old Testament Studies in the University
of London

Dear Professor Hooke,

The fourteen men who have contributed to this volume represent a far greater number of your friends and admirers, colleagues and disciples, who join in congratulating you on the attainment of your ninetieth birthday.

The Society for Old Testament Study has sponsored this publication, because of the pride and joy that it takes in one who is not only a former President but one of its most esteemed and best loved members. But the range of your interests is such that the Society felt it proper to invite contributions to the volume from outside the Old Testament field. We know that your own interest in the Old Testament springs not only from its great intrinsic worth but also from the rich promise it contains of good things to come ; and some of these good things find their place here along with the promise which they fulfil.

Our manifold indebtedness to you is something of which we are all deeply conscious. Some of the debts are acknowledged—but by no means repaid !—in the pages which follow. You have stimulated our thinking, you have stretched our minds, you have kindled or fostered our love for sacred learning—and what learning is not shown to be sacred when it is taught by you ? But above all, you have enriched our lives with your friendship, and for this we can never be sufficiently grateful.

On this happy occasion we join in assuring you and Mrs. Hooke (for we always think of you both together) of our affectionate greetings and heartiest good wishes.

Yours very sincerely,

F. F. BRUCE,
Editor.

SAMUEL HENRY HOOKE:
A PERSONAL APPRECIATION

By W. R. MATTHEWS

To stand back and contemplate objectively a friend whom one has known intimately for many years is difficult, still more when the purpose is to describe his personality in words. Hooke's achievement in scholarship can be estimated, by those who are competent, from his writings ; and this *Festschrift* to celebrate his ninetieth birthday is a fitting testimony to the esteem in which he is held by his peers ; but the evidence for his quality as a man and his influence on other men is diffused in the experiences of innumerable individuals, many of whom are dead, whose lives have been enriched by contact with him. This appreciation is submitted as the impression of one such individual, who came to know him when he became Samuel Davidson Professor in the University of London, that is when important years of his career were past. I had almost written " the formative years," but that would be false, for one of his most astonishing characteristics is his capacity for growth, mental and spiritual. All his years, up to the present, have been formative, and still, when one meets him again after an interval, one wonders what new insights, or it may be what temerarious conjectures, he has to impart.

One of his former students recently remarked to me that he had an astonishing zest for new experiences, always welcoming opportunities for seeing fresh places, meeting strange people, and considering new ideas. She attributed this to his " temperament " and, no doubt, his original endowment had something to do with his adventurous spirit ; but I think it was closely connected with his faith, which might be described as an " expectant " faith— always looking for some manifestation of the divine. It is worthy of note that, throughout his life, his adventures of body and mind have been closely allied with his study of the Bible. In the last decade, he has given rein to his adventurous spirit. In 1958 he went to Ghana as visiting Professor in University College

I

Divinity Department, and while there he conducted a refresher course for clergy, giving twelve lectures in nine days : in 1962 he visited Southern Rhodesia, where he lectured on the Dead Sea Scrolls and on Ancient Babylon. Too often, a devotion to the study of the text of Scripture has appeared to lead to stagnation of mind and repression of enquiry : in Hooke it has had precisely the opposite effect. He has found in it an inexhaustible subject for enquiry and contemplation, believing that yet more light and truth can break forth from the Scriptures.

With such a man it is almost irrelevant to trace in him influences from his childhood and youth, yet they have, of course, some interest. He has, I think, always regarded his undergraduate days in Oxford as a crisis time in his development, for it was then that he finally broke from the Plymouth Brethren and became an Anglican, becoming confirmed by Bishop Gore. Some legacy from that repudiated past, however, he carried forward into his later life. His detailed knowledge of the text of the English Bible (which he seemed to have almost by heart) was, I suppose, largely acquired then. Though Hooke never ceased to be an Anglican, after his confirmation, questioning and even crisis was not banished from his later experience. There was, indeed, a period during my friendship with him when he seemed to tremble on the brink of agnosticism. He has always been, I would say, a man of faith, but it is an adventurous faith, intellectually as well as morally, for it never evades questions or is content with dogmatic answers. As his latest writings plainly indicate, this intermittent " Sturm und Drang " has been succeeded by calmer weather.

His years in Canada had a more obvious influence upon his later personality. He has always looked back upon his Canadian years as a time of great happiness and of widening mental horizons. He found satisfaction in the work and evidently left a mark upon the university. Life in a new country, and a growing one, had great attraction for him and friendships which he made with colleagues and pupils were a delight to him ; many of them are still kept alive. The Student Christian Movement was one of his interests and left its impress upon him, as it did on so many of his generation. I wish I had known him then, for he was evidently at his best and happiest. There are still memories of his sometimes puckish interventions in Student Christian Movement discussions, as, for example, his comment on the institution of a prayer room at a conference, that he sometimes himself felt the need for a " swearing room "—which, it is said, called forth a limerick from the great Dr. Streeter. I suppose that a by-product of these Student Christian conferences was the development of his facility in light verse, which has delighted so many of his friends in these later years. And perhaps this is the place to refer to his love for poetry and his all too rare exercises in a serious vein. Some verses, which he has sent at Christmas-time to a chosen few, are precious expressions of his deeper thoughts. Had he devoted himself to literature, he might have been a considerable poet and could certainly have written at least one remarkable novel of a semi-autobiographical kind. Perhaps there are manuscripts still in his drawer which may yet be given to the world.

The first impression which Hooke made on me (and, no doubt, on many others) was that of unbounded energy, intellectual and physical. I can recall scarcely any other man of my acquaintance who has such intellectual power, combined with such various interests. He is the fortunate possessor of a ready and tenacious memory, which enables him, as it were, to have the wares demanded always at hand. And, like the scribe instructed in the Kingdom, he brings out of his store things new and old without difficulty or delay. I have sometimes thought that it would be hard to mention any subject which he had not studied at some time. When he was appointed Davidson Professor, he was in Zurich, studying psychology under C. G. Jung, whose theories and clinical results seemed to him important, at a time when this was not so generally agreed as it is at present. His versatility and readiness to teach almost anything seems to have been manifested in Canada. During the war (1914–18), he was Professor of Oriental Languages and Literature in the University of Toronto, but in the absence of many of the professorial staff he took over the subject of Constitutional History. History repeated itself in the last war, when he taught the sixth form at Blundell's School, on the invitation of his friend Neville Gorton, then headmaster. My informants are uncertain of the full list of the subjects which he taught, but they are sure that they included Religion, English Literature, Classics, and Philosophy. Nor did he confine himself to classwork. He had a room where discussions and informal talks were carried on as an important part of the work. It was characteristic that he was not content with teaching boys, but started a group to study the New Testament for members of the staff. This will not surprise those who know him, for wherever he is, he always becomes the centre of a knot of students of the New Testament, and the result at Blundell's seems to have been very much what it has been elsewhere. Many were fascinated and testified that the gospels and epistles had come alive for them as never before. All were interested and some trembled for their orthodoxy, thinking him a lovable heretic.

Canada gave scope for his physical energy. He was, I am told, a skater of renown, and bought an island in a Canadian lake for five pounds, on which he built a house with his own hands. On the endless Canadian roads, he perfected that skill in motor driving which he retained up to an advanced age. I shall not soon forget a drive with him from Oxford to Cambridge and back to pay a visit. It started after lunch and brought us back in time for him to give a brilliant lecture after dinner. " Rapid but safe " might describe his method—at least we had no accident. Of his performances in golf, continued year after year, I am not competent to speak, but they have amazed many much younger players.

I can think of no better description of him than the hackneyed quotation " Gladly would he learn and gladly teach." To him, teaching and learning are two phases of one activity and, from the day when I first met him (and doubtless long before that day) to the present time, he has been doing it. For twenty years, he and I collaborated in short courses for teachers in secondary schools, under the auspices of the Board of Education. Our subject was Religious Knowledge, which is wide enough to constitute a liberal education, if properly handled. These courses, which were residential and lasted a fortnight, are among my happiest memories. Several causes contributed to their happiness: the lively and intelligent men and women who were our students, the pleasant setting of an Oxford or Cambridge College in the long vacation, but for me, most of all, the daily companionship with Hooke and the opportunity of sharing his thought. I am sure that, whenever I have been present with him, he has shown himself to be a truly great teacher. Perhaps I may be allowed to refer to an experience which illuminates one side of Hooke's personality and, perhaps, something more than that. In some of those years of our collaboration, Hooke's own religious beliefs were passing through a stage of disturbance and revision, which ultimately issued, as we know, into a deeper and more comprehensive Christian faith. But there was a period when his negations seemed to be alarming and I wondered whether some of our students might not be shaken, for Hooke never concealed his thoughts, though he never attempted to impose them on others. I need not have been anxious, for something happened which I have never completely understood. In two of those years, students wrote to me, testifying to the profound religious influence which the course had had upon them. As one said, " We came expecting a series of lectures, but at the end they turned into a retreat." May it not be that the attempt to study the Bible with a sincere desire to find the truth, and to do that as a group, is, at least for educated persons, the best and most lasting evangelism ? Hooke, instead of being a disturbing factor, had a major influence in this experience.

With regard to his university teaching, I cannot speak from direct personal knowledge. Undergraduates are notoriously critical of their teachers and it is not surprising that some of his university students were not enthusiastic admirers, though all whom I have met respected his learning. Some, perhaps, grew a little weary of " the ritual pattern," for I have been told that a few irreverent youths used to call him " old Myth-and-ritual," but most of those who were inclined to criticize did so on the familiar ground that his lectures did not have the examinations in view. His lectures were too interesting. To be sure of passing the exam, one had to resort to a dull teacher. Like nearly all great teachers, Hooke was happiest when he could forget syllabuses and pursue the subject wherever it led him.

But enough on such matters : we must bring to an end this attempt to delineate a remarkable and complex personality. We are reduced, after all, to piling up abstract terms, which cannot truly convey the living man to one who does not know him. But we must use them and we must say of him that he is a man of complete intellectual integrity, who has devoted great powers of mind and imagination to the study of religion and to teaching. He has never ceased or slackened in his devotion to truth, nor has he ever forgotten that the themes of the Bible are of profound interest and importance to every human being. Along with this, and, perhaps, deeper than this, is his loving-kindness, his active interest in persons and his care for them. In all his activities throughout a long life, he has collected a number of friends who desire to keep in touch with him and for whom he has a loving concern. Aided by his like-minded wife, he has avoided that penalty of advancing years, growing detachment and aloofness from life, as old friends and acquaintances pass away from this world. So far from diminishing, his circle of friends enlarges with the passage of time, so that on his ninetieth birthday he is still young in heart and mind.

OLD TESTAMENT THEOLOGY AND ITS METHODS

By A. A. ANDERSON

DURING the last few decades there has been an increasing interest in Biblical studies including Biblical theology. The revival of Biblical theology, however, has created suspicions in many circles, and both the interest and the concern seem to be based on reasonable grounds. During recent years the Christian Church has been involved, to a greater or lesser extent, in a reconsideration of its life and faith, and therefore it is only natural that there should be a growing interest in the Bible which is inseparably linked with the life and faith of the Church. Yet this renewed emphasis on Biblical theology has raised doubts in some quarters because the methods used in theology may have been questionable at times, and in the more recent years the writings of Wilhelm Vischer, in particular, have added to the uneasiness of mind. Most Old Testament scholars would agree that if allegorical interpretation and unlimited typology were allowed unrestrained freedom, then years of patient and fruitful work in Biblical studies would be cast aside in favour of ingenious imagination. There have been times when the historical development in the Old Testament was disregarded, and when the differences between the two Testaments tended to be eliminated or obscured.[1] Consequently it is understandable that a renewed emphasis on Biblical theology has aroused some scepticism, and it seems that in order to dispel any doubts, attempts have been made to establish Biblical theology as a scientific discipline. Thus in a recent article [2] we read that " Biblical theology is a scientific discipline, which as such is not concerned with the validity or otherwise of the theological content of the Bible, but only seeks to understand it and give as accurate an account of it as possible." The same writer goes on to state that " the question the Biblical theologian has to answer is not whether the theology

---

[1] Cf. P. Wernberg-Møller's article " Is there an Old Testament Theology ? " in *Hibbert Journal*, LIX (1960–1), pp. 21–9.
[2] P. S. Watson, *The Expository Times*, LXXIII (1961–2), p. 200.

of the Bible is true, but what the theology of the Bible is." [3]
There is no doubt that we ought to be as scientific as possible in
our approach to the Old Testament but the warning by N. W.
Porteous [4] is most fitting : " It is not scientific to adopt a
method which turns into something else the proper object of a
particular science." Thus there is the possibility that some
" scientific " theologies of the Old Testament have actually
ceased to be theologies.

Many theologies of the Old Testament have been published
during the recent years but some of them appear to be either
a history of Israel's religion or a systematic exegesis of Old
Testament material arranged according to different themes.
W. A. Irwin [5] has argued that the difference between an Old
Testament theology and a history of the religion of Israel is to
be found in the arrangement of material, the selection of facts,
and the mood of the author. This may be true of some Old
Testament theologies but in other instances the difference may
practically disappear. If this is so, are we not parading a history
of religion as a theology ? Have we not deprived theology
of its proper task ? It seems that the real problem of Old
Testament theology is whether it should be a purely descriptive
science or should it go beyond mere classification and description ?
If the latter alternative were impossible, then it is doubtful that
theology could ever be anything but a kind of history of religion,
whatever the method or arrangement. But if so, should this
discipline be called theology ? This then brings us to the definition
of Old Testament theology or Biblical theology. It seems to us
that the definition of Biblical theology ought not to be arbitrary,
even if the motives are praiseworthy, but it must be closely
linked with the nature of the Bible which is the basis of Biblical
theology. We may also add the proviso that theology ought
to be as systematic and objective as possible without destroying

---

[3] P. S. Watson, *op. cit.*, p. 200.

[4] *Oudtestamentische Studiën*, VIII (1950), p. 5.

[5] *The Journal of Religion*, XXV (1945), pp. 244–6. Irwin realizes that the
difference between theological and historical treatments of Israel's religion is
rather small and that it " reduces to little more than one of reshuffling the cards :
of telling the same story topically instead of chronologically ! " (*op. cit.*, p. 246).
To H. H. Rowley the distinction is clear : for a history of Israel's religion *all*
religious ideas and practices demand full consideration, while for an Old Testament
theology " all that is not of the essence of the faith of Israel is irrelevant " (*The
Faith of Israel* (1956), p. 17). This suggestion appears to be very reasonable but
the only question is whether some relevant material may not have been disregarded.

or changing in the process the characteristics of our sources, *i.e.*, the Old and New Testaments. P. S. Watson defines theology as " logically ordered and coherent discourse about God, a systematic account of His nature and attributes, His relation to the world and man, and so forth." [6] If this definition is accepted, then it is obvious that the Bible is not such a theology although it may provide material for such a task. Some scholars have doubted, however, that what the Bible says about God can be reduced to an orderly, consistent, and harmonious system, and they may well be right.[7] It seems to us that Biblical theology is not the beginning of Biblical studies but rather the " crown " of it all. It cannot dictate or prescribe to other related disciplines what their conclusions ought to be, but it must make a full use of all the information provided by archaeology, historical research, comparative religion, critical linguistic and philological study of the Bible, and other cognate subjects. The theologian must not disregard facts or distort the information provided by the above-mentioned studies, yet he cannot rest with mere information and description ; he has to seek for a meaning in the Bible, and not only for a meaning but also for a Person. This then appears to be one of the chief differences between theology and all kinds of histories of religion ; the former being primarily concerned with a *Person*, the latter with ideas about God, etc. The theologian starts out with a presupposition that " the *Theos* or God, from whom theology derives its name, has revealed himself or made himself known to human beings, and indeed that he does so still." [8] The theologian who disregards the conclusion drawn from this statement, namely, that God is also his " contemporary," has lost sight of one of the fundamental features of the Bible. Nevertheless, the theologian must accept all the guidance which other scientific disciplines can give him, but he must go beyond science or its methods. One could scarcely label theology as being unscientific because it attempts to deal also with what lies outside the reach of scientific methods. Theology deals ultimately with God who cannot be subjected

---

[6] *Op. cit.*, p. 195 ; cf. also E. Jacob, *Theology of the Old Testament* (1958), p. 11.

[7] Cf. A. S. Herbert's article " Is there a Theology of the Old Testament ? " in *The Expository Times*, LXI (1949–50), p. 361.

[8] A. R. Vidler, *Essays in Liberality* (1957), p. 31. The same author points out that by the methods of abstraction, analysis, and classification we may get to know a lot *about* a person " without ever getting to know him as a unique individual and without ever taking in what he has to say to us " (*op. cit.*, p. 32). Cf. also D. Cairns, *A Gospel without Myth ?* (1960), pp. 213–8.

to repeated experiments or tests ; on the contrary, it is God who tests, in a sense, the theologian. Theology deals with a God who is the same now as he was in the past and who will remain unchanged also in the future. The theologian ought not to be primarily concerned with abstractions but rather with the relationships between God and man. It is possible that the type of approach, as outlined above, may be regarded as too subjective ; but irrespective of any criticism, the fact remains that the belief in a living, personal God is the basis of the Bible as well as of the Christian Church, and it seems to us that this same presupposition must be valid also for Biblical theology. It has been said that " the task of the Biblical theologian is to give a clear, comprehensive, and coherent account of what the Bible has to say, and then to hand it over to the dogmatic (or ' systematic ') theologian, whose business it is to interpret, expound, and draw out its implications for the Church of his own time. As scientific discipline, Biblical theology has a purely descriptive task, but it fulfils a normative rôle in the realm of dogmatic theology." [9] It is difficult to see, however, how a theology which is purely descriptive can provide a norm for dogmatic theology or anything else. If the Bible spoke with one voice on all points, then descriptive method and a suitable classification could supply the desired norm, but unfortunately this is not the case. Consequently we must introduce a criterion or criteria already in Biblical theology because the " biblical theologian, to the degree to which he is a theologian (which includes a systematic point of view), does not present pure facts to us ; he gives theologically interpreted facts." [10] Furthermore, it seems undesirable to create a gulf between Biblical and dogmatic (or " systematic ") theology. If there is no give and take between the two, then the Church is left at the mercy of the dogmatician while the Biblical theologian, as a theologian, is cut off from the life of the Church.

In order to gain a better understanding of the problems of the Old Testament theology, we shall return to its basic source, the Old Testament. Although some scholars [11] have regarded the Old Testament as a record of man's groping after God, it is clear that the Old Testament itself claims to be primarily a

[9] P. S. Watson, *op. cit.*, p. 200.

[10] P. Tillich, *Systematic Theology*, I (1960), p. 40.

[11] Cf. R. H. Pfeiffer, *Religion in the Old Testament* (1961), pp. 8 ff.

record of God's revelation. Whether we accept or reject the possibility of revelation, the fact remains that for the writers of the Old Testament or the Bible as a whole, God was a reality who has made himself known to his people. It is true that the question of revelation is beset by numerous problems, but since it plays such an important rôle in the Scriptures, we cannot avoid it. It seems to us that revelation is in the first place the self-giving of God, yet man's reception of this self-manifestation of God forms an integral part of the revelation.[12] Although revelation is in the first place an encounter with God,[13] it also involves communication.[14] There are, practically, no limits to the possible media of revelation but God's self-manifestation in history occupies a very special place in the Old Testament. There may be also more than one way in which God may communicate with man, and although some of the more recent approaches to this problem are rather attractive,[15] yet we must remain open also to other possibilities. Most scholars seem to be agreed that revelation involves both divine and human elements, and wherever the human factor is present, infallibility and inerrancy are out of the question. The Bible itself is not the revelation but rather a human, although inspired, record of revelation, as well as an account of what men did with it and because of it. Since there are in the Old Testament different views concerning God and his actions, as can be expected, we would follow H. H. Rowley in recognizing a progressive revelation, " not that it is a record of man's progressive search for God, but that it is the record of man's growing experience of God, and progressive response to God."[16] That is to say that it was not God who did not reveal himself perfectly but the selfgiving of God was conditioned by the limitations of the receiver.

The record of revelation has been preserved not only in the Old Testament or the Bible as a whole, but also in the religious community which lived and still lives the life that sprang from that revelation.[17] It was that community which treasured the

---

[12] Cf. P. Tillich, op. cit., p. 40.

[13] Cf. J. K. S. Reid, The Authority of Scripture (1957), p. 180.

[14] Cf. E. Brunner, Revelation and Reason (1947), p. 84 ; see also the article by Carmino de Catanzaro, in Anglican Theological Review, XLIV (1962), pp. 261 f.

[15] For the rôle of images in revelation cf. A. Farrer, The Glass of Vision (1948), and A. Richardson, The Bible in the Age of Science (1961), pp. 142 ff.

[16] The Relevance of the Bible (1942), p. 35. Cf. also A. S. Herbert, op. cit., p. 362.

[17] Cf. W. N. Clarke, An Outline of Christian Theology (1916), pp. 12 ff.

record of God's self-manifestation and preserved it ; the same community also adapted the record of revelation to its needs according to its religious life and spirit. The life kindled by the revelation of God has not come to an end but we see it continued, at least, in the Jewish community and the Christian Church.

It is possible to study the Old Testament from no less than three main points of view, the Jewish, Christian, and non-religious ; but it seems to us that for the Christian theologian there is only one approach—the Christian one. This does not mean that the Christian theologian is given a blank cheque or that he can indulge in what has been called " exegetical hocus-pocus." [18] The Christian, like anyone else, is bound to take into account the findings of Old Testament scholarship as long as the latter does not make dogmatic pronouncements which are outside its proper sphere. For the Christian Church the Old Testament does not exist on its own, because there is a sequel to it, i.e., the New Testament. This does not make the Old Testament into what it is not or into a Christian book in the sense that it was " written with reference to, and for, the Christians and can therefore be understood only by them " [19]— although this may have been and, perhaps, still is, the view in certain circles. The people of Israel lived in their own right and the Old Testament is their witness to God's revelation. What they experienced and believed, however, had a significance not only for their own times and their own direct descendants but also for the Christian Church. The Christian theologian holds that the God who can make himself known to the whole of mankind " has done so, above all through his dealings with a particular people (the Hebrews) and in a particular course of events which culminated in the ' advent ' or coming of Jesus Christ." [20] Therefore in both Testaments we are dealing with the same God and his relationship with man and the world.

It seems to us that for a Christian theologian to be " neutral " or " disinterested " is an impossibility. N. W. Porteous has reminded us that theology has to do with the knowledge of God, which does not mean " mere cognition but involves the emotions and the will no less than the intellect " [21] and apart from a

[18] P. Wernberg-Møller, op. cit., p. 29.
[19] P. Wernberg-Møller, op. cit., p. 24.
[20] A. R. Vidler, op. cit., pp. 32–3.
[21] Op. cit., p. 4.

personal " engagement with the truth we cannot ourselves have knowledge of God in the Biblical sense of the expression. . . ." [22] In other words, a disinterested or non-religious approach to the Bible and Biblical theology is at some disadvantage because, e.g., " we know what the word ' horse ' or ' red ' means if we have seen a horse or the colour ' red ' but not otherwise " ; [23] and the same must be true, at least to some extent, of many religious terms which remain largely unintelligible to us unless we have some acquaintance with that which they represent. One can hardly grasp the full significance of statements such as " God is holy " or " God is forgiving," etc., unless one has encountered the holy God and known his forgiveness. We would hesitate to affirm that a non-religious approach to the Old Testament is impossible or that it must be necessarily fruitless but it is doubtful that this approach could give us the *full* religious and theological significance of the Bible, even though most of the religious terms are used to describe also human relationships, thus giving even to the non-religious person some idea of what is meant by the respective religious terms.

For the Christian neither the Old nor the New Testament can stand on its own because they form two indispensable parts of the whole, *i.e.*, the Bible, and one is not really complete without the other since both Testaments bear witness to the same God. To disregard one or the other would mean (at least for the Christian theologian) to judge a case on the basis of only a part of the relevant evidence. Therefore also both the Old and the New Testament theologies are only means to an end which is Biblical theology, and even the latter cannot fulfil its proper task without the co-operation of systematic theology. Only by taking into account both the Bible and the past and present life of the Church as a whole, we can hope to approach our goal : the knowledge of God. Theology must tend to be normative or it would lose sight of its true service. " Theology, as a function of the Christian Church, must serve the needs of the Church " [24] in being its guide. At this point the objection may be raised that if this is the purpose of theology, then it ought not to be included in the curriculum of a university. Yet since we do not possess, and probably never will, *the* theology of

---

[22] *Op. cit.*, p. 5.
[23] *Op. cit.*, pp. 5–6.
[24] P. Tillich, *op. cit.*, p. 3.

the Old Testament or the Bible, the Faculty of Theology is concerned, among other things, with the history of theology or with the historical development of Biblical theology. Thus the theologian is free to pursue his rightful task in the service of the Church while the Faculty of Theology is cleared of the charge of being unscientific.

The statement that Biblical theology must be normative, needs a further qualification and we cannot improve on the observation made by N. W. Porteous : " Error can scarcely be avoided, yet it need not be deadly error, so long as it is not allowed to harden into dogma but is kept in the moving stream of life." [25] On the one hand, we must be honest and realistic in our treatment of the Old Testament but on the other hand, we are searching for the " knowledge of God " not simply to enjoy an intellectual exercise but in order that this religious truth could be embodied in actual life. Therefore we cannot escape from the need for some " norm " which would be the best guide we can find yet neither final nor sacrosanct.[26] It is also doubtful whether there is any other person better fitted to deal with this problem than the Biblical theologian who is both aware of the scholarly work in Biblical and cognate studies, and also equipped to deal with the information provided (as far as that is possible for one individual). In Biblical studies no one can work in isolation and there may be times when even the historian and the linguist may have to consult the theologian, and the latter will most certainly profit from the work of the former. Similarly the Biblical and systematic theologians have to work together. "The two cannot live in separation from each other because each is essential to the other," [27] since the Biblical witness is only a part, although the most essential part, of the testimony to God's self-manifestation. The systematic theologian draws also upon the other part, i.e., the life of the Church. Without this religious life of the community the Bible might have become a glorified form of a Gilgamesh Epic. The Bible must criticize and challenge the religious community but on the other hand, the religious life and faith of the group may provide a criterion for the Biblical theologian.

So far we have dealt with the nature of the Old Testament and the task and responsibilities of the Biblical theologian, but

[25] *Peake's Commentary on the Bible* (1962), 120b.
[26] Cf. G. E. Wright, *God who Acts* (1952), p. 116 ; G. A. F. Knight, *A Christian Theology of the Old Testament* (1959), p. 7.
[27] J. D. Smart, *The Interpretation of Scripture* (1961), p. 25.

next we shall consider the content of theology. Since Biblical
theology is based upon the Bible, the content of the former must,
in some way at least, be influenced by the latter. According to
the usual definitions of theology, its content must be a systematic
account of God's nature, attributes, etc.[28] This is, of course,
possible and it is followed out in a number of Old Testament
theologies [29] but the question is whether such an arrangement is
not foreign to the Biblical material ? The " classical " arrangement God-Man-Salvation [30] may be a useful one but it appears
to have been forced upon the Old Testament rather than derived
from it. G. E. Wright [31] points out that in the Bible the various
doctrines, such as that of God, man, sin, etc., are " so interrelated
in a historical context that they cannot be separated and
examined entirely as independent objects of reflection." Wright's
own suggestion, *Theology as a Recital*, is a great step forward
and he may be right in stressing that " the Bible is not primarily
the Word of God, but the record of the Acts of God, together
with the human response thereto," [32] although we must not take
" the Word " and " the Acts " as mutually exclusive or uncon-
nected. In Wright's opinion the subject-matter of theology is
" the confessional recital of the unique events of Biblical history
together with the inferences and interpretations. . . ." [33] The
reconstruction of the nature and attributes of God, although
legitimate in itself, would lead us away from history and from
sharing in the historical events which are so essential to the
Biblical faith. Therefore one feels attracted to Wright's suggestion, even though he does not claim originality for this
approach, as well as to von Rad's treatment of Old Testament
theology with its emphasis on *Heilsgeschichte* or history of
salvation. Yet the *Heilsgeschichte* is not identical with the facts
of history, [34] and the acts of God can hardly be separated from

[28] Cf. J. Baker, *Theology*, LVIII (1955), p. 254 ; see also H. Schultz, *Old
Testament Theology*, I (1898), pp. 5 ff.
[29] Cf. A. B. Davidson, *The Theology of the Old Testament* (1925) ; P. Heinisch,
Theology of the Old Testament (1950).
[30] Cf. L. Koehler, *Old Testament Theology* (1957).
[31] *God who Acts* (1952), p. 111.
[32] *Op. cit.*, p. 107. Cf. also C. R. North, *Scottish Journal of Theology*, II (1949),
p. 113, who writes : " . . . revelation in the Old Testament was mediated through
history, so that it cannot be disengaged from history without reducing it to
something like a valley of dry bones."
[33] *Op. cit.*, p. 107.
[34] Cf. Eichrodt, *Theology of the Old Testament*, I (1960), pp. 512 ff. See also
J. Barr's masterly article on von Rad's *Old Testament Theology*, in *The Expository
Times*, LXXIII (1961–2), pp. 142–6.

the Israelite world of faith. We are not presented with bare historical data but with history interpreted theologically and therefore it is difficult to avoid contact with the realm of religious concepts.

J. N. Schofield quotes R. H. Kennett as saying that " every story and saying in the Bible has been retained for a purpose and that the message, the theology, becomes clear when we understand that purpose " ; [35] and it seems to us that the main purpose of the Bible, and so ultimately of God's revelation, is to make known to man what is God's way for him and what is God's judgement upon man's own way of life. We use the term " way of life " in its widest possible sense to cover all the varied relationships of man. Here again we are indebted to N. W. Porteous who has pointed out that Old Testament theology " has to proceed by concentrating its attention upon man, since revelation becomes visible in the human response to it." [36] This is not intended as a replacement of theology by anthropology but simply as an attempt to follow the Old Testament example by emphasizing that all human relationships depend ultimately upon man's relationship with God. Thus in describing the way of man as it is and as it ought to be, in the light of God's revelation, we are actually giving an indirect account of God's nature, attributes, and will. At least one of the functions of the Bible is to bring man into a right relationship with God, and this is achieved by sharing in God's mighty acts of salvation and by walking in his ways, which is imperative if we are to have communion with God. The great events of Exodus, *e.g.*, were related, so it seems, not for the sake of entertainment but that the people of Israel might recognize the loving-kindness of God to *them* and that they might walk in God's ways in a spirit of grateful obedience. The Exodus events were not primarily a sign pointing to some eternal truth but rather the eternal God acting graciously in the life of his people. It is not merely an account of what God did for the fathers but an event which must be shared by each successive generation by acknowledging the blessings of the acts of God and by accepting their responsibilities to God.

Thus an Old Testament theology could start with the basic relationship between God and the World, Mankind, Israel, and

[35] *The Modern Churchman*, n.s., V (1962), p. 239.
[36] *Peake's Commentary on the Bible* (1962), 120d.

Man, and follow this with the dependent relationships. It is unlikely that we shall find the perfect system of arrangement, but a scheme that overlaps least and takes into account the whole evidence of the Old Testament, would appear the best. Each relationship ought to be traced through our sources in historical order, or as far as that is possible, to show what each relationship is in the light of God's revelation, how it is maintained or broken, and finally what is its significance for us in relation to the evidence of the New Testament and the life and faith of the whole Church. This then seems to be the task of Old Testament theology.

We have already mentioned the need for some criterion and it seems to us that there are several possible criteria although none of them can be regarded as an absolute standard or an infallible rule. The basis of the Bible is the self-manifestation of one and the same God whose actions must be consistent with his unchanging character. This is a presupposition but without it the Christian religion could hardly exist. It is also true that we can perceive a certain development in the Old Testament and that there are differences in its testimony, yet on the other hand, the Old Testament is not a haphazard collection of writings whose only common link is their accidental preservation in the same literary corpus. In spite of the diversity in the Old Testament, there is also a unity ; " if God was revealing Himself, then there should be some unity about the revelation, since it was the same Being Who was being revealed." [37] One may, perhaps, say that there emerges from the Old Testament an impression of the relationships between God and man, and the application of the principle of consistency may provide us with a pointer as to which relationships are more likely to express what ought to be. Here we have to add also the witness of the New Testament or the revelation in Christ in particular, and H. H. Rowley seems to be right when he states : ". . . all that we learn of God in the Old Testament that is not in harmony with the revelation given in Christ is not of God. It represents the misunderstanding of God by sincere men, whose view was distorted by the eyes through which they looked upon Him." [38] None would deny, least of all the above-mentioned author, that also the revelation of God in Christ has come to us through

[37] H. H. Rowley, *The Unity of the Bible* (1953), p. 8.
[38] H. H. Rowley, *The Relevance of the Bible* (1942), p. 33.

human channels and therefore the account of it is not infallible. Although there are problems in the Gospels as well as in the rest of the New Testament, yet the outline of the revelation of God in Jesus Christ seems to be reasonably plain. The use of this criterion does not authorize us to read the New Testament into the Old but it may point out what relationships in the latter may be a contribution to our relationship with God and our understanding of it. There may be certain things in the Old Testament which are superseded in the New, *e.g.*, some aspects of the Israelite cult, yet the relationship involved even in these elements may still have significance beyond the Old Testament and its times.

Another criterion is the life and faith of the Church as a whole, both in its past and its present, because the witness to the revelation is found not only in the Bible but also in the religious community. Since the canon of the Bible is closed, the latter has become, in a sense, static while the life of the Church is or ought to be dynamic because " the living and continuing revelation is inseparably connected with the living God." [39] This means that we can expect a development in the life and faith of the Church but the Bible must continually challenge the life of the Church although at the same time the life of the religious community may provide a criterion for the evaluation of the witness of the Old Testament or the Bible as a whole. It is evident that we cannot escape from the subjective element but even an imperfect tool is better than none at all, and some criteria there must be if the Bible is to become relevant to the needs of every generation.

We may make use also of the principle of selectivity by which we mean not an arbitrary choice of material but the selectivity which is at work already in the Old Testament itself. We see that certain relationships are transformed, while others are abandoned or limited, and in those elements which were continued and made " permanent " in Israel's faith we may find the relationships as they ought to be. Furthermore, the " nonessential " elements are not to be rejected or disregarded but it is the duty of the theologian to understand and explain this divergent evidence as far as possible, and it may well be that this task may produce some positive contribution to the Theology of Relationships.

[39] G. Aulén, *The Faith of the Christian Church* (1961), p. 39.

Finally, we may refer to the criterion mentioned by O. J. Baab,[40] namely, that there must be a conformity with the discoveries of the scientists. Since theology deals not only with God but also with his relationships with the world, man, etc., there may be certain aspects where theology and science overlap. This criterion does not mean that science is made the final authority on all matters of theology or religion but in its proper sphere the work of the scientist may be an indispensable guide. In as far as science helps us to understand how man and the world function, it can also help us towards a better understanding of our relationships with God. These criteria must function together and even though they are deficient for their task, yet they enable us to arrive at a theology of Relationships which is both descriptive and normative. By " normative " we do not mean a dogmatic system which is above all criticism but rather a challenge which demands our decision ; it offers to men the possibility of hearing the living word of God, which may be accepted or rejected but not ignored.

[40] " Old Testament Theology : its Possibility and Methodology," in *The Study of the Bible Today and Tomorrow*, edited by H. R. Willoughby (1947), p. 418.

THE PROPAGANDA FACTOR IN SOME ANCIENT NEAR EASTERN COSMOGONIES

By S. G. F. BRANDON

THE mark of a truly seminal thinker is surely to be found in the influence that his ideas have had upon the subsequent development of the subject to which he has devoted himself. Judged by such a criterion, S. H. Hooke must justly be acclaimed one who has not so much contributed to his chosen field of study as given to it a " new look." The present writer can vividly recall the new interest which was stimulated within him for Old Testament study by his original reading of the symposium *Myth and Ritual*. Myth suddenly took on a fresh significance, affording new insights into familiar material and suggesting further lines of exploration. Conscious that such stimulus has in his own case borne some fruit that has not been quite to the taste of him who sowed the seed, he rejoices especially in this opportunity to honour a great scholar, to whose seminal thinking he knows that he owes so much. If all the many complex ingredients that go to make up the following study could be resolved back into their original form, it would doubtlessly be found that not a few stem ultimately from the impetus supplied, directly or indirectly, by the work of S. H. Hooke.

That the world had a beginning, in fact was created, is an idea so deeply rooted in the human mind that it may truly be regarded as instinctive. Indeed, even in those cultures where the time-process has been conceived as cyclic, instead of linear, so that a series of worlds or world-ages has been contemplated, the idea of a beginning to each constituent of the series has virtually implied an act of creation. However, despite the wide occurrence of the concept and its long establishment, on reflection it appears to be a really strange notion for man to have acquired. For, to think that the world had a beginning involves a truly mighty act of the imagination—it means thinking that the firm earth, with its seemingly eternal hills and ever-flowing seas, once did not exist and only came into being at a specific point in the past. When the strangeness of this notion is fully savoured, the question naturally arises : what prompted man originally to conceive of so extraordinary a situation which nothing within the range of his normal experience was likely to have suggested to him ?

Of the dawning of the concept of creativity the present writer has written at length elsewhere, concluding that in the preliterary era of human culture there is certain evidence explaining the inception of the idea of the origin of organic beings, but not of man's physical environment, *i.e.*, of his world.[1] The earliest known cosmogonies of mankind, however, are found in the literatures of certain ancient Near Eastern peoples, and it is the purpose of this essay to interrogate these in an endeavour to discover whether any common factor operated in their production.

What on *a priori* grounds might reasonably be considered as the most likely, because it seems to be the most obvious, cause of cosmogonic speculation, is, however, quickly found on investigation to have played a very insignificant rôle in the earliest of the cosmogonies with which we are concerned. This is aetiological interest ; as we shall see, the desire to explain the origin of things, stemming from a natural curiosity, appears to have been only a subsidiary motive in these cosmogonic systems, and the real impulse to their composition came from interests of a very different kind.

Egypt and Sumer provide our earliest evidence of cosmogonic thought, the documents concerned in each instance dating from about the middle of the third millennium B.C. and each clearly incorporating still older traditions. We shall turn our attention first to the Egyptian examples, not because of any belief in their chronological priority but in view of their obvious attestation of a motive that may be discerned operating effectively, but not so overtly, elsewhere.

The two earliest extant documents of Egyptian thought, besides being approximately contemporaneous, contain each cosmogonic statements which evidently amount to rival claims about the respective precedence of two gods, namely, Atum and Ptah. These documents, moreover, emanate from two different religious centres, the one coming from 'Iwnw, the Biblical Ōn,

[1] See his book *Creation Legends of the Ancient Near East* (Hodder and Stoughton, London, 1963) (Chapter I.

which the Greeks knew as Heliopolis, and the other from Memphis, both places being situate in Lower Egypt and close to each other. The Heliopolitan document, now known as the *Pyramid Texts*, comprises long series of hieroglyphic texts which were inscribed on the interior walls of the pyramids of certain pharaohs of the Fifth and Sixth Dynasties to facilitate their safe passage after death from this world to the next. These texts, which were evidently compiled by the priesthood of Heliopolis, constitute an amorphous collection of hymns, prayers, and incantations, deriving from a rich and complex mythology, some parts of which are evidently of great antiquity.[2] The Memphite writing, which has been preserved to us in a copy made of a much earlier document at the command of the pharaoh Shabaka (716–695 B.C.), is much shorter in length and it appears to be the text of a kind of " mystery-play ", designed to demonstrate the unique sanctity of Memphis as the scene of certain acts of primordial significance.[3]

Since these two documents appear to contain rival cosmogonies, as we have already noted, a primary requisite in seeking to appreciate their significance is that of determining which represents the earlier tradition. This can only be done on grounds of internal evidence, and it will be convenient to anticipate here a finding which, as we shall see, is clearly evident from a study of the text of the so-called Shabaka Stone. It is that this text is concerned to prove that Ptah, the god of Memphis, created Atum, the god of Heliopolis.[4] Now, since in the *Pyramid Texts* Atum's rôle as the Creator is stated without any trace of consciousness of the Memphite claim, it would seem reasonable to conclude that the Heliopolitan cosmogony was composed so long before that of Memphis as to be completely unconcerned about rebutting any rival claim against the primordial status of the Heliopolitan deity, Atum. Moreover, on comparison it would appear that the Memphite cosmogony is a more sophisticated composition, and it seems concerned to exhibit the superiority

---

[2] On the *Pyramid Texts* generally see H. Bonnet, *Reallexikon der aegyptischen Religionsgeschichte* (Berlin, 1952), pp. 620a–623b ; S. A. B. Mercer, *The Pyramid Texts* (New York, 1952), I, pp. 1 ff.

[3] Cf. K. Sethe, *Dramatische Texte zu altägyptischen Mysterienspiegeln,* I (" Das ' Denkmal memphitischer Theologie,' der Schabakostein des Britischen Museums "), in *Untersuchungen zur Geschichte und Altertumskunde Aegyptens,* Band X (Leipzig, 1928), pp. 2–5 ; H. Junker, *Die Götterlehre von Memphis* (Berlin, 1940), pp. 6–16 ; Brandon, *Creation Legends*, pp. 29–43.

[4] See below p. 32.

of its metaphysic over the primitive crudities of Heliopolitan thought.[5]

These inferences indicative of the priority of the Heliopolitan system are consistent with other evidence that points to the importance of Heliopolis as both a political and cult centre in the Predynastic period.[6] On the other hand, it is known that Memphis was founded at the beginning of the First Dynasty (c. 3100 B.C.) to be the capital of a newly united kingdom.[7] Accordingly, the concern shown in the Shabaka text to demonstrate the priority of Ptah to Atum, and the primordial status of Ptah's chosen abode, is easily intelligible as coming from a newly created political centre seeking to establish its position against the prestige of the venerable city which it had superseded.

The way in which the Memphite theologians sought to counter the traditional prestige of Heliopolis and at the same time assert the authority of their own city and its tutelary deity is truly notable, because it constitutes our earliest and most striking evidence of the appreciation of what might be termed the ecclesiastical significance of cosmogony. The Memphite case was developed along two lines, one of which has already been briefly mentioned, namely that Ptah was the creator of Atum. Now, the priesthood of Heliopolis had already achieved a remarkably profound conception of their god Atum when they described him as " he who exists of himself " ($hpr(r)$ $d\check{s}.f$).[8] But it would appear that the unique nature which they thus attributed to Atum became a problem when they went on to ascribe to him the creation of what they regarded as the two primordial constituents of the universe, i.e., air and moisture, personified respectively as the deities Shu and Tefnut. Thinking instinctively in terms of sexual reproduction, they were obliged to resort to what is to us a very crude piece of imagery in order to explain how a sole male deity generated other gods : " Atum became

[5] See below p. 24. R. Anthes in *Mythologies of the Ancient World* (New York, 1961), pp. 63–4, does not consider these points when he denies that there is any anti-Heliopolitan polemic in Memphite theology.

[6] Cf. Bonnet, pp. 543–5 ; K. Sethe, *Urgeschichte und älteste Religion der Ägypter* (Leipzig, 1930), pp. 87–116 (104–28) ; A. H. Gardiner, *Egypt of the Pharaohs* (Oxford, 1961), pp. 84–6, 427 ; S. Schott, *Mythe und Mythenbildung im alten Aegypten* (Leipzig, 1945), pp. 10–20.

[7] Cf. Sethe, *Urgeschichte*, pp. 179, 180 (217), 181–2 (219), 182–4 (221–2), *Dramatische Texte*, p. 5 ; Schott, p. 68 ; Bonnet, pp. 446b–447b ; W. B. Emery, *Archaic Egypt* (Harmondsworth, 1961), p. 122.

[8] *Pyr.* 1587b.

as one who masturbates (*twšƶw*) in Heliopolis. He put his phallus in his hand, to excite desire. The son and the daughter were born, the brother and the sister : Shu and Tefnut." [9] Having thus achieved the production of this primordial pair, the other deities which made up the Heliopolitan divine Ennead were easily accounted for—Shu and Tefnut gave birth to Geb (earth) and Nut (sky), who in turn produced Osiris and Isis, Set and Nephthys.[10] To meet this Heliopolitan cosmogonic scheme, which thus attested Atum's status as the unique Creator, the Memphite priests made two counter-assertions which, while not denying the creative activity of Atum, represented the Heliopolitan god as the creature and agent of Ptah :

> Ptah, who is upon the Great Throne . . . ;
> Ptah Nun, the Father, who [begot] Atum ;
> Ptah Naunet, the Mother, who bore Atum ;
> Ptah the Great (*wr*), who is the Heart and who is the Tongue of the Ennead ;
> [Ptah] . . ., [. . .] who gave birth (*mš*) to the gods ; . . . . .[11]

> His (Ptah's) Ennead is before him as teeth and lips, (being) the semen and the hands of Atum. The Ennead of Atum indeed came into being through the semen and the fingers of Atum. But the Ennead (of Ptah) is the teeth and lips in this mouth, which pronounced the name of all things, from whom came forth Shu and Tefnut who created (*mš*) the Ennead.[12]

The other line adopted to controvert the claims of Heliopolis not only introduces us to a fundamental concept of Egyptian cosmogonic thought, but it unwittingly constitutes the first recorded instance of a well-known ecclesiastical *trait*, of which notable examples are to be found in many other religions, including Christianity.

The Heliopolitan thinkers had apparently envisaged the primordial state of things, before the process of creation began, as a featureless expanse of motionless water which they called Nun—a concept surely inspired by the annual phenomenon of the Nile's inundation.[13] From this primeval deep in the " first

[9] *Pyr.* 1248a–d. Cf. Brandon, *Creation Legends*, pp. 22–3.
[10] Cf. Brandon, *Creation Legends*, pp. 23.
[11] Cf. Sethe, *Dramatische Texte*, pp. 46–50 ; Junker, *Die Götterlehre*, pp. 16–20 ; J. A. Wilson in *ANET*, p. 5a ; Brandon, *Creation Legends*, pp. 32. Naunet is the female counterpart of Nun.
[12] Cf. Sethe, *Dramatische Texte*, pp. 57–9 ; Junker, *Die Götterlehre*, pp. 55–8 ; Wilson in *ANET*, p. 5a ; Brandon, *Creation Legends*, pp. 35–6.
[13] Cf. Bonnet, pp. 535b–536b ; S. A. B. Mercer, *The Religion of Ancient Egypt* (London, 1949), pp. 261–2 ; A. de Buck, *Die Egyptische Voorstellingen betreffende

time." Atum had emerged to begin his work of creation. But, in order to perform this, the god had to have some firm foothold above the waters of Nun. Hence arose the concept of the primeval hill, which was also surely suggested by the phenomenon of the Nile's annual flooding of its valley—as the waters gradually subside the higher features of the land re-appear. The temple at Heliopolis claimed to mark the site of the first land that had emerged from the primeval waters, thus providing a foothold for Atum as the following text commemorates: " Atum-Khepre, thou wert high (*kꜣ*) as (the) Hill (*kꜣꜣ*). Thou didst appear as (the) *bn*-bird of the ben-stone in the House of the *bn*-bird in Heliopolis." [14] The Memphite theologians were equal to the challenge afforded by this unique character of Heliopolis, and they negated it by identifying their god with the whole land that had emerged from the primeval waters of Nun. The claim is made in a characteristically Egyptian idiom: " Horus stood (as king) over the land. He it is who united this land, named with the great name ' Ta-tenen (*tꜣ-tnn*), South-of-his-Wall, Lord of Eternity.' He is this Horus, who appears as king of Upper and Lower Egypt who united the Two Lands in the Wall Nome (*i.e.*, Memphis), in the place where the Two Lands are united." [15] The key-term here is " Ta-tanen," which was a title of Ptah, the god of Memphis and signified " the land that raises itself " or " the land arising." [16] According to the context of the passage, Ptah is identified with Horus, the mythical prototype of the king who united the two parts of Egypt, besides being the personification of the whole land that had come forth from the waters of Nun.[17] Thus is the ancient claim of Heliopolis to be the site of the primeval hill tacitly set aside by this lordly declaration that Ptah is both the whole land itself and he who effected its historic unification.

It is reasonable, as we previously noted, to suspect that this

den Oerheuvel (Leiden, 1922), pp. 16–17, 18–22 ; S. Sauneron et J. Yoyotte in *Sources orientales*, t. I (Paris, 1959), p. 22.

[14] *Pyr.* 1652a–b (text in K. Sethe . *Die altaegyptischen Pyramidentexten*, I, p. 372). Cf. Mercer, *The Pyramid Texts*, III, pp. 778–80 ; Brandon, *Creation Texts*, pp. 18–19. The *bn*-bird was the sacred bird of Heliopolis, and the ben-stone was an obelisk-like stone in the temple there. Cf. Bonnet, p. 100 ; de Buck, pp. 23–34.

[15] Cf. Sethe, *Dramatische Texte*, p. 32 ; Wilson in *ANET*, pp. 4b–5a.

[16] The epithet " Ta-tenen " is rendered by Sethe as " das sich (aus dem Urgewässer) erhebende Land," *Urgeschichte*, p. 183 (222), see *Dramatische Texte*, pp. 46–50. Cf. M. Sandman-Holmberg. *The God Ptah* (Lund, 1946), pp. 19, 31–42 ; de Buck, pp. 49–62.

[17] Cf. Brandon, *Creation Legends*, p. 31.

P.F.—3

attempt of the Memphite priesthood to claim for their city a
greater sanctity than that of Heliopolis may have been prompted
by the creation of Memphis as the capital of the newly established kingdom of Upper and Lower Egypt : in other words, that
religious sanction was sought for the achievements of political
eminence in terms of cosmogonic significance. Whether such a
motive had operated at another ancient cult-centre, namely,
Hermopolis, which was also distinguished by the possession of a
notable cosmogony, is not certain. There is some evidence that
this Upper Egyptian city may have enjoyed some temporary
political prominence; [18] but, however that may be, from a
remote period Hermopolis was associated with a mysterious
company of eight primordial beings who had played some crucial
rôle in the process of creation. This Ogdoad is significantly
referred to in an inscription of king Nacht-nebôf (378–341 B.C.)
as " the gods of the primeval age of the hill," or as " the Great
Ones of the primeval age." [19] Their cosmogonic work seems to
have been that of providing an egg, out of which Re the sun-god
emerged, to be the demiurge. This belief is attested in a salutation
to Re, dating from the New Kingdom period :

> Thou art ascended on high, (coming forth) from the secret egg, as
> the child of the Eight.[20]

And the location of this primordial event is alluded to in an
inscription of the late sixth century B.C. concerning the sun-god :

> . . . thy habitation, at the beginning, was the hillock of Her-
> mopolis. Thou didst touch the earth in the Isle of the Two Knives.
> Thou didst raise thyself from the waters, out of the secret egg, with
> Amunet in attendance.[21]

From these scattered references the lineaments of a cosmogony
may be discerned that makes Hermopolis the site of the primeval
hill ; but it differs from the Heliopolitan and Memphite systems

---

[18] Cf. K. Sethe, *Amun und die Acht Urgötter von Hermopolis* (Berlin, 1929),
pp. 41–2 (40) ; J. Spiegel, *Das Werden der altaegyptischen Hochkultur* (Heidelberg,
1953), pp. 185–9.

[19] Cf. G. Roeder, *Hermopolis, 1929–1939* [Ausgrabungen der Deutschen
Hermopolis-Expedition in Hermopolis, Ober-Aegypten] (Hildesheim, 1959),
p. 173 (12(*b*)).

[20] Ostracon in the Museum at Cairo, in Sauneron et Yoyotte, I, p. 61 (19*a*).

[21] In Sauneron et Yoyotte, I, p. 61 (19*b*). Cf. p. 80, n. 28. Amunet is the
female counterpart of Amun.

by its association of a mysterious Ogdoad with the initial act of creation, which involves the concept of a kind of cosmic egg that contained the actual demiurge, who was the sun-god. That this myth was not merely a piece of esoteric speculation, but was also a strongly held belief that could be advantageously exploited by the authorities of Hermopolis to attract pilgrims to the temple there is evidenced in a particularly illuminating way. In his tomb inscription a priest of Hermopolis, Petosiris, who lived about 320 B.C., in commemorating the restoration-work which he had accomplished at the temple there, refers to the many religious antiquities which could be viewed by the pilgrim—they included the primeval hill, as an island in a sacred lake, and relics of the shell of the primordial egg.[22]

That cosmogonic significance became an accepted criterion of status and authority in ancient Egypt is attested by the example of Thebes, which was made the capital of the land in the New Kingdom period, with its patron deity, Amun, exalted by the Theban princes as the state-god *par excellence*. Being a late-comer in the field of cosmogonic pretension, the city, or rather the priesthood of Amun, had to take account of the established cosmogonies. Accordingly, since the innate disposition of the Egyptian mind was to conserve, not destroy, Theban cosmogony became a synthesis of the earlier traditions largely by way of identification, which was greatly facilitated by the fact that Amun was already connected with the Ogdoad of Hermopolis.[23] A significant instance of this process is found in a papyrus which dates from the time of Rameses II (*c.* 1301–1234 B.C.). Amun is being addressed : " The Ogdoad (of Hermopolis) were the first of thy forms until thou didst complete those (other forms), for thou art the Unique One. Thy body is wholly hidden among the Great Ones. Thou art hidden as Amun at the head of the gods. Thou changest thy form into Ta-tenen (of Memphis), in order to bring forth the primeval gods in thy first being as the Primeval God." [24] Thebes is, correspondingly, proclaimed as the site of the primeval acts of creation : " Thebes (*wst*) is the pattern (*mtr*) to all other cities. The water and the land were in her at the First Time. Then came sand to set the bounds to the

---

[22] Cf. Brandon, *Creation Legends*, pp. 49–50.
[23] Cf. Brandon, pp. 46–7, 52–3.
[24] *Leiden Papyrus*, I, 350, Hymn 80, trans. in G. Roeder, *Die aegyptische Religion in Texten und Bilden*, I (Zürich, 1959), p. 293 ; cf. Sauneron et Yoyotte, I, p. 68 (*C*).

fields and to create her foundations upon the hill. Thus the earth came into being. Then men came into being, in order to found every city in her true name. They were each denominated ' city ' (as Thebes), and they were under the oversight of Thebes, the Eye of Re." [25]

This ecclesiastical exploitation of cosmogony can be traced even further down the long course of Egyptian history, for notable evidence of it occurs in the inscriptions in the Ptolemaic temple at Edfu [26] and in those of the temple of Esna, dating from the Roman period. [27] Indeed, when the main Egyptian cosmogonic statements are considered, ranging as they do from the third millennium B.C. down to the early centuries of the present era, it would appear that each is essentially linked with some particular sanctuary, whose prestige it is intended to establish and promote.

The cosmogonic tradition of ancient Mesopotamia comprises two distinctive types which, with some minor qualifications, may be designated respectively as Sumerian and Babylonian. The former, which is, of course, the older, finds expression in a variety of myths which explain the divine origin of various things, animate or inanimate, including mankind. [28] In most of these the god Enki figures as the creator, although he is never actually represented as the demiurge. [29] Enki's cult-city was Eridu, which was evidently one of the oldest of the Sumerian cities ; [30]

[25] *Op. cit.*, Hymn 10, in Roeder, I, p. 287 ; cf. Wilson in *ANET*, p. 8a. Cf. Brandon, *Creation Legends*, pp. 52–4.
[26] Cf. E. A. E. Jelinková, " The Shebtiw in the Temple at Edfu," in *Ae.Z.*, 87 (1962), pp. 41–54.
[27] Cf. S. Sauneron, *Quatre Campagnes à Esna, Esna I* (Le Caire, 1959), pp. 69, 77, 79, 99–100, 113–14. Cf. Sauneron et Yoyotte, I, p. 73 (30).
[28] Cf. Brandon, *Creation Legends*, pp. 66–88.
[29] According to Professor S. N. Kramer (*Sumerian Mythology*, Philadelphia, 1944, pp. 39, 114, n. 41, *Mythologies of the Ancient World*, New York, 1961, p. 103) the goddess Nammu was the original creatrix, being also the personification of the primeval waters : this latter identification is disputed by T. Jacobsen in *JNES*, V (1946), p. 139. The name En-ki signifies " the lord of the earth," but Enki was essentially regarded as a water-deity ; cf. C. F. Jean, *La Religion sumérienne* (Paris, 1931), p. 35. An early Sumerian text refers to Enlil as performing the primordial act of separating the interlocked heaven and earth, after the manner of Shu's act in Egyptian cosmogony : cf. Brandon, pp. 68–80 and the references there given.
[30] According to the Sumerian King List (cf. *ANET*, p. 264b), kingship first descended from heaven at Eridu. Cf. A. Parrot, *Archéologie mésopotamienne* (Paris, 1946), pp. 270–1 ; V. G. Childe, *New Light on the Most Ancient East* (London, 1953), pp. 11, 13.

however, although the building of Enki's shrine there is commemorated, there are no indications in the surviving texts of any
attempt on the part of the Eridu priesthood to exploit such
cosmogonic significance after the manner of that which was done
in Egypt. Indeed the only two apparent instances of the Sumerian
use of cosmogonic texts to further political or ecclesiastical pretension either ignore or reduce the status of Eridu, while exalting
that of other cities, although Enki is the chief actor in each of
the episodes concerned. Thus in one of these texts Enki is
represented as visiting Ur as a kind of culture hero in the
primordial age to lay the foundations of its greatness,[31] while
in the other it is related how Enki travels to Nippur to obtain
the blessing of the god Enlil on the temple that he has built for
himself at Eridu.[32]

If cosmogony was, accordingly, not notably utilized as a means
of ecclesiastical propaganda in Sumer, its value as such was fully
recognized and exploited by the priesthood of Marduk, the patron
god of Babylon. The celebrated Creation Epic, known generally
as the *Enuma elish*, attests the ability of the Babylonian theologians to match the ingenuity of the various Egyptian priest-
hoods in representing their divine patron as the demiurge and
the sanctuary, which they served, as the most sacred place on
earth by virtue of its primordial significance.

The theological tradition, which the Babylonians inherited,
precluded any possibility of claiming that Marduk was, chronologically, the first or original god. Even Anu, the god of heaven,
was recognized as the grandson of two primordial beings, Ti'âmat
and Apsû, respectively personifications of the bitter and sweet
waters. And Marduk, in his turn, was admitted to be the son of
Enki, who was the son of Anu.[33] However, the Babylonian
theologians were equal to this difficulty. They represented
Marduk as not only exceeding the other gods in stature and
ability,[34] but as standing forth as their sole champion when they
are threatened with destruction by the monstrous Ti'âmat. But
that is not all. Marduk is depicted as shrewdly exploiting the

---

[31] See Kramer, *Sumerian Mythology*, pp. 59–62.
[32] See Kramer, *Sumerian Mythology*, pp. 62–3. " La finale, voyage d'Enki
à Nippur, montre la réele suprématie d'Enlil même sur un dieu comme Enki,"
M. Lambert in *RA*, IV (1961), p. 186.
[33] *Enuma elish*, Tab. I, ll. 16–20, ll. 79–85 (in *ANET*, pp. 61a, 62a).
[34] Tab. I, ll. 87–100 (in *ANET*, p. 62a). Cf. G. Furlani, *Miti babilonese e
assiri* (Firenze, 1958), pp. 80–1.

text.

critical situation. He offers to save the other gods on one condition, to which they readily agree :

> If I indeed, as your avenger,
> Am to vanquish Tiamat and to save your lives,
> Set up the Assembly, proclaim supreme my destiny !
> When jointly in Ubshukinna you have sat down rejoicing,
> Let my word, instead of you, determine the fates.
> Unalterable shall be what I bring into being ;
> Neither recalled nor changed shall be the command of my lips.[35]

After fashioning the universe from the body of the vanquished Ti'âmat, Marduk assigns their places therein to the three great deities of the traditional pantheon, who were his elders, thus further emphasizing their dependence upon him :

> He (Marduk) crossed the heavens and surveyed the regions.
> He squared Apsu's quarters, the abode of Nudimud,
> As the lord measured the dimension of Apsu.
> The Great Abode, its likeness, he fixed as Esharra,
> The Great Abode, Esharra, which he made as the firmament.
> Anu, Enlil, and Ea he made occupy their places.[36]

Having created mankind to serve the gods,[37] the Epic then describes how the great gods, the Anunnaki, built for Marduk, as a token of their gratitude, a mighty temple at Babylon :

> The Anunnaki applied the implement ;
> For one whole year they molded bricks.
> When the second year arrived,
> They raised high the head of Esagila equaling Apsu.[38]

Thus is the *Enuma elish* a brilliant piece of propaganda designed to provide a transcendental sanction for the supremacy of Babylon and its god in terms of cosmogonic significance. Although a late-comer to an established pantheon, Marduk's precedence is skilfully depicted as being meritoriously deserved and willingly accorded, while his sanctuary at Babylon is invested with a unique and glorious prestige.

[35] Tab. II, ll. 123–9 (in *ANET*, p. 65*b*, trans. E. A. Speiser). Cf. A. Heidel, *The Babylonian Genesis* (Chicago University Press, 1951), p. 29, n. 60.
[36] Tab. IV, ll. 141–6 (in *ANET*, p. 67*b*). On the meaning of " Esharra " see Brandon, *Creation Legends*, p. 102, n. 4. " Nudimud " and " Ea " are other names of Enki.
[37] Cf. Brandon, *Creation Legends*, pp. 104–8 for a discussion of the passage concerned and its problems ; see also *Man and his Destiny in the Great Religions* (Manchester University Press, 1962), pp. 85–7.
[38] Tab. VI, ll. 59–62 (in *ANET*, pp. 68*b*–69*a*). Furlani, p. 100, thinks that the building is located in the heavens : " Il poeta la chiama Babele, poiché si tratta del prototipo celeste della Babele terrena."

In process of time it would appear that in Israel also the propagandistic potentialities of cosmogony were realized. How far this realization was prompted by knowledge of Mesopotamian or Egyptian precedents cannot be determined. Many attempts have been made to trace various *motifs* of the Hebrew creation legends to foreign sources, especially Mesopotamian ; but, whatever may be the extent or nature of Hebrew indebtedness in this respect, it would seem most likely that an appreciation of cosmogonic significance in Israel stemmed from some general acquaintance with the fact itself that other cosmogonies did exist and were significant. In Israel, however, a very different religious situation resulted in a very different use of cosmogony ; for there the need was not to establish the precedence of rival sanctuaries, but to promote the policy of a religious party within the state.

In seeking to establish and maintain Yahweh as the God of Israel against the competition of deeply rooted tribal cults and the attractions of Canaanite religion, the Yahwist prophets were led to condemn ancient mortuary beliefs and practices which presupposed some significant form of *post-mortem* survival for the individual person. In turn they became themselves the protagonists of a doctrine of Man that limited the significance of human life to this world, assigning to the individual a miserable *post-mortem* existence in the gloomy realm of Sheol, which was tantamount to virtual annihilation or even worse.[39] About the ninth century B.C. some unknown Yahwist thinker sought to provide a kind of *rationale* to this doctrine, and, significantly, he resorted to cosmogony, or, perhaps more accurately, to the composing of an account of the origin and destiny of mankind.[40] This account, which in its essential part runs from *Genesis* ii. 4b to iii. 24, depicts the Primordial Man as fashioned out of the earth by Yahweh, and animated by him, so that he owes his very being solely to his divine Creator. Yahweh had apparently intended him, and his wife, to live continuously in idyllic conditions. But the divine plan is thwarted by human disobedience, and Adam, by learning the secret of reproducing himself, makes himself subject to death, thus fulfilling the warning given to him by his Creator.[41] As the progenitor of the human race, Adam also incurs a destiny that is inherited by each generation of his

[39] Cf. Brandon, *Man and his Destiny in the Great Religions*, pp. 120–3.
[40] Cf. Brandon, *Man and his Destiny*, pp. 122–9 ; *Creation Legends*, pp. 121–2.
[41] Cf. Brandon, *Creation Legends*, pp. 132–9.

descendants. Hence, in a superbly dramatic narrative, the Yahwist explains the mortal nature of man, and, since man is formed of the earth and returns to it again, nothing significant survives to be tended and perhaps venerated in some mortuary cultus.[42] Thus, by this skilful narration of the creation and fall of Adam, the Yahwist doctrine of Man, deemed necessary in the interests of an essentially ethnic religion, was given a most impressive justification which was destined to exercise a powerful influence, not only upon Jewish belief, but also upon the formation of Christian soteriology.

The significance of the so-called Priestly cosmogony (*Genesis* i. 1–ii. 4*a*) from the point of view of our present interest is less easy to determine. It is uncertain whether the composition was intended to replace some earlier cosmogonic statement that had prefaced the Yahwist account of the Creation and Fall of Man,[43] and also whether it was an *ad hoc* compilation or an already existing tradition, possibly deriving from the liturgy of some New Year festival.[44] Dating, as it does, from the post-Exilic period, it would be possible to see in it tacit refutations of other cosmogonies. Thus, for example, whereas the cosmological situation clearly reflects that of the *Enuma elish*, the creation of the firmament to divide the waters is achieved by the utterance of a divine *fiat* in contrast to the primitive conception of Marduk's fashioning of the solid canopy of the sky from the body of the primeval monster, Ti'âmat.[45] Then, the statement in i. 4 that, before creating the sun, God had separated the light from the darkness, could be interpreted as an assertion, with an implied reference to the dualistic cosmogony of Iran, that God pre-existed and controlled those two opposing forces which in Zoroastrianism were identified respectively with Ahura Mazdāh and Ahriman.[46] That the Priestly cosmogony could thus contain a kind of veiled polemic against other systems, with which the Jews had become familiar during the Exile, is indeed possible ; but it must be admitted in view of the implied subtlety of the

[42] Cf. Brandon, *Man and his Destiny*, p. 129.
[43] Cf. Brandon, *Creation Legends*, pp. 146–7.
[44] Cf. S. H. Hooke, *In the Beginning* (Oxford, 1947), p. 36 ; Geo Widengren in *Myth, Ritual and Kingship* (edited by S. H. Hooke, Oxford, 1958), p. 175 ; G. W. Anderson in *The Old Testament and Modern Study* (edited by H. H. Rowley, Oxford, 1951), pp. 291–3 ; E. O. James, *Myth and Ritual in the Ancient Near East* (London, 1958), pp. 169–70.
[45] Cf. Brandon, *Creation Legends*, pp. 149–50.
[46] Cf. Brandon, pp. 148–9, 194–9.

refutations, that it is unlikely that such was the purpose of the composition.   A more probable instance of the operation of the propaganda motive is to be found in the *raison d'être* which this account of divine creation provides for the sanctity of the sabbath ; for Priestly concern for the proper observation of the sabbath is only too obvious in the detailed legislation on the matter which emanated from this circle of religious orthodoxy.[47]

To complete our survey of the motivation of the main cosmogonies of the ancient Near East we must briefly notice the evidence that is relevant of Iran and Greece.

The very complex problem of understanding what was the nature of Iranian religious belief before its reform by Zarathustra still greatly exercises those who specialize in this field of research. However, there does seem to be a general consensus of opinion that a dualistic cosmogony of some kind predated Zarathustra, and that his utterances on the subject, as recorded in the *Gathas*, were built upon this inheritance, with certain minor amendments required by his concept of Ahura Mazdāh.[48]   Since Zarathustra does not seem to have been connected with any city or sanctuary, the *Gathas* understandably contain no indication of an intent, such as we have met elsewhere, to locate certain primordial events at a specific place.   The most obvious evidence of the exploitation of cosmogonic significance in Iran dates from a much later period, namely, that of the Sassanian rulers (A.D. 208–651), although its origins undoubtedly lie further back in the past.   About this time it would appear that Zarathustra's description of the primordial principles as " twins " was felt increasingly to raise a problem concerning the implied common origin of these principles.[49]   To meet this problem certain thinkers sought for some ultimate source which would account for such a joint derivation.   They found what they sought in the concept of Zurvān, an ancient deity (perhaps a kind of high-god) who was in effect a personification of Time.[50]   Accordingly, the generation

[47] *Gen.* ii. 1–3.   Cf. J. Skinner, *Genesis* (*ICC*, Edinburgh, 1912), pp. 35–9 ; E. Kutsch in *RGG* (3 Aufl.), V, 1259.
[48] Cf. Brandon, *Man and his Destiny*, pp. 259–268 ;   *Creation Legends*, pp. 194–9, where a full documentation will be found.
[49] Cf. R. C. Zaehner, *The Dawn and Twilight of Zoroastrianism* (London, 1961), pp. 175–84.
[50] On Zurvān see R. C. Zaehner's massive study *Zurvān, a Zoroastrian Dilemma* (Oxford, 1955), and his *Dawn and Twilight of Zoroastrianism*, chapters 8–11. See also G. Widengren, *Hochgottglaube im alten Iran* (Lund, 1938), pp. 266–310 ;

of Ohrmazd, the good principle, and of Ahriman, the principle of evil, was explained in a myth which told how Ahriman originated from the doubt that once clouded Zurvān's mind as he offered sacrifice for a thousand years for the birth of the son that was to be Ohrmazd.[51] Two sons were consequently born, and they created according to their natures : Ohrmazd, all that was beautiful and good ; Ahriman, all that was ugly and evil. This Zurvanite doctrine was rejected as heresy by the orthodox Zoroastrians, who in their opposing cosmogonic systems represented Zurvān as either an assistant of Ohrmazd in his work of creation or as an aspect of him.[52]

Greece seems to provide the exception to what has appeared to be a common motive for cosmogonic composition in the other cultures of the ancient Near East. For, so far as we are informed by the extant evidence, cosmogony seems never to have been used to substantiate or promote the claims of any Greek sect, city or sanctuary. With the exception of a few very brief and obscure cosmogonic references that occur in Homer,[53] such evidence as we have of Greek interest in cosmogony reveals that tendency to rationalization that was so soon to produce the systems of the Milesian philosophers. Thus with Hesiod, whose writings are largely devoted to cosmogonic themes and clearly draw upon much traditional material, an incipient rationalism inspires all that he relates about the origin of things.[54] Perhaps the most significant evidence from our point of view is of a negative kind, namely, that none of the great religious centres of Greece claimed to derive its authority or sanctity from its being the site of some great primordial event of creation. This apparent obliviousness to the value of cosmogonic significance is particularly notable in the case of two of the most important sanctuaries. At Delphi a stone was shown as marking the *omphalos* or navel of the earth ; yet the significance of the fact was only the subject of a jejune tale. The famed association of

---

J. Duchesne-Guillemin, *Zoroastre* (Paris, 1948), pp. 95–103, *The Western Response to Zoroaster* (Oxford, 1958), pp. 58–60 ; U. Bianchi, *Zamān i Ohrmazd* (Torino, 1958), pp. 95–117, 130–46. Cf Brandon, *Man and his Destiny*, pp. 261–2, 280–2, 291–5.

[51] For various versions of this Zurvanite myth see Zaehner, *Zurvān*, pp. 419–34, also pp. 60–6 ; cf. *Dawn*, pp. 212–13, 227–8.

[52] Cf. Brandon, *Creation Legends*, pp. 203–7, for references.

[53] *Iliad*, XIV, 200–4, 244–6, 256–61 ; XXI, 194–7 (cf. XVIII, 483–5). Cf. Brandon, *Creation Legends*, pp. 162–6.

[54] Cf. Brandon, pp. 166–83.

Eleusis with Demeter, the corn-goddess, might well have been exploited in some legend of the origin of agriculture ; instead the cult-legend of the sanctuary there was concerned only to account for the origin of its annual mystery-rites.[55] It is doubtlessly consistent with this apparent lack of concern about the propaganda value of cosmogony that the Greeks never claimed a high antiquity for themselves, and that they were content to look elsewhere, particularly to Egypt, for the beginning of things.[56]

From our survey it would, accordingly, appear that generally in the ancient Near East cosmogonies were not the products of a detached interest in accounting for the origin of things, but *ad hoc* compositions motivated by ecclesiastical ambition or theological policy. In effect they constitute the most ancient witnesses to the human disposition to seek for the sanction of precedents and not to rest content with an existential situation.

[55] Cf. Brandon, pp. 161–2.
[56] Cf. Brandon, pp. 48, 183, 210.

PROMISE AND FULFILMENT IN PAUL'S PRESENTATION OF JESUS

By F. F. BRUCE

PROFESSOR HOOKE's questing mind has, over the years, ranged far and wide in the field of Near Eastern religion, but he is a biblical scholar first and last. One of his earliest books, *Christ and the Kingdom of God*, was devoted to the central theme of the biblical revelation; and if, in the years that have followed, he has deservedly gained a worldwide reputation as exponent-in-chief of myth and ritual and the cultural pattern of the ancient Near East, he has in his latest book (his latest to date, that is) brought the glory and honour of this rich kingdom into the city of God by making his researches yield their contribution to the unfolding of the pattern of divine revelation in the Old and New Testaments.

In the pattern of Biblical revelation the teaching of Paul occupies an important place. Professor Hooke sees " the full extent of the expansion of the pattern of revelation of which Paul was made the vehicle " in Col. i. 12–23, where " all the implications of the new image of the Head and the body are brought out. Here the Second Man, the Last Adam, is placed in the centre of God's new creation, and all the disorder and broken images caused by the failure of the first Adam fall into place, all discords are resolved, all things in heaven and earth are reconciled. In order that such a consummation might become possible it was necessary, and the divine pleasure, that in him through whom all this work of restoration was to be accomplished, all the fullness, the Pleroma, should dwell." [1]

Paul's Christology was part of his gospel which, by his own account, came to him " through a revelation of Jesus Christ." Evidently there was nothing in this revelation which clashed, as he saw it, with the historical facts of the ministry of Jesus,

---

[1] *Alpha and Omega*, pp. 255 f. (Above I have referred to this book as Professor Hooke's " latest to date "; that was true when this paper was written in September 1962; but since then his Pelican Book *Middle Eastern Mythology* has appeared.)

as he had opportunity of ascertaining these during the two weeks that he spent with Peter in Jerusalem in the third year after his conversion. Indeed, with regard to the historical facts, he himself declares his agreement with the original apostles : " whether then it was I or they, so we preach and so you believed " (I Cor. xv. II). The idea that Paul had no interest in the historical facts of the ministry rests on what I can only regard as a misinterpretation of what he says about knowing Christ " after the flesh " in 2 Cor. v. 16. He is not there contrasting his own knowledge of Christ with the knowledge of Christ possessed by the apostles who had been with him during the earlier ministry ; he is contrasting his present knowledge of Christ with his own uninformed conception of him in the period before his conversion. The New English Bible brings out the force of his words quite clearly : " With us therefore worldly standards have ceased to count in our estimate of any man ; even if once they counted in our understanding of Christ, they do so now no longer." As so often in his epistles, when he says " us " and " our " in this passage, he means primarily " me " and " my."

A further, and important, source of Paul's Christology is to be found in the Old Testament. When once Paul came to recognize Jesus of Nazareth as the Messiah of Israel and the exalted Lord, he was bound to recognize him as one to whom the Old Testament scriptures bore witness. The conception of Jesus as the fulfiller of prophecy was common to Paul and those who were " in Christ " before him ; already before Paul's conversion it had begun to provide " the sub-structure of New Testament theology," [2] for in fact there is ample evidence that it goes back to the thinking and teaching of Jesus himself.

When Paul paid his first visit to Thessalonica, according to the narrative of Acts, he attended the Jewish synagogue and on three successive sabbaths " argued with them from the scriptures, explaining and proving that it was necessary for the Christ to suffer and to rise from the dead, and saying, ' This Jesus, whom I proclaim to you, is the Christ ' " (Acts xvii. 2 f.). Not long afterwards, when he arrived in Corinth, he acted in the same way ; according to the longer reading of the Western text, " he went into the synagogue and argued every sabbath, *inserting*

[2] The sub-title of C. H. Dodd's *According to the Scriptures* (1952).

the name of the Lord Jesus, and persuaded both Jews and Greeks "
(Acts xviii. 4). Even if the added phrase is not part of the
original text, it may very well give a true picture of Paul's procedure. The insertion of a name in the course of the reading to
make it plain who is being referred to is a targumizing practice,
as may be gathered from the insertion of " Messiah " in the
Targum of Jonathan as a gloss on " my servant " in Isa. xlii. 1,
xliii. 10, lii. 13. But to gloss an Old Testament passage with the
title " Messiah " was one thing ; to gloss it with the name of
Jesus was quite another matter. Yet the inserting of Jesus'
name in this way would have expressed, in the simplest and most
telling fashion, Paul's conviction that Jesus was the central subject of the Hebrew Bible. That this was indeed his conviction
is evident from his epistles. It is the purpose of this paper to
select seven elements in Paul's presentation of Jesus as the
Christ, and see how he finds them all anticipated in the Old
Testament.

I. THE SON OF DAVID

In the exordium of the Epistle to the Romans, where Paul
introduces himself as " an apostle, set apart for the gospel of
God," he goes on to say that this gospel, which God had
" promised beforehand through his prophets in the holy scriptures," has to do with " his Son, who was descended from David
(ἐκ σπέρματος Δαυείδ) according to the flesh and designated Son
of God in power according to the Spirit of holiness by his resurrection from the dead, Jesus Christ our Lord " (Rom. i. 2–4).
These words perhaps echo an early credal summary of the
doctrine of Christ. The belief that Jesus was a descendant of
King David certainly did not originate with Paul ; it was part
of the primitive Christian message which he " received." The
Davidic descent of Jesus plays but a minor part in Paul's epistles,
just as Jesus himself laid no weight upon it, although he did not
repudiate the designation " son of David " when others gave it
to him. The phrase ἐκ σπέρματος Δαυείδ recurs in a later credal
summary in 2 Tim. ii. 8—" Remember Jesus Christ, risen from
the dead, descended from David, as preached in my gospel." [3]
Paul adduces Old Testament justification for the belief in Jesus'

[3] κατὰ τὸ εὐαγγέλιόν μου, as in Rom. ii. 16, xvi. 25.

Davidic descent in Rom. xv. 12, where Isa. xi. 10 is quoted as a prophecy of the extension of Christ's rule over the Gentiles by the preaching of the gospel :

> " and further Isaiah says,
> ' The root of Jesse shall come,
> he who rises to rule the Gentiles ;
> in him shall the Gentiles hope.' "

Indeed, the very application to Jesus of the title χριστός presupposes that his descent from David was so commonly accepted as not to be a matter for dispute or demonstration.[4]

The opening words of Ps. cx. regularly received a messianic interpretation in New Testament times and were current as a *testimonium* in the early Church. It was common ground to Jesus and the scribes of his day that the personage referred to as " my lord " in Ps. cx. 1 was the expected Messiah (Mk. xii. 35 ff. and parallels). It was in language drawn partly from Ps. cx. 1 that Jesus made the claim for which the Sanhedrin pronounced him worthy of death : " you will see the Son of man sitting at the right hand of Power . . ." (Mk. xiv. 62).[5] When Paul in Rom. viii. 34, possibly again echoing a primitive confession, speaks of " Christ Jesus . . . who is at the right hand of God," when in 1 Cor. xv. 25 he affirms that Christ " must reign until he [God] has put all his enemies under his feet," and when in Eph. i. 20 he refers to the power which God exerted when he raised Christ " from the dead and made him sit at his right hand in the heavenly places," we cannot fail to recognize the allusion to Ps. cx. 1, " Yahweh says to my Lord, ' Sit at my right hand, till I make your enemies your footstool.' "[6] The Davidic king to whom this divine oracle is addressed is identified by Paul and the other New Testament writers with Jesus, " who was descended from David according to the flesh." But he is identified at the same time with the figure of Ps. viii. 4 ff., under whose feet all things have been placed by God.

---

[4] God's fulfilment in Jesus of the " holy and sure blessings " promised to David is expounded in Paul's synagogue address at Pisidian Antioch (Acts xiii. 23 ff.), with reference to Ps. ii. 7, Ps. xvi. 10, and Isa. lv. 3.

[5] Cf. also the use of Ps. cx. 1 in Acts ii. 34 f. ; Heb. i. 13, etc. ; 1 Pet. iii. 22 ; Rev. iii. 21.

[6] Cf. also Col. iii. 1, " seek the things that are above, where Christ is, seated at the right hand of God." The wording of Ps. cx. 1 is not reproduced in Phil. ii. 9, but the same sense is recognizable : " God has highly exalted him and bestowed on him the name which is above every name " (see pp. 44f., 50).

II. The Son of Man

Christ must reign, says Paul in 1 Cor. xv. 25, till God has put all his enemies under his feet (the last of these enemies, he adds, is death). Then he quotes an Old Testament *testimonium* in support of his statement : " For God has put all things in subjection under his feet." This is a direct quotation of Ps. viii. 6 (apart from the change of the second person " thou " to the third person " he "). There is an allusion to the same scripture in Eph. i. 22 (" he has put all things under his feet ") and in Phil. iii. 21, where Paul speaks of the power by which Christ is enabled " even to subject all things to himself."

This suggests that the section of Ps. viii. beginning with the question in *v.* 4—" what is man that thou art mindful of him, and the son of man that thou dost care for him ? "—was applied to Christ at an early stage in Christian history. It might scarcely be relevant to adduce in this connexion Jesus' own quotation of *v.* 2 (" Out of the mouth of babes and sucklings thou hast brought perfect praise ") during his last week of ministry in the temple court at Jerusalem (Matt. xxi. 16), because the appropriateness of that quotation depends not on its context in Ps. viii. but on the situation in which it was uttered. But *vv.* 4–6 are cited effectively in Heb. ii. 6–8 to show how Jesus as the Son of man was temporarily made " lower than the angels " in order that ultimately the whole universe should become subject to him. The application of these verses to Jesus, found both in Paul's writings and in the Epistle to the Hebrews, may have been taken over by both authors from early Christian usage, although each develops the application along lines of his own. While the primary Old Testament source of Jesus' own use of the designation " Son of man " is probably Dan. vii. 13, it was natural that other Old Testament passages containing the expression " son of man " should have been interpreted of Jesus in the primitive Church.

The " son of man " in Ps. viii. 4 ff. is, of course, Adam or mankind ; the words " Thou hast given him dominion over the works of thy hands " (*v.* 6) are manifestly based on Gen. i. 26–28, where man is divinely appointed to rule the animal creation. But Paul (like the writer to the Hebrews) applies the psalmist's language not to the first Adam but to the second. Here we touch on Paul's conception of Jesus as the heavenly man, the last Adam

—a conception highly relevant to his Christology, and indeed to his whole philosophy of God and the world, but one which cannot be expounded within the compass of this paper. The " son of man " passage in Dan. vii. 13 has left few traces in Paul's epistles.[7] In Phil. ii. 7 f., where he speaks of Jesus as " being born in the likeness of men " and " being found in human form " (ἐν ὁμοιώματι ἀνθρώπων γενόμενος . . . σχήματι εὑρεθεὶς ὡς ἄνθρωπος), we may indeed recognize a reflection of k̲ᵉbar 'enāsh [8] in Dan. vii. 13 ; but the affinities of Phil. ii. 6 ff. are much more with another Old Testament passage than with Dan. vii. 13 f.[9] Again, the association of " clouds " with the parousia of Jesus in 1 Thess. iv. 17 goes back to Dan. vii. 13 where the " one like a son of man " is seen coming " with the clouds of heaven " ; but Paul's reference to the clouds is probably more directly dependent on such sayings of Jesus as those found in Mk. xiii. 26, xiv. 62.

When, however, Paul speaks of the parousia " of our Lord Jesus with all his saints " (1 Thess. iii. 13), his words not only echo Zech. xiv. 5 but may also reflect the close association of the " one like a son of man " in Daniel's vision and " the saints of the Most High " in the interpretation of the vision (Dan. vii. 27). So too, when he says to his Corinthian converts, " would that you did reign, so that we might reign with you ! " (1 Cor. iv. 8), and reminds them that " the saints will judge the world " (1 Cor. vi. 2), he is speaking of a royal and judicial function which can be theirs only through their relationship with the Son of man. It is the vision of Dan. vii. that lies behind his language here, as indeed it lies behind most of the New Testament passages which speak of reigning with Christ as the sequel to suffering with him (e.g., Rom. viii. 17, 2 Tim. ii. 11 f.).[10] The " one like a son of man " who receives dominion from the Ancient of Days attains this glory through suffering,[11] as the " saints of the Most High "

---

[7] Dan. vii. 13 probably underlies the statement in Paul's Aeropagitica (Acts xvii. 31) that God " will judge the world in righteousness by a man whom he has appointed " (ἐν ἀνδρὶ ᾧ ὥρισεν) ; a more literal rendering of k̲ᵉbar enāsh would have been meaningless in that environment.

[8] LXX and Theodotion ὡς υἱὸς ἀνθρώπου.

[9] The exaltation of Christ in Phil. ii. 9–11 may be linked in sense with Dan. vii. 14 (as with Ps. cx. 1), but the wording of Phil. ii. 10 f. is dependent on Isa. xlv. 23 (see p. 50).

[10] Our Lord's own words in Luke xxii. 28–30 (cf. Matt. xix. 28) must have influenced apostolic teaching on this subject.

[11] Cf. what is said in Ps. lxxx. 17 about " the man of thy right hand, the son of man whom thou hast made strong for thyself."

P.F.—4

who are associated with him in his rule have endured the fierce
assaults of the " little horn " (Dan. vii. 21). When Jesus spoke
of the Son of man as destined to " suffer many things and be
treated with contempt " (Mk. ix. 12), he implicitly identified the
Son of man with the Isaianic Servant of Yahweh ; but Daniel's
Son of man was from the start intended to be identical with the
Servant.

III. THE SERVANT OF YAHWEH

The figure of the obedient and suffering Servant of Yahweh,
as portrayed in Isa. xlii.–liii., made a contribution of the first
importance to the early Christians' understanding of the mission
of Jesus.[12] In many sectors of the apostolic Church it was the
Servant Songs (and especially the fourth, Isa. lii. 13–liii. 12)
that provided the first theological interpretation of his passion
and triumph.[13]

The Servant Songs, however, do not play as prominent a
part in the Pauline epistles as they do in a number of other New
Testament books. Yet their influence on Paul's argument here
and there is unmistakable. It is evident that he attached
evangelical significance to the fourth Servant Song and its
context [14] from his quotation of Isa. liii. 1 in Rom. x. 16—" they
have not all heeded the gospel ; for Isaiah says, ' Lord, who
has believed what he has heard from us ? ' " This follows almost
immediately upon a quotation from Isa. lii. 7, " How beautiful
are the feet of those who preach good news ! " [15] The good
news of deliverance for Zion is naturally interpreted of the
greater deliverance proclaimed in the Christian gospel.

Again, in Rom. xv. 21 Paul justifies his policy of bringing the
gospel to unevangelized territory by quoting Isa. lii. 15 in the
LXX form, " They shall see who have never been told of him,

[12] And, I should add, to Jesus' own understanding of his mission. The terms
in which this case has frequently been argued have been subjected to criticism
by C. K. Barrett in *New Testament Essays : Studies in memory of T. W. Manson*
(edited by A. J. B. Higgins, 1959), pp. 1 ff., and by M. D. Hooker, *Jesus and the
Servant* (1959).

[13] Cf. Acts iii. 13 ff., viii. 32 ff. ; Heb. ix. 28 ; 1 Pet. ii. 21 ff.

[14] The New Testament writers were under no obligation to anticipate B.
Duhm's precise delimitation of the four Servant Songs.

[15] Cf. Isa. xl. 9. The New Testament use of εὐαγγέλιον and its cognates goes
back to the repeated εὐαγγελιζόμενος of Isa. xl. 9 (LXX). Cf. Mark's quotation
of Isa. xl. 3 as a *testimonium* of " the beginning of the gospel " (Mark i. 1–3).

and they shall understand who have never heard of him." The quotation is not made for illustrative purposes only; Paul attaches eschatological significance to his ministry as apostle to the Gentiles,[16] which in his eyes forms part of the mission of the Servant.[17] More impressive confirmation of this appears in Col. i. 24, where Paul rejoices in his sufferings for his converts' sake, because (as he says) " in my flesh I complete what is lacking in Christ's afflictions for the sake of his body, that is, the church." [18] Paul, in other words, affirms his readiness to fill up in his own person as large a measure as possible of the " messianic birth-pangs " still outstanding, in order that his fellow-Christians may be relieved of the suffering which would otherwise fall to their lot before the parousia of Christ.

How does the portrayal of the Isaianic Servant contribute to Paul's presentation of Christ himself ? " Christ died for our sins," says Paul, " according to the scriptures " (1 Cor. xv. 3)—this is part of what he tells us he had " received." If we enquire more particularly how Christ died for our sins, Paul will tell us that God " for our sake . . . made him to be sin (ἁμαρτίαν ἐποίησεν) who knew no sin, so that in him we might become the righteousness of God " (2 Cor. v. 21). The expression ἁμαρτίαν ἐποίησεν may best be understood if we bear in mind that the same Hebrew word does duty for both " sin " and " sin-offering." Paul expresses the same thought in Rom. viii. 3, where he speaks of God as " sending his own Son in the likeness of sinful flesh and as a sin offering " (περὶ ἁμαρτίας). The phrase περὶ ἁμαρτίας regularly appears in the LXX in the sense of " sin-offering " ; but for our purpose its most striking Old Testament occurrence is in Isa. liii. 10, where the Servant's life is given περὶ ἁμαρτίας (Heb. 'āshām).

But the appointment of Christ to be a sin-offering on his people's behalf has as its object " that in him we might become the righteousness of God." Similarly in Rom v. 19 Paul describes the effect of the work of Christ by saying that " through the one man's obedience the many will be made righteous " (δίκαιοι κατασταθήσονται οἱ πολλοί). Here again Christ is said to fulfil what is predicted concerning the Servant : " by his knowledge

---

[16] Cf. J. Munck, *Paul and the Salvation of Mankind* (E.T., 1959), pp. 36 ff.

[17] Cf. Barnabas and Paul's application of Isa. xlix. 6 to themselves at Pisidian Antioch (Acts xiii. 47).

[18] Cf. T. W. Manson, *Ministry and Priesthood : Christ's and Ours* (1958), pp. 29 f. ; S. H. Hooke, *Alpha and Omega*, pp. 253 ff.

shall the righteous one, my servant, make the many to be accounted righteous; and he shall bear their iniquities " (Isa. liii. 11). Paul in Rom. v. 19 departs from the LXX text by adding the definite article before "many," and thus does more justice to the force of the Hebrew text of Isa. liii. 11.

When Paul speaks of Jesus as having been " delivered up for our trespasses and raised for our justification " (Rom. iv. 25), the general sense of his statement is similar to that of other passages in his epistles where the influence of Isa. liii. has been traced. The use of the verb " delivered up " ($\pi\alpha\rho\epsilon\delta\delta\theta\eta$) may be compared with the use of the same verb (in the imperfect tense $\pi\alpha\rho\epsilon\delta\delta\delta\tau o$) in 1 Cor. xi. 23, where Paul, transmitting a narrative which he himself had received, tells how the Eucharist was instituted by Jesus " in the night in which he was to be delivered up " (for his betrayal by Judas, to which most translators find a reference here, was but one incident in his being " delivered up "). In Isa. liii. 6 the LXX says of the Servant, " the Lord delivered him up to our sins " ($K\acute{\nu}\rho\iota o\varsigma$ $\pi\alpha\rho\acute{\epsilon}\delta\omega\kappa\epsilon\nu$ $\alpha\grave{\nu}\tau\grave{o}\nu$ $\tau\alpha\hat{\iota}\varsigma$ $\dot{\alpha}\mu\alpha\rho\tau\acute{\iota}\alpha\iota\varsigma$ $\dot{\eta}\mu\hat{\omega}\nu$), while in the last clause of v. 12 its wording is almost identical with that of Rom. iv. 25, except that a different word is used for "trespasses" (Paul's word here is $\pi\alpha\rho\alpha\pi\tau\acute{\omega}\mu\alpha\tau\alpha$): $\delta\iota\grave{\alpha}$ $\tau\grave{\alpha}\varsigma$ $\dot{\alpha}\nu o\mu\acute{\iota}\alpha\varsigma$ $\alpha\grave{\nu}\tau\hat{\omega}\nu$ $\pi\alpha\rho\epsilon\delta\delta\theta\eta$, says the LXX (" because of their trespasses he was delivered up "), deviating notably from the Massoretic text, " he made intercession for the transgressors." The sense of the Massoretic text is reproduced in Rom. viii. 34 (in a context where it has already been suggested that we have a pre-Pauline credal summary) : " Christ Jesus, who died, . . . who indeed intercedes for us." [19]

But of all the places in the Pauline corpus where the prophet's portrayal of the suffering Servant can be traced, the most outstanding is Phil. ii. 6–11, where the humiliation and exaltation of Christ are set forth as an incentive to Christians to exhibit the same attitude of self-forgetfulness as he did. If, as E. Lohmeyer and others have maintained, this passage is a pre-Pauline hymn, Paul has made it his own by incorporating it in his argument. Here we have the theme of humiliation followed by exaltation, of suffering followed by vindication, as we have it in the third and fourth Servant Songs. In so far as the language

---

[19] The Targum of Jonathan in Isa. liii. describes the Servant-Messiah as making entreaty for trespasses not only in v. 12 but also in vv. 4 and 11. But in the Targum he is not a *suffering* Servant-Messiah.

of Phil. ii. 6–11 echoes the Isaianic language, it by-passes the LXX and appears to represent an independent rendering of the Hebrew. Jesus takes the form of a δοῦλος (not παῖς) ; and when he is said to have "emptied himself . . . unto death" (ἑαυτὸν ἐκένωσεν . . . μέχρι θανάτου) in vv. 7 and 8, we may have, as Wheeler Robinson thought, a literal representation of the Hebrew wording in Isa. liii. 12, *he'erāh lammāweth naphshō*.[20]

IV. THE SON OF GOD

The substantive παῖς, used by the LXX to denote the Servant of the Lord (Heb. *'ebed Yahweh*), is sufficiently elastic to cover the senses of "servant" and "son." But when Jesus is called the Son of God, as he is throughout the New Testament, the word used is υἱός. In so far as an Old Testament background for υἱός in this connexion is to be sought, Ps. ii. 7 comes readily enough to mind. From Ps. ii. 7 in itself, it might be inferred that "Son of God" was a title which the Davidic Messiah bore by virtue of his office ; but it is clear that when Jesus at his baptism heard himself addressed in the words "Thou art my beloved Son," he understood them in no merely official sense. For him his awareness of a unique filial relation on his part to God was the central and controlling element in his religious consciousness. This appears not only in the few passages where he speaks of himself as "the Son" (among which the logion preserved in Matt. xi. 27 and Luke x. 22 is prominent),[21] but still more in those places where he calls God his Father, whether speaking to him or speaking of him.[22] We need not doubt that when Paul and the other New Testament writers call Jesus the Son of God, their intention is to give the words the same meaning as they had for Jesus himself.

There is, however, another Old Testament passage which has been discerned behind some of Paul's references to Jesus as the Son of God. "He who did not spare his own Son, but gave him up for us all, will he not also give us all things with him ? " (Rom. viii. 32). The first clause of this sentence (as Origen saw) is such a clear echo of God's words to Abraham in Gen. xxii. 16

---

[20] H. W. Robinson, *The Cross in the Old Testament* (1955), pp. 103 ff.

[21] Cf. also Mark xiii. 32.

[22] Especially Mark xiv. 36 (to which John xviii. 11 provides a remarkable parallel).

("you have not spared your son, your only son . . .") that one might well ask whether Paul makes any further allusion to the "binding of Isaac," as a foreshadowing of the sacrifice of Christ. H. J. Schoeps has dealt with this question in some detail ; [23] but while his own conclusion is that the narrative of Gen. xxii. "has provided the very model for the elaboration of Pauline soteriology" (for which conclusion he appeals to the expiatory value attached in rabbinical tradition to the sacrifice of Isaac), he concedes that "Paul himself has not yet explicitly drawn out the typology Isaac-Christ." He is disposed to adopt the suggestion that Rom. iii. 25—"whom God has set forth" ($\pi\rho o\acute{\epsilon}\theta\epsilon\tau o$)— is linked with Gen. xxii. 8—"God will provide ($\check{o}\psi\epsilon\tau a\iota$) a lamb . . ."—but the link is precarious in the absence of any such verbal similarity as there is between Rom. viii. 32 and Gen. xxii. 16. Two other New Testament writers refer more explicitly than Paul does to Abraham's sacrifice of Isaac (Heb. xi. 17–19 ; Ja. ii. 21–23) ; but neither of them relates it to the sacrifice of Christ. Pseudo-Barnabas was the first Christian writer of many to do this (vii. 3).[24]

V. CHRIST OUR PASSOVER

The sacrifice of the Servant and the sacrifice of Isaac are not the only Old Testament sacrifices which Paul regards as fulfilled in Christ. The general sacrificial terminology of Eph. v. 2, "Christ loved us and gave himself up for us, a fragrant offering and sacrifice to God," is drawn from the recurring Old Testament description of a sacrifice which is acceptable to God (found about forty times in the Pentateuch and four times in Ezekiel).[25] But one specific sacrifice is mentioned in 1 Cor. v. 7 f., where Paul, urging his readers to maintain ethical purity in their fellowship,

[23] *Paul* (ET, 1961), pp. 141 ff. See the careful examination of his arguments by C. K. Barrett in *From First Adam to Last* (1962), pp. 26 ff.
[24] *Test. Levi* xviii. 6, in the course of the passage about the new priest (a Christian passage, surely), says : "The heavens will be opened, and from the sanctuary of glory shall come upon him sanctification, with the father's voice as from Abraham to Isaac" (most probably a reference to the heavenly voice at the baptism of Jesus). M. Black ("The Messiah in the Testament of Levi xviii," *Expository Times* LX (1948–49), pp. 321 f.) relates this to the one utterance by Abraham to Isaac recorded in the Bible—the sacrificial utterance of Gen. xxii. 8.
[25] Cf. Phil. iv. 18, where Paul uses this terminology to describe the Philippian church's gift to him.

says : " Christ, our paschal lamb, has been sacrificed.   Let us,
therefore, celebrate the festival, not with the old leaven, the
leaven of malice and evil, but with the unleavened bread of
sincerity and truth."

The association of Christ with the paschal lamb was inevitably
suggested to early Christians [26] by the fact that his death took
place at the Passover season, if not indeed (as the Johannine
account implies) at the very time when the lamb was sacrificed.
Paul's argument is that, since the paschal sacrifice was followed
immediately by the festival of unleavened bread (cf. Lev. xxiii.
5–8), so Christians ought to manifest their appreciation of the
death of Christ by a perpetual " festival "—a life permanently
purified from the " leaven " of sin and marked by moral and
spiritual integrity.

The presentation of Christ as the paschal lamb and of Christian
life as the consequent festival of unleavened bread is bound up
with a whole series of typical analogies drawn between the
beginnings of Israel's national history and Christian experience,
of which Paul himself supplies a notable example in 1 Cor. x. 1–11.

VI. THE WISDOM OF GOD

That Christ is " the wisdom of God " is asserted by Paul in
1 Cor. i. 24, 30, in a context where the crucifixion is specially
emphasized.   This is an intentional paradox on Paul's part,
because by every worldly standard the crucifixion was an
exhibition of foolishness and weakness.   But it is plain from other
Pauline passages that the conception of Christ as the wisdom of
God has its roots in the Old Testament, with reference not only
to redemption but also to creation and providence.

With regard to creation, the outstanding Pauline passage is
Col. i. 15–18, where Christ is said to be the one in whom all
things were created and in whom all things cohere.[27]   In other
words, he is given the rôle which is claimed by Wisdom in Prov. viii.
22 ff., where she speaks of herself as the Creator's assessor and
master-workman when he brought the universe into being.   But

---

[26] Cf. the description of Christ in 1 Pet. i. 19 as " a lamb without blemish or
spot," coupled with the admonition " gird up your minds " in verse 13 (cf. Ex.
xii. 5, 11).
[27] Cf. 1 Cor. viii. 6.

Paul is employing no mere literary personification, but referring to the eternal Son of God, who in the fulness of time became man as Jesus of Nazareth. Wisdom is " the beginning " of Yahweh's way in Prov. viii. 22 ; Christ is " the beginning " *par excellence* in Col. i. 18. In relation to the old creation he exercises the right of heritage which is his as the Father's first-begotten ; in relation to the new creation he exercises a parallel privilege because of his priority in resurrection.

With regard to providence, we note the passage where Paul says that the Israelites in the wilderness " drank from the spiritual rock which followed them, and the Rock was Christ " (1 Cor. x. 4). In current Jewish thinking the rock from which Israel drank in the wilderness was associated with Divine Wisdom. According to Wisd. xi. 1–4 it was Wisdom, their helper and defender in the wilderness, who supplied them with " water . . . out of flinty rock, and slaking of thirst from hard stone." Even more explicitly Paul's older contemporary, Philo of Alexandria, says : " The flinty rock is the wisdom of God from which he feeds the souls that love him." [28] Paul goes further : that rock, he says, was Christ himself, who accompanied his people in the wilderness.[29] This conception may have found support in those Old Testament passages where God promises his people that the angel of his presence will go before them in all their wanderings until he brings them into the promised land (Ex. xiv. 19 ; xxiii. 20 ff. ; xxxii. 34 ; xxxiii. 2, 14 ; cf. Isa. lxiii. 9). But since Paul links the presence of Christ with the provision from the rock, we can hardly fail to associate his thought with the near-contemporary references to the rock in connexion with Divine Wisdom.

Where did Paul get the idea of identifying Jesus with the Wisdom of God ? The idea is not original to him, for we find it elsewhere in the New Testament, notably in Hebrews and in the Johannine literature. The description of Jesus as the ἀπαύγασμα of the divine glory in Heb. i. 3 is plainly related to the similar description of Wisdom in Wisd. vii. 25. The influence of Prov. viii. 22 ff. is clearly traceable not only in Col. i. 15 ff. but also in Heb. i. 2 f. and John i. 2 f., where Christ is similarly presented as

[28] *Leg. Alleg.*, II, 86.
[29] Cf. Jude 5, where the original text is probably that which reads : " Jesus, who saved a people out of the land of Egypt, afterward destroyed those who did not believe."

the one through whom the worlds came into being, and in Rev.
iii. 14, where the enthroned Christ speaks in the rôle of " the
Amen, . . . the beginning of God's creation."

When we find a new idea of this character in so many streams
of early Christian thought, it is most natural to look for its
origin in the teaching of Jesus himself. Some of the utterances
of Jesus have been classified as " Wisdom sayings " ; of these the
" comfortable words " of Matt. xi. 28 ff. come most readily to
mind, with their well-known resemblance to Ben Sira's epilogue
(Sir. li. 23 ff.). In inviting men to come to him and take his yoke
upon them, Christ " does not summon men to Wisdom, as a
mere expert or teacher or even pupil of Wisdom, but . . . like
Wisdom, calls men to himself. He speaks in the name of Wisdom,
indeed as Wisdom herself." [30]

VII. THE LORD

The important contribution of Ps. cx. 1 to primitive Christian
Christology has already been observed. In that passage the
invitation " Sit at my right hand till I make your enemies your
footstool " is " Yahweh's utterance to my lord " (*'ādōn*). But
the psalmist's acknowledgment of the Messiah as his lord is not
the same thing as giving him the ineffable name of Yahweh.
The vast majority of Jewish scribes would have agreed that " my
lord " was the Messiah ; but they would have dismissed as
blasphemy the suggestion that he was entitled to be put on a
par with Yahweh, let alone be given Yahweh's name. Yet Paul
does not hesitate to take this further step, and he is not the only
New Testament writer to do so.[31] That Jesus was addressed as
" Lord " in the Aramaic-speaking Church is sufficiently proved
from the currency of the invocation *Marana-tha*, an invocation
so primitive that it was taken over by the Greek-speaking
Christians (cf. 1 Cor. xvi. 22 ; *Didache* x. 6). Among Greek-speaking Christians this title, κύριος, was identical with the form which
in the LXX does duty regularly for Yahweh as well as for *'ādōn*.
But it was not primarily this linguistic accident that made those

[30] R. Otto, *The Kingdom of God and the Son of Man* (ET, 1943), p. 172.
[31] Cf. the application of Isa. viii. 13 (" Yahweh of hosts, him you shall
sanctify ") in 1 Pet. iii. 15 (" sanctify in your hearts Christ as Lord "), and the
quotation of Ps. cii. 25, words addressed to Yahweh, in Heb. i. 10 as words
addressed to Christ.

50 PROMISE AND FULFILMENT

early Christian writers apply to Jesus Old Testament passages which plainly referred to Israel's God. What moved them to do so was the impact which Jesus himself made on their lives—an impact so unparalleled that it made men who had been brought up as faithful monotheistic Jews give Jesus, inevitably and spontaneously, the glory which belonged to the one God.

We see this process in Paul's substitution for " the day of the Lord " such synonymous expressions as " the day of Christ," " the day of Jesus Christ," " the day of our Lord Jesus Christ." We see it in his quotation of Joel ii. 32—" everyone who calls upon the name of the Lord will be saved "—in Rom. x. 13, in a context which suggests that Jesus is the Lord referred to, since he has just said that salvation belongs to those who confess Jesus as Lord (v. 9). Yet Yahweh stands in the Hebrew text. We see it most unambiguously in Phil. ii. 9–11, where Paul affirms that God has given Jesus " the name which is above every name, that in the name of Jesus every knee should bow, . . . and every tongue confess that Jesus Christ is Lord." Here he applies to Jesus the words of Isa. xlv. 23, " To me every knee shall bow, every tongue shall swear "—words spoken by him who has said immediately before : " I am God, and there is no other." The " name which is above every name " can only be κύριος in that plenary sense in which it stands for Yahweh. Yet, says Paul, it is God himself who has bestowed this name on Christ, and his own glory is not diminished but enhanced thereby.[32] In Professor Hooke's words, " it is the image of the Servant that Paul has before him, and all that he has been saying to the Philippians about the self-emptying of the Servant is the exposition of the glory of the Son, and so the passage closes with the Father's conferring on the Son the ineffable Name. . . . In John's gospel xvii. 5 the Son prays, ' And now, O Father, glorify thou me with thine own self, with the glory which I had with thee before the world was,' and here Paul declares that it has been done. This is the climax of Paul's exposition of the glory." [33]

But let Paul (more suo) have the last word. " For," says he, " all the promises of God find their Yes in him. That is why we utter the Amen through him, to the glory of God " (2 Cor. i. 20).

[32] If the passage is a pre-Pauline hymn, the implications are obvious.
[33] *Alpha and Omega*, p. 259.

THE ARK IN THE PSALMS

By G. HENTON DAVIES

THERE is only one explicit reference to the *'aron* in the Psalter. In Ps. cxxxii. 8 [1] we read :

> Arise, O Yahweh, into thy resting place,
> Thou and the ark of thy strength
>
> ('*attah wa'aron 'uzzekha*).

It is clearly important that this one reference to the Ark in the Psalter is textually beyond doubt, but it is also strange, especially in view of the increasing recognition of the cultic significance of the Psalter,[2] that the word *'aron* comes but once in the Psalter.

There are of course other places in the psalms where the presence of the Ark is implied, though the commentators are by no means agreed. Thus Kirkpatrick [3] finds a reference to the Ark in ten other psalms, and a possible eleventh, but in three only of these eleven psalms does Gunkel [4] find a reference to the Ark. Weiser finds references to the Ark in many more psalms in connexion with the theophany in the cult.[5]

The commentators are agreed that in several places the Ark must be assumed. But is it possible to be more precise ? The question is whether there are any clues in the cultic terms of the Psalter which point to the Ark.

Ps. cxxxii. 8 presents us with the first clue by its use of the word *'oz* in connexion with the Ark.

---

[1] It is well known that the cultic significance of this Psalm has been emphasized in several recent studies : S. Mowinckel, *Psalmenstudien* II, pp. 107–126 ; A. Bentzen, " The cultic use of the story of the ark in Samuel," in *JBL*, LXVII (1948), pp. 35–53 ; H. J. Krauss, *Die Königsherrschaft Gottes im alten Testament* (1951), pp. 51–59 ; J. R. Porter, " The Interpretation of II Samuel VI and Psalm CXXXII," in *JTS*, new series, V (1954), pp. 161–73.

[2] It is hardly necessary to point out that acceptance of the cultic interpretation of the Psalms does not necessarily involve acceptance of the theory of a New Year Festival in Israel.

[3] A. F. Kirkpatrick, *The Book of Psalms* (Cambridge Bible, 1903) ; cf. Pss. ix. 11 (12), xv. 1, xxiv., xliv. 9 (10), xlvii. 5 (6), lxiii. 2 (3), lxviii. 1 (2), lxxviii. 61, xcvi. 6, (?) xcix. 5, ci. 2.

[4] H. Gunkel, *Die Psalmen* (1926). Cf. Pss. xxiv, lxviii. 1, lxxviii. 61.

[5] A. Weiser, *Die Psalmen* (1950), p. 21.

The words, " Thou and the ark of thy strength," confirm the
view that another almost certain reference to the Ark is to be
found in Ps. lxxviii. In this historical psalm *vv.* 60 and 61 read :

> And he forsook the tabernacle of Shiloh,
> The tent of dwelling with man,
> And he surrendered his strength (*'uzzo*) to captivity,
> And his beauty (*tiph'arto*) into the enemy's hand.

This would appear to be a clear reference to the fall of Shiloh
and to the capture of the Ark as recounted in 1 Sam. iv.–v. 1,
and this is how most commentators interpret the reference.[6]
Buttenwieser,[7] however, thinks that these verses in Ps. lxxviii.
refer to the overthrow of Samaria by Assyria in 722 B.C. He also
believes that the words " their strength " (*'uzzo*) and " their
glory " (*tiph'arto*) are descriptive not of the sacred Ark (stationed
at Shiloh in ancient days), as generally understood, but of the
" tabernacle of Shiloh," just as in Ezek. xxiv. 21 " the pride of
your strength " and the " delight of your eyes " are descriptive
of " my sanctuary "—that is, the Temple of Jerusalem. Buttenwieser bases his argument upon certain difficulties in the Psalm,
by slight rearrangements of the order of the verses, and by
inferring from the Greek and Aquila [8] " that instead of the
singular they read plural suffixes in their Hebrew copies."

Buttenwieser's opinion, like his manipulations of the text,
appears singularly unconvincing, and it is preferable to adopt
the common view that Ps. lxxviii. 60 f. indeed refers to the fall
of Shiloh, and to the capture of the Ark. Widengren interprets
this section of Ps. lxxviii. in mythological terms.[9]

[6] Cf., *e.g.*, J. J. S. Perowne, *The Book of Psalms* (1878) ; F. Delitzsch, *The
Psalms* (1888) ; J. Wellhausen, *The Book of Psalms*, E.Tr. (1898) ; B. Duhm,
Die Psalmen (1899) ; Kirkpatrick, *op. cit.* (1903) ; T. W. Davies, *The Book of
Psalms* (Century Bible, 1906) ; C. A. Briggs, *The Book of Psalms* (ICC, 1908) ;
R. Kittel, *Die Psalmen* (KAT, 1922) ; H. Gunkel, *Die Psalmen* (1926) ; H.
Schmidt, *Die Psalmen* (HAT, 1934) ; J. Calès, *Le Livre des Psaumes*[7] (1936) ;
H. Herkenne, *Das Buch der Psalmen* (1936) ; W. O. E. Oesterley, *The Psalms*
(1939) ; C. Lattey, *The Psalms* (Westminster Version, 1944) ; A. Cohen, *The
Psalms* (Soncino, 1945) ; A. E. Leslie, *The Psalms* (1949) ; E. Podechard, *Le
Psautier* (1949–54) ; A. Weiser, *Die Psalmen* (1950) ; E. J. Kissane, *The Book
of Psalms* (1953) ; W. S. McCullough, in *The Interpreter's Bible*, IV (1955).
All the above references *ad loc.* Also BDB, pp. 739*a*, 802*a* ; cf. A. Lauha, *Die
Geschichtsmotive in den Alttestamentlichen Psalmen* (1946), pp. 109 f.

[7] M. Buttenwieser, *The Psalms* (1938), p. 132.

[8] Cf. *Septuaginta*, edited by A. Rahlfs : Ps. lxxvii. 61, ἰσχὺν αὐτῶν . . . αὐτῶν.
So Aq. ; Vg. *eorum . . . eorum*. But αὐτοῦ B + $.

[9] Widengren (*Sakrales Königtum im Alten Testament*, pp. 64–6) has recently
pointed out that lxxviii. 60–1 with its account of destruction of land and temple

Fortified then by these two references to the Ark in the Psalter, both of which use the noun 'oz with suffixes, it occurs to me to point out that a similar interpretation is possible in some of the other forty-three occurrences of 'oz in the Psalter. In lxxviii. 61 'oz and tiph'ereth are in parallelism. In xcvi. 6, they also appear together: 'oz w'thiph'ereth b'miqdasho, " Strength and beauty are in his sanctuary." [10] As usual the commentators make various suggestions, but in lxxviii. 61 the first word 'oz refers to the Ark. It would be reasonable to suppose that the same is true of xcvi. 6, as some commentators in fact suggest. So the words, " Strength and beauty are in his sanctuary," mean in terms of cultic reality [11] that the Ark is in its place.

But this verse in Ps. xcvi. 6 occurs again in 1 Chron. xvi. 27 in the form 'oz w'hedwah bim'qomo. Why bim'qomo replaces b'miqdasho is clear,[12] but why tiph'ereth has given way to hedwah is not clear to me.[13] The vital word 'oz remains, and again the reference could be to the Ark, because Ps. xcvi. is part of " the composite anthem which the Chronicler introduces to celebrate the translation of the Ark to Zion (1 Chron. xvi. 8 ff.)." [14] 'Oz in Ps. xcvi. 6 and 1 Chron. xvi. 27 then probably means the Ark.[15]

---

is an illustration of that condition of chaos which comes as a result of God's departure from his people. The various Old Testament features described by Widengren have parallels in the Tammuz and Ishtar cult, and Widengren quotes the Old Testament passages and parallels as the background for the conception of a sleeping, waking, risen God. He is also able to cite various points, e.g., use of '*adonai*, in favour of his view of the material. It seems to me, however, that he has disregarded the historical basis of lxxviii. 60-1, when he regards " Might " as simply descriptive of the power of Yahweh.

[10] Briggs, op. cit., ad loc., thinks of the " ancient pillars Jachin and Boaz in the porch of the temple . . ." ; Kittel, op. cit., Barnes, op. cit., ad loc., of personal attendants upon God in heaven (presumably) ; cf. Oesterley, op. cit., ad loc., and T. W. Davies, op. cit., ad loc., Leslie, op. cit., ad loc., presumably suggests a reference to Yahweh's worshippers ; Weiser, op. cit., ad loc., attendants of God in a theophany. But to Father Lattey, op. cit., ad loc., the words " probably refer primarily to the ark of the covenant, as in lxxviii. 61 . . ." Cf. Mowinckel, op. cit., II, p. 158, n. 2. So possibly Podechard, op. cit., at lxxviii. 61.

[11] For the phrase see Mowinckel, op. cit., III–VI, Chapter I. Table of contents : " poetische Fiktion oder kultische Realität." Sometimes Mowinckel uses the word " Aktualit ät "(II, p. 16, and cf. " von erlebten Dingen," ibid., p. 16). Bentzen, op. cit., p. 41, speaks of " actualizations." Hence the phrase " cultic actuality " as a medium for the interpretation of the Psalms, etc.

[12] Cf. Gunkel, op. cit., Ps. xcvi. 6, ad loc. ; also Calès, op. cit., xcvi. 6.

[13] But cf. Kirkpatrick, op. cit., ad Ps. xcvi. 6.

[14] Kirkpatrick, ibid., p. 576.

[15] The first stichos of these verses, " Honour and majesty are before him," is also capable of interpretation in terms of " cultic reality." What are the " honour and majesty " which are " before God ? " The word " before," " in

The reference to " thy mighty ark " (*^aron 'uzzekha*) in Ps.
cxxxii., may well serve as a point of departure for another place,
viz., Ps. cv. 4 = 1 Chron. xvi. 11.

> Seek Yahweh and his strength (*'uzzo*),
> Seek his face perpetually.[16]

H. Hupfeld [17] says that the Rabbis and ancient commentators
interpreted " his strength " of the Ark, and that I think is the
right view.[18] Again the choice is poetic fiction or cultic reality.
It should not be forgotten that cv. 4, like xcvi. 6, appears in
1 Chron. xvi. where the Ark is translated to Zion. The context in
1 Chron. confirms the suggestion that once again *'uzzo* here is
really a reference to the Ark. That is confirmed rather than
denied by *panim* in the parallel stichos. The liturgical character
of the psalm is emphasized by the commentators,[19] and the
verbs *darash* and *biqqesh* are the words employed for a visit to a
sanctuary. Surely the cultic reality applies not only to the
journeys to the sanctuary, but to the object of the visit also ?

Though some commentators, like Gunkel, claim that *biqqesh*
(with or without *panim*) and *darash* are also used in a more
spiritual sense, the concrete actual context of the passage is
against this poetic fiction, and so I consider that the reference
to the Ark is fairly certain.

front of," suggest something in a definite place in front of God, or of the sanctuary,
or of the Ark. B.D.B. " especially of majesty of יהוה " is difficult to follow. How
is Yahweh's majesty in front of Him ?   The words *hod w^ehadar* occur together
seven times. In xxi. 6 they are divinely bestowed upon the king ; in xlv. 4
they clearly refer to the king, however the text is to be read.   In civ. 1 and
cxi. 3 they are used of God, and in Job xl. 10 in a reproach to Job. The suggestion
is clear. The words describe attributes of royalty, whether of God or man ;
cf. Ps. viii. 2, cxlv. 5, cxlviii. 13, 1 Chron. xxix. 11 ; Jerem. xlviii. 18, Zech.
vi. 13, Hab. iii. 3, 1 Chron. xxix. 25, and Dan. xi. 21. May not the first stichos of
Ps. xcvi. 6 and 1 Chron. xvi. 25 be a cultic description of the king standing in his
place in front of the temple ?   The whole verse then describes the presence of
king and Ark in the sanctuary.

[16] In both Ps. cv. 4 and 1 Chron. xvi. 11, LXX and $ read " and be strength-
ened." So Barnes *op. cit., ad loc.* Commentators take it as follows (*ad loc.*) :
H. Hupfeld, *Die Psalmen* (1860), " Stärke " and " Angesicht " ; Kirkpatrick,
" His strength cannot here mean the Ark as in lxxviii. 61 " ; Briggs, ". . . the
strength of his lifted hands and outstretched arms " (is this explanation better ?) ;
Gunkel, " Herrlichkeit " and " Antlitz " ; Schmidt, " Macht " and " Antlitz " ;
Calès, " puissance " and " face," though he does not exclude LXX reading ;
Herkenne, " Macht " and " Antlitz " ; Cohen, " as a power to save " ; Weiser,
" Macht " and " Antlitz " ; Kissane, " might " and " face."

[17] H. Hupfeld, *op. cit.*, Ps. cv. 4 *ad loc.*

[18] So Lattey, *op. cit., ad loc.*, who translates " His praise."

[19] *E.g.*, Kittel, *op. cit., ad loc.*, ". . . der Psalm ist sicher für den Kultus
bestimmt " ; Weiser, *ad loc.*, " Kulthymnus der Bundesgemeinde."

Again Mowinckel [20] points a parallel between Ps. cxxxii. and Ps. lxxxi., in that they both deal in varying form with the theme of the renewal of the covenant. Further Mowinckel supposes that Ps. lxxxi. belongs to the cultic moment when the procession has reached the temple, and the Ark has been once more restored to its place. Is it then merely a coincidence that the Psalm begins : "Sing aloud unto God, our strength" (*harninu le'lohim 'uzzenu*) ?

Surely "our strength" points to the Ark.

The same conclusion applies, as it seems to me, to Ps. lxiii. 3

> *ken baqqodesh ḥᵃzithikha*
> *lir'oth 'uzzᵉkha ukhᵉbodᵉkha*

So in the holy place have I beheld thee,
Looking upon thy strength and thy glory.[21]

Since beholding and looking generally mean seeing, and since *baqqodesh* probably means sanctuary here,[22] it is surely not unreasonable to claim that "thy strength" and "thy glory" means something that could be seen in or from the temple court. Furthermore the speaker in the Psalm is probably the king, and he would have had a nearer view.[23] Even the commentators are more prepared to find a reference to the Ark in this passage.[24]

---

[20] *Op. cit.*, II, pp. 152–6 ; and cf. A. R. Johnson, *Sacral Kingship in Ancient Israel* (1955), p. 61 n.

[21] Hupfeld : "von geistlichen Schauen." Cheyne (*The Book of Psalms*) reads : "Do I long for thee " ; so probably Kissane. Kirkpatrick mentions the Ark as "the symbol of God's Presence, of his strength and glory," but commits himself no further. Calès speaks of "sa puissance, symbolisée dans les cherubins de l'Arche." Oesterley, *op. cit.*, refers to Num. x. 35, 36 and 1 Sam. iv. 3–8 in reference to his statement : ". . . it is clear that the divine presence was conceived of as connected with some concrete object." Briggs : "in the contemplation of public worship." So essentially Kittel, T. W. Davies, Gunkel, Graetz, Ehrlich, G. Muller, W. R. Taylor in *Interpreter's Bible*. But cf. Peters, *op. cit.*, *ad loc.* : "emblems." Some of these also emend the text in some way. Weiser (*ad loc.* and p. 21) supposes a theophany which may be connected with the Ark. Kissane : "manifestation of God's omnipotence . . ."

[22] Buttenwieser denies this and translates, "Oh, that I may behold thee in grandeur revealed " ; but cf. lxviii. 25.

[23] Cf. Leslie, *ad loc.*, who refers to the king on his bed near the Ark, mentioning the name of Yahweh.

[24] Similarly Ps. lxxxiv. 8. The reference to seeing God in Zion must be interpreted in the light of the reference to Yahweh of Hosts in the following verse, Yahweh of Hosts being the name of the Ark, as will be mentioned later. A. R. Johnson interprets lxxxiv. 8 as : "in all the accompaniment of worship." Presumably this does not exclude the Ark.

Psalm lxviii. is a difficult psalm to interpret.[25] Whether it be composed in the main of two psalms, one early and one late,[26] or whether it be a collection of fragments of psalms,[27] or " a catalogue of incipits of poems," [28] or whether the psalm is a cultic unity, it may fairly be claimed that a processional motif is apparent in most parts of the psalm.[29] It is, for example, the neglect of this processional motif with its related themes, which leads Buttenwieser to ascribe the illustration of Yahweh's march through the desert in *vv.* 6–7 to one psalm, 68A, and the account of a procession to or into the sanctuary in *vv.* 23–27 to another psalm, 68B. The idea of the processional theme makes such a division in the psalm unnecessary.

If Ps. lxviii is a processional psalm, and is, as Johnson suggests, " the necessary context to psalm xxiv, with its theme of Yahweh's kingship and its obviously processional background centring in the Ark," [30] then it is natural to ask if the Ark is mentioned in the psalm ? There are allusions to the Ark, or to the so-called Song of the Ark in Ps. lxviii. 2–4 (1–3), but they are not intended to indicate the processional station of the Ark. There are, however, two passages in the psalm which clearly describe a procession, and a comparison of these passages may throw light on the question where the Ark appeared in the procession.

In *vv.* 16–19 (15–18) there is a description of a procession as it wends its way into the sanctuary. Then again in *vv.* 25 and following (24 and following) there is another description of a procession.[31] It is worth while setting down the order of the procession as this occurs in each passage.

[25] *E.g.*, Buttenwieser, *op. cit.*, pp. 30–4, and cf. W. F. Albright, *Archaeology and the Religion of Israel*, pp. 129, 211 : " Ugaritic parallels show that his [*i.e.*, Buttenwieser's] sharp cleavage between 68A and 68B is not warranted . . ."

[26] For Ps. lxviii. see Samuel Iwry, " Notes on Psalm 68," in *JBL*, LXXI (1952), pp. 161–5, and the literature there cited ; especially : Cassuto, *Tarbiz*, XII (1941), pp. 1–27 ; and W. F. Albright, " A Catalogue of Early Hebrew Lyric Poems (LXVIII)," *HUCA*, XXIII (1950–1), p. 23 ; also A. R. Johnson, *op. cit.*, pp. 68–77.

[27] Cf. Iwry, *op. cit.*, p. 163 : " Cassuto breaks up the whole psalm into twenty fragments which are strung together on the basis of a supposed central idea." Schmidt (*ad loc.*) thinks of sixteen pieces ; Leslie (" A Hymnbook of Enthronement Songs ") fifteen all told.

[28] So Albright, *op. cit.*, and Iwry, *op. cit.* ; Weiser, and cf. Peters, *op. cit.*, p. 50.

[29] So Schmidt, *ad loc.* ; cf. Calès, *ad loc.*, " Chant de Procession." Cf. Johnson, *op. cit.*, p. 68, and Peters, *op. cit.*, p. 58.

[30] Johnson, *op. cit.*, p. 74.

[31] Johnson, *op. cit.*, p. 74, describes these verses as " a more detailed account of the procession itself."

16–19	25 ff.
18. The Chariots of God.	25. The Processions of God.
	26. Singers and instrumentalists.
18b. The Lord is among them as in Sinai, in the sanctuary.	27. The companies blessing God from Israel's Spring.
	28. Benjamin, the sanctuary tribe, Judah, the royal tribe, the Princes of Zebulun and Naphtali.
19. Thou hast gone up on high.[32]	
19. Captives bearing tribute.	30. Kings bearing tribute.

There are obvious points of parallel between the two descriptions. In the first description the reference to God appears in 18b between the chariots and the captives. This suggests that we should look for a similar reference to God between Zebulun and Naphtali on the one hand, and the kings bearing tribute on the other. What does come between is the enigmatic verse, 29 (28):

> Thy God hath commanded thy strength;
> Strengthen, O God, that which thou hast wrought for us.

At first sight the sequence is not apparent, but the overall comparison of the two passages suggests that the description of the procession continues even in this enigmatic verse. How then are the words: "Thy God commanded thy strength," etc., a processional feature? In other words, does this verse hide a parallel to the phrase: "Thou hast gone up on high," in the previous passage? But first the text calls for attention. For the perfect, we must read the imperative,[33] and then we must read either "God," or as Johnson so happily suggests,

---

[32] For the significance of ʻalah, cf. Johnson, op. cit., pp. 66 ff., 88. If ʻalah passages like lxviii. 19 and xlvii. 6 also refer to the Ark, then the Elyon-Yahweh syncretism is even more striking and complete.

[33] So Heb MSS, LXX, Vulg. Jer. (some MSS) Syr. Targ. So Hupfeld, op. cit., Perowne, op. cit., Wellhausen, op. cit., Duhm, op. cit., Cheyne, op. cit. Kirkpatrick, op. cit., "O God, command thy strength," and so T. Witton Davies, op. cit., "Be strong, O God, that hast wrought for us," i.e., taking the verb paʻalta as intransitive. Briggs, op. cit., Gunkel, op. cit., following Ewald, Olshausen, Kittel.
    Kittel, Schmidt, Calès, Herkenne, Buttenwieser,
          "Muster thy power, O God,
           Show thy might in what thou doest for us."
    Lattey, Leslie, Weiser, Kissane.

" My God." [34] The suffix " thy " attached to " God " does not, I think, belong to the following word, but is an erroneous anticipation of the same suffix in the following word.[35] Apart from this one point, it is quite clear that Johnson's brilliant division of the text is to be followed.[36] This gives the following result :

> Command, O my God, thy strength,
> The divine strength with which thou hast wrought for us.
> How hast thou undertaken on account of Jerusalem !
> To thee kings are bringing their presents.

If that be the right text, the question remains : How is this text a processional feature ? I suggest that in the words " thy strength " we find once more a reference to the Ark, and in the first stichos of the verse the quasi-rubric for the location point of the Ark in the procession. The words mean : " This is the place in the procession which God has commanded the Ark should take." If this interpretation of the passage is possible, we have gained a more complete parallel to the earlier description of the procession, and saved the unity of the psalm at that point.[37]

It may be added that the word 'oz appears several times in Ps. lxviii. ; cf. vv. 34, 35 (bis), 36, and it may well be that the underlying thought of the Ark as the strength of Yahweh has prompted these other metaphorical references.

[34] Johnson (with other modifications) :
> " Issue thy command, O my God,
> As befitteth thy might."

[35] M.T. " thy God " means that Israel is suddenly addressed in a context in which God is consistently addressed. The reading, justified also on other grounds, corrects this. Delitzsch, op. cit., retains M.T.

[36] Johnson, op. cit., p. 75, notes.

[37] The actual order of the tribes—Benjamin, Judah, Zebulun, and Naphtali is very interesting. The question is why are Zebulun and Naphtali next, this is, in front of the Ark ?

The similarity of Ps. lxviii to the Song of Deborah reminds us of the bravery of Zebulun and Naphtali described in Deborah's Song. In the prose version, however, Jdg. iv. 10–14, suggest that only Zebulun and Naphtali fought in the battle, and that they followed Yahweh into battle (?) " Is not the LORD gone out before thee ? " Was it traditional in (not very) later ritual, as represented by Ps. lxviii., to commemorate the bravery of Zebulun and Naphtali by giving them the place of honour immediately in front of the Ark ?

Further, is it possible that the humiliation of the land of Zebulun and Naphtali in Isa. ix. 1 could refer indirectly to the loss of this place of honour in the ritual procession consequent upon the division of the kingdom ? Isa. ix. 2, the people that walked in darkness have seen a great light. Does the verse mean that Zebulun and Naphtali will be restored to their former glory ?

In both passages, Jdg. iv. and Isa. ix., the nearness of these tribes to the warring Yahweh and the new light is very striking.

A similar processional passage helps to confirm the interpretation in Ps. lxviii. In Ps. lxxvii. 11–16, after recalling Yahweh's works of old, the speaker continues :

> O God, in the sanctuary is thy way,
> Who is a God great as God ?
> Thou art the God doing marvellous deeds,
> Thou hast made known among the peoples thy strength.

Apparently the writer turns from history to temple and then back to history and to Israel's history in quick succession, and so the unity of the passage is destroyed. Indeed most commentators preserve the unity by translating *baqqodesh* as " in holiness," and so avoid a reference to the sanctuary.[38] But if the reference is to the sanctuary,[39] then too the making known of " thy strength " is a cultic occasion in the sanctuary [40] best explained in connexion with the Ark.

[38] Cf. Hupfeld, " Heiligkeit," following Symmachus, Syr. and Targum. The word *baqqodesh* appears in Ex. xv. 11, but, to say the least, the reference to the sanctuary cannot be excluded in Ex. xv. 11, because the sanctuary is otherwise so largely a theme of that temple hymn. " Holiness," Cheyne (also " uniqueness ") : 1 Sam. vi. 20 (" this holy God " refers to the Ark of Yahweh in the Beth-Shemesh incident). So Kirkpatrick, Barnes : " In sanctity "—Briggs. Cohen, Leslie, Kissane, Gunkel : " Yahweh, erhaben ist dein Weg." Kittel : " O Gott, dein Weg ist erhaben," as though *baqqodesh* is the equivalent of *gadol*. Similarly Schmidt, Calès, Lattey, Herkenne : " Welterhabenheit," " Unvergleichlichkeit." Buttenweiser : " Sublime are thy ways."

[39] " In the sanctuary." So LXX, Vg, Jerome and " early Jewish authorities " (Briggs) ; Weiser.

[40] The usage of *qodesh* (nominal form), in the Psalter is as follows : *qodesh* six times : cxxxiv. 2 " in or to the sanctuary " ; xxix. 2 = xcvi. 9 *behadrath qodesh* of some feature of temple worship, cf. cx.3 (? many MSS, Symmachus, Jerome *behareve* for *behadre*) ; lxxxvii. 2 of Zion ; xciii. 5 of Yahweh's house. All these six references have to do with the sanctuary. *Baqqodesh* five times and always of sanctuary. So R.V. *Miqqodesh* once and of sanctuary. *Qodshi* three times : of Zion ii. 6 ; of oil lxxxix. 21 ; and lxxxix. 36, " Once have I sworn by my holiness," *i.e.*, Yahweh swears by himself. The possibility exists that the words mean " Once for all (A.R. Johnson) have I sworn in my sanctuary." The same problem arises in regard to *dibber beqodsho* in lx. 8 ; cviii. 8 (see below). *Qodshekha*, *qodshekha* eight times as gen. of quality. Thrice of temple, twice with (sanctuary) *har* ; once each of *debir*, *ruah*, and *shem*. *Qodsho* eighteen times : sixteen times as gen. of quality, including four times with *shem*, thrice with (sanctuary) *har* ; twice with *zekher* ; once each with *hekhal*, *sheme*, *meqom* (= sanctuary), *kisse'*, *me'on* (heaven), *debar* and *zeroa'* ; and twice of the sanctuary : lxxviii. 54 (" border of his sanctuary ") and cii. 20 (" height of his sanctuary "). *Beqodsho* three times including cl. 1, " in his sanctuary," and lx. 8 and cviii. 8, " God has spoken in his holiness," *i.e.*, a quasi-oath-formula ; cf. *qodshi* above. But the sentence could refer to the giving of a cultic oracle in the sanctuary : " God has spoken in his sanctuary." *Leqodsho* once : " Judah became his sanctuary " (cxiv. 2). The noun is used with one or two exceptions in connexion with the sanctuary, and means the sanctuary when it is not merely a genitive of quality.

Reference should also be made to Pss. xx. and xxi.[41] which describe a king going to combat, and returning therefrom ; with references to *'oz* in xxi. 2, " O Yahweh, in thy strength the king shall rejoice," and, again in xxi. 14, " Arise, Yahweh, in thy strength " (*rumah YHWH b*ᵉ*uzzekha*). Thus Ps. xxi. requires a reference to the triumphant Ark for its full understanding.

It is possible then to find references to the Ark in the Psalter under the word *'oz* as well as in other places where the Ark may be implied without being mentioned, as in Ps. xxiv.

There are at least four other clues which, though they may not be investigated here, nevertheless deserve mention :

(*a*) Reminiscences of the Song of the Ark.

In the Song of the Ark in Num. x. 35–36, the Ark is bidden : " Arise, O Yahweh " (*qumah YHWH*) ; " Return, O Yahweh " (*shubah YHWH*).

Is it then not possible that if *qumah YHWH* refers to the Ark in Numbers, some of the six repetitions of *qumah YHWH* in the Psalms,[42] may not also refer to the Ark ? Especially when it is realized that the sixth of these references occurs in Ps. cxxxii. 8, and is addressed to Yahweh and the Ark of his strength. Similarly the two references *qumah* ᵉ*lohim*.[43]

Is it not equally possible, if *shubah YHWH* in Num. refers to the Ark, that some of the three occurrences of the phrase in the Psalms also refer to the Ark ?[44] The *qumah* and *shubah* formulae occur together in vii. 7–8.

(*b*) In 2 Sam. vi., the story of the bringing of the Ark to Jerusalem, the phrase " before the ark " in *v*. 4 is followed by the phrase " before Yahweh " in *v*. 5. The phrases mean exactly the same thing in this context.[45] Similarly in *vv*. 14, 16, 17 and 21 (*bis*) " before Yahweh " can only mean " in the presence of," " in front of," the Ark.

It is therefore reasonable to ask whether the words " before Yahweh," especially when they occur in cultic contexts, do not presuppose the Ark ? " Before Yahweh " appears some 225

[41] Cf. A. R. Johnson, *op. cit.*, pp. 122–4.
[42] Pss. iii. 8, vii. 7, ix. 20, x. 12, xvii. 13, cxxxii. 8 ; and cf. xliv. 27 and xxxv. 2. For another interpretation of the use of some of these passages for a Risen God, see Widengren, *op. cit.*, p. 68.
[43] lxxiv. 22, lxxxii. 8.
[44] vi. 5, xc. 13 ; and cf. vii. 8, lxxx. 15.
[45] Cf. also 2 Sam. vi. 9. Similar identifications of Yahweh and the Ark may be found in the following passages : Josh. vi. cf. *vv*. 6 and 8 ; cf. Ex. xxx. 6 and xxx. 8.

times in the Old Testament and in many places it does not, and cannot, have anything to do with the Ark. On the other hand in the narratives [46] and laws of the Ark,[47] the phrase is obviously related to the Ark. " Before Yahweh " in the Psalms comes only five times and " before the king, Yahweh " once in xcviii. 6. Of these five references, it has been claimed that xcvi. 6 already conceals a reference to the Ark, so that " before Yahweh " and " he has come " in xcvi. 13 cover the further references to the Ark in the same Psalm. In turn the interpretation of xcvi. 13 controls that of xcviii. 9 (and cf. *v.* 6). References to the Ark are equally possible in xcv. 6, as the " object " of adoration, and in cxvi. 9, describing the king's place in front of the Ark in a procession. The reference in cii. 1 is too general for a decision.

Similarly *liph‘ne* (*ha*)*’elohim* appears some seventeen times in the Old Testament including Pss. lvi. 14, lxi. 8 and lxiii. 4, all three being cultic contexts, and the context of lxiii. 5 making a reference to the Ark almost certain. The third and fourth clues relate to the use of the words " glory " and " face," but consideration of these is not possible within the space afforded here.

It is a high privilege indeed to offer this essay in thankfulness and appreciation of the learning and humanity and friendship of this former President of the British Society for Old Testament Study, and now the present-day doyen of British Old Testament scholars, who has contributed so much to the understanding of the Bible and the thought and worship of ancient Israel, and who has been so constant in his encouragement of the following generations of students.

[46] *E.g.*, Num. x. 33 ff., Num. xiv. 44, Josh., *passim*, 1 Sam. iv. 1–vii. 1 and 2 Sam. vi., xi., xv., and 1 Kings viii.

[47] *E.g.*, Ex. xxv. 10–22=xxxvii. 1–9, and Deut. x.

SACRED NUMBERS AND ROUND FIGURES

By G. R. DRIVER

THE figures making up the chronological " prophecies " in *Daniel*
have long given trouble, but an almost forgotten pamphlet of
Cornill [1] offers a reasonable solution of most of them ; much of
his exposition, however, is so obscurely expressed and one or two
points are so doubtful that a fresh statement, as brief and lucid
as possible, seems desirable. [2]

I

Jeremiah had foretold a state of desolation and ruin for 70
years after the destruction of Jerusalem and the deportation of
the Jews to Babylon in 586 B.C.,[3] that after this period God
would fulfil his " good word " to the holy city,[4] and that finally
a " new covenant " would be made and Jerusalem rebuilt.[5]

These 70 years began in 586 B.C. ; [6] the period, however,
defined by the author of Daniel from " the commandment to
restore and to rebuild Jerusalem " announced by Jeremiah to the
rebuilding of Jerusalem authorized in the edict which Cyrus
issued in 538 B.C., the first year of his reign, and the appointment
of Joshua son of Jehozadak as the " anointed priest," *i.e.* as the
first high-priest after the restoration in 537 B.C., was not 70 years
but " seven weeks," [7] *i.e.* seven " weeks of years " or 49 years
(586–537 B.C.).

Then " after three score and two weeks shall an anointed

---

[1] Namely *Die Siebzig Jahrwochen Daniels* (Königsberg, 1889). I am much
indebted to the Librarian of Edinburgh University for the loan of a copy of this
work, the only one which I have traced in any public library in this country,
and to the Rev. Prof. N. W. Porteous for having arranged the loan.

[2] I must also express my thanks to the Rev. Dr. N. H. Snaith and Mr. G.
Yates for checking a number of calculations for me, and making several suggestions
which I have incorporated in the text.

[3] Jer. xxv. 11.

[4] Jer. xxix. 10.

[5] Jer. xxxi. 31, 38.

[6] Thiele, *Mysterious Numbers of the Hebrew Kings*, 163–4.

[7] Dan. ix. 25.

one, though innocent, be cut off " ; [8] this would be Onias III, the last but one high-priest of the Zadokite line prescribed by Ezekiel, murdered in 171 B.C., *i.e.*, 62 " weeks (of years) " = 434 years after the restoration of Jerusalem in 538 B.C. This calculation, however, is incorrect. The error seems to be due to having incorrectly taken 605–4 B.C., the year of Nebuchadnezzar's accession, as the starting point ; [9] for 434 years from that date come to 170 B.C., which is near enough to the murder of Onias III for the purpose. The figure, however, must be wrong ; for the author of *Daniel* clearly intends the 7 " weeks " = 49 years mentioned in *v.* 25 to precede and to be additional to the 62 " weeks " = 434 years of *v.* 26.

Then " the people of the prince that shall come shall destroy the city and the sanctuary . . . ; and he shall enter into a firm agreement with the chief men for one week, and in the midst of the week he shall put an end to sacrifice and oblation " ; [10] this prince would be Antiochus IV, who overran Palestine and after coming to an agreement with the " chief men (*hārabbîm*)," *i.e.*, various apostate Jewish leaders, entered Jerusalem, suspended the services in the Temple and desecrated the altar on 25 Kislew 168 B.C.[11] This outrage was committed " in the midst of the week," [12] *i.e.*, approximately 3½ years after that in which Onias III had been murdered and so half-way through a " week " of 7 years. This state of affairs was to continue " even till the consummation," [13] *i.e.* for another 3½ years till the end of the " week " of 7 years in 164 B.C.

Thus the " seventy years " from 586 B.C., as foretold by Jeremiah, are treated as 70 " weeks " of years, *i.e.*, 70 × 7 = 490 years, " to finish the transgression and to make an end of sin " ; [14] they would therefore terminate, if the figures were correct, in 96 B.C. The Temple and the altar, however, were re-dedicated on 25 Kislew 165 B.C.[15] and Antiochus IV died in 164 B.C. ; and with his death the persecution of the Jews came to an end.

[8] Dan. ix. 26.
[9] Jer. xxv. 1 ; see pp. 74 f. Actually, although Nabopolassar had died in August, 605 B.C., Nebuchadnezzar being absent from the country did not ascend the throne till September, 604 B.C. (Wiseman, *Chronicles of Chaldaean Kings*, 23–8).
[10] Dan. ix. 27–28.
[11] 1 Macc. i. 54–59.
[12] Dan. ix. 27.
[13] Dan. ix. 2.
[14] Dan. ix. 24.
[15] 1 Macc. iv. 52–53.

The error becomes patent when the figures are tabulated :

(i) 586–537 B.C. = 7 " weeks " of years = 49 years
(ii) 538/7–171 B.C. = 62 " weeks " of years = 434 years (!)
(iii) 171–164 B.C. = 1 " week " of years = 7 years
  ─   ───────────────
              70 " weeks " of years = 490 years

I. 7 " weeks " = 49 years
   reckoned from " the word of the
   Lord to Jeremiah " [16] or " the going
   forth of the commandment to
   restore and rebuild Jerusalem " [17]
   in   .   .   .   .   .   . 586 B.C.
   till the appearance of " an anointed
   one, a prince," [18] i.e. Cyrus, who
   issued an edict allowing the Jews to
   return and restore Jerusalem and
   rebuild the Temple in his 1st year [19]
   in   .   .   .   .   .   . 538/7 B.C.
                                          ───────────
                            i.e.,   49 years ;

II. 62 " weeks " = 434 years
    reckoned from the issuing of the
    same edict in   .   .   .   . 538 B.C.
    until " an anointed one shall be cut
    off without trial," [20] i.e. until Onias
    III was murdered in   .   .   . 171 B.C.
                                          ───────────
                    i.e., (not 434 but)   367 years ;

III. 1 " week " = 7 years divided into
        3 periods
    (i) reckoned from the murder of Onias
        III in (the summer of)   .   . 171 B.C.
        until " the prince of the people shall
        come and destroy the city and the

[16] Dan. ix. 2.   [18] Isa. xlv. 1.
[17] Dan. ix. 25.   [19] Ezr. i. 1–4.
          [20] Dan. ix. 26.

sanctuary," [21] *i.e.*, until Antiochus IV desecrated the Temple and the altar in the winter of . . .	168 B.C.	
		3½ years ;
(ii) from the desecration of the Temple and the cessation of " the sacrifice and the oblation in the midst of the week " in the winter of . .	168 B.C.	
till the Maccabaean victories, the re-dedication of the Temple and the altar in the winter of . . .	165 B.C.	
		3 years ;
(iii) from the re-dedication of Temple and altar in the winter of . .	165 B.C.	
until " the consummation and that which shall be determined shall be poured upon the author of the desolation," [22] *i.e.* until Antiochus perished in the summer of . .	164 B.C.	
		½ year
	i.e.,	7 years

Briefly, I : the figures are correct and call for no comment beyond remarking that Jeremiah's 70 years have become $(7 \times 7 =)$ 49 years ; II : the total figure is patently incorrect, being $(7 \times 62 =)$ 434 instead of 367 years ; [23] III : the figures are correct, although " the midst of the week " only approximates to the middle point of the 7 years in which it falls.

II

Hebrew and Jewish chronology from the earliest times down to the destruction of Jerusalem in A.D. 70 was based not so much on scientific principles as on traditional lists which were often defective or corrupt. The reasons why the records were so

---

[21] Dan. ix. 26.   [22] Dan. ix. 27.   [23] See p. 72.

imperfect were several : lack of exact information, damage to manuscripts and corruption of the text in the course of transmission and the misreading or misunderstanding of symbols and ciphers for numbers.[24] Consequently scribes and even serious historians were tempted to make good the gaps as best they could by conjecture. In this work they were obsessed with several preconceptions, which could but have a disastrous effect on the accuracy of the figures which they transmitted to posterity.

The first of these preconceptions was the value of " sacred " numbers. The principles underlying the choice of these numbers rested on the facts of nature and of life. For the pre-exilic period the basic figures were 12 and 40. The latter represents half the greatest number of years which a man could hope to live [25] and which indeed the ancient Persians were thought to live,[26] his whole working life or an entire generation of men ; [27] this was taken as the length of the desert wanderings [28] and the desolation of Egypt,[29] and as the average for the tenure of the high-priestly office, although it was obviously unduly high. Similarly, the former is the number of the stations of the moon and of the months of the year ; it therefore easily comes to be regarded as a " sacred " number.[30] With the exile different numbers came into use ; these were 70, 10, and 7. The first represents the normal span of a man's life, as both the Psalmist [31] and Solon [32] say. The second has equally significant associations, notably as the approximate difference in the number of the days in the solar and lunar years as observed by the ancient Hebrews ; also, the Egyptians had a week of 10 days and the Greeks divided the month into equal periods of 10 days, the lamb for the Passover was selected on the 10th day of Nisan [33] and the day of Atonement fell on the 10th day of the 7th month (Tishri) [34] and the commandments

---

[24] Driver in *Textus*, I, 125–8.
[25] Ps. xc. 10 (fourscore years).
[26] Herodotus *Histories*, III, xxii. 3–xxiii. 1, where, however, the Ethiopians, capable of bending a bow beyond the strength of ordinary men, are said to reach 120 years (cf. Gen. vi. 3).
[27] Ps. xcv. 10.
[28] *E.g.*, Amos ii. 10 ; v. 25 (see G. A. Cooke, *Ezekiel*, 53).
[29] Ezek. xxix. 12–13.
[30] König in Hastings' *Dictionary of the Bible*, III, 563–4.
[31] Ps. xc. 10 (threescore years).
[32] Herodotus, *Histories*, I, xxxii. 2.
[33] Ex. xii. 3.
[34] Lev. xxiii. 27, xxv. 9.

were known as the "ten words of the Law." [35] A "sacred" character would thus be stamped on this number. Further, the Hebrew numerical system was decimal, presumably because of the 10 fingers of the hands, which made it a mathematically convenient number.[36] The third, too, had astronomical authority; it was the number of the planets and of several groups of stars as known to ancient observers, of the phases of the moon and of the days of the week, of which traces lingered also in the Assyro-Babylonian calendar.[37] Thus it too easily imposed itself on the imagination as "sacred." [38] Both 7 and 70 were also commonly employed in the Old as in the New Testament as round or typical figures, the former for small and the latter for large numbers,[39] and eventually 7 and multiples of 7 prevailed. So also the Covenanters at Qumrân adopted them, for example in having 7 principal feasts each following the other at intervals of 7 weeks in their liturgical calendar,[40] in recognizing 7 sovereign angels and reciting 7 angelic blessings on the Sabbath, called the "seven words of majesty" or "wonder." [41] The "sacred" associations of these last numbers, having proved themselves irresistible to apocalyptists and theologians, passed from them even to sober historians.

The basis on which the length of the exile as announced in advance by the prophets must have been reckoned now becomes clear. Jeremiah put it at 70 years [42] as the normal span of a man's life in order to indicate that no one alive at the time, not even the youngest child carried in the arms, might expect or be expected ever to come back. Ezekiel chose 40 years,[43] which was the length of a generation, implying thereby that none of the contemporary generation would live to see the restoration ; and he assigned the same number of years, obviously for the same reason, to the anticipated desolation of Egypt.[44]

Numerous examples of simplifying numbers by adapting

---

[35] Ex. xx. 2.
[36] König, *ibid.*, 564.
[37] Langdon, *Babylonian Menologies and the Semitic Calendar*, 73, 83–7.
[38] König, *ibid.*, 562–3.
[39] Cf. van Goudoever, *Biblical Calendars*, 243–50, where numerous instances of "sacred" numbers in the Bible are collected.
[40] Milik *ap.* Vermès, *Scrolls in English*, 44.
[41] Strugnell in *Vetus Testamentum, Supplementum*, VII, 322–3.
[42] Jer. xxv. 12, xxix. 10 ; cf. 2 Chron. xxxvi. 20–1.
[43] Ez. iv. 6.
[44] Ez. xxix. 11–14.

them to the nearest multiple of one or other of these " sacred "
numbers can be found in sober historical works ; and the
transition from pre-exilic to post-exilic practice is seen when
both St. Paul and Eusebius arbitrarily convert the scriptural
and therefore traditional 480 (40 × 12) into 490 (70 × 7) years
for the length of time from the departure out of Egypt to the
establishment of the kingdom under David.[45] The process is
finally reduced to absurdity when Josephus changes the duration
of the temple at On (170 B.C.–A.D. 73), in order to obtain multiples
of 7, from 243 to 343 (7 × 7 × 7) years.[46]

Caution, however, must be observed before dismissing all
multiples of seven as artificial or fictitious ; for they may be
factual. For example, Egypt was ruled by the French-sponsored
dynasty of Mehemet Ali for 70 years (A.D. 1805–75) and then
passed under Franco-British and eventually sole British control
for another 70 years (A.D. 1875–1945).

The second preconception was the value of gêmaṭr^{e}yâ, that
is the use of the sum of the numerical value of the letters of the
alphabet spelling a word, to obtain or convey information. The
beginnings of this practice have been traced to the Old Testament,[47] and examples of it can be found both in the Scrolls and
in the New Testament, where the arrangement of the genealogy
at the beginning of the first Gospel [48] and the number of the beast
are evidence of its popularity,[49] and it becomes extremely
common in Rabbinic literature. Its only result was to put
chronology, when it was applied to it, hopelessly out of gear.

Four other causes of chronological uncertainty may here be
mentioned. The first is the lack of any clearly defined starting
point, which is reckoned backwards on figures which will often
have been dubious or conjectural. The second is that the New
Year may be reckoned either from the spring or from the autumn
according to the calendar, the sacred or the secular, which is
being used ; and the date of the ancient New Year on either
method of reckoning diverges by approximately 3 months from
that of the modern calendar. The third is the doubt whether
the year in any given calculation is lunar or lunisolar or solar.

[45] See pp. 70 f.
[46] In *War*, VII, x. 4, § 436 (see Eisler *ap.* Thackeray, *Josephus* [Loeb], III,
627).
[47] See pp. 83 f., 86f.
[48] See p. 84.
[49] Rev. xiii. 18.

The fourth is the difficulty of discovering whether the number of years for which a man has held office is calculated from the date of his entering on it or from the following New Year's Day. No ancient writer explains which method he is adopting in either of these cases. The fifth is the uncertainty whether the first and last terms in a calculation are included or excluded. For example, that Jesus implied 4 months between sowing and harvest [50] and that certain Rabbis in the following century counted 6 months from seed-time to harvest [51] involved no essential discrepancy ; these included both the first and the last months (Marcheswan, Kislew, Tebet, Shebat, Adar, Nisan), while Jesus counted only the 4 intervening months (Kislew, Tebet, Shebat, Adar).[52] The same difficulty arises in calculating the number of years between any two given dates ; for either method, inclusive or exclusive of the first and last years, may be employed.

The chronology of Hebrew or Israelite history is not the subject of the present study ; but something must be said about it because some, if not all, of these principles begin to operate in this period and continue to have considerable influence even in the exilic and post-exilic periods down to the end of the Second Commonwealth.

The author of *Kings* assigns 480 years from the departure out of Egypt to the building of the temple in the 4th year of Solomon ; [53] and the number of the years of the kings of Judah from that event to its destruction in 586 B.C., when added up, is 430 years, which with 50 years for the Exile also amounts to 480 (40×12) years.[54] This coincidence of 480 years for both periods is as surprising as it is unlikely ; and not only can the method by which this sum is reached be shown to be entirely artificial, but also other historians give different figures.[55]

The basis of the calculation is the number of the high-priests in the two periods and the length of the tenure of office of the individual priests ; these are both assumed to have been practically the same in each period. The priests of the first

---

[50] Jn. iv. 35.
[51] P. Talmud, *Ta'anith*, i. 64a.
[52] Cf. Strack and Billerbeck, *Kommentar zum Neuen Testament*, II, 439–40 ; and Galling, *Biblisches Reallexikon*, 3–4 (showing how the dates for agricultural operations vary with the altitude of the districts concerned).
[53] 1 Kings vi. 1.
[54] See pp. 71, 75 ; cf. Curtis in Hastings' *Dictionary of the Bible*, I, 403.
[55] See pp. 70 f., 85 f.

period are given as 12 (Aaron, Eleazar, Phinehas, Abishua, Bukki, Uzzi, Zerahiah, Meraioth, Amariah I, Ahitub I, Zadok I, Ahimaaz), and those of the second period are also given as 12 (Ahimaaz, Azariah I, Johanan, Azariah II, Amariah II, Ahitub II, Zadok II, Shallum, Hilkiah, Azariah III, Seraiah, Jehozadak).[56] If then the first period is reckoned at 480 years, each of the 12 high-priests will have held or will have been supposed to have held office for 40 years, although the 40 years of Ahimaaz will obviously have fallen partly in the earlier and partly in the later period so that he will not have in fact have held office for a full 40 years in either period ; clearly therefore 480 years is a round figure approximating to the supposed sum of the years of office of the 12 high-priests. Further, that 12 high-priests running can each have held office for 40 years is in itself highly improbable : and the improbability is only increased when the age at which each high-priest is likely to have succeeded to the office and the uncertainty of human life in the ancient East are taken into consideration. Not that even the kings of Israel and Judah were allowed such an average of years on the throne ; but many of them died by violence.

Doubts regarding these figures become insistent when those found in other ancient authorities are considered. For example, Josephus reckons now 592 and now 612 years from the departure out of Egypt to the building of Solomon's temple [57] and 477 years from David to Nebuchadrezzar ; [58] and he assigns 13 high-priests to the earlier and 18 to the later period.[59] These, like other, discrepancies are most easily explained by assuming that he is taking over figures which he has found in his sources without critically examining them ; [60] but he will certainly not have been in a position to undertake such a task. These divergent figures also suggest that the author(s) or compiler(s) of *Kings* may have omitted any high-priest whose term of office was brief or unimportant in order to obtain a round or sacred number of years. St. Paul [61] estimates the time from the departure out of Egypt to the beginning of David's reign at $40+450=490$ (7×70) years ;

        [56] I Chron. v. 29–41 [vi. 3–15] ; see Curtis, *Chronicles*, 128–9.
        [57] In *Antiquities*, VIII, iii. 1, § 1 (592 years) and XX, x. 1, § 230 (612 years) ; cf. *Contra Apionem*, II, ii. 19.
        [58] In *War*, VI, x. 1, § 439.
        [59] In *Antiquities*, XX, x. 1, § 230.
        [60] Cf. Niese in *Hermes*, XXVIII, 194–229.
        [61] In Acts xiii. 17–22.

and Eusebius,[62] whose figures for the reigns of the kings of Judah, adapted from the Old Testament, allow 430 years from the commencement of the building of the First Temple to its destruction, says that " after the number of 70 years Cyrus became king of Persia and remitted the captivity of Judah and allowed those who wished to go back to their own land and to raise up the temple again," where he treats the founding of the Second Temple in 536 B.C. as identical or simultaneous with its dedication in 516 B.C. and so is able to make the period from the founding of the First Temple to the completion of the Second Temple one of 490 (7 × 70) years.[63]

Another curious point is this : Solomon spent 7 years on the building of the temple and 13 on that of " his own house," *i.e.* 20 years on these two operations, and then consecrated the buildings ; [64] and similarly the number of years from the founding of Zerubbabel's temple in 536 B.C. to its dedication in 516 B.C. was also 20 years. Have the figures of the former period, of which no direct knowledge may have been available, been adapted to those of the latter, which will have been reasonably certain ?

An equally artificial and improbable scheme was constructed for the period of the exile onwards ; for the same number of high-priests was reckoned from the captivity in 586 B.C. to the virtual extinction of the Zadokite line with the murder of Onias III in 171 B.C., namely 12 (Jozadak, Jeshua, Joiakim, Eliashib, Joiada, Jonathan, Jaddua, Onias I, Simon I, Onias II, Simon II, Onias III).[65] Ancient historians, however, variously estimated the number of years (415) in this period ; for example, Josephus (writing in the first century A.D.) counted 15 high-priests to whom he would seem to have assigned 415/6 years [66] and R. Jôsê ben Ḥalaftâ (who lived in the second century A.D.) made it, in accordance with his " reduced chronology " for the Persian age, only 261 years.[67]

Here again the rough average for the high-priestly tenure of

---

[62] In *Praeparatio Evangelica*, X, xiv. 4–5 (503*b–c*).

[63] Actually, according to the Biblical figures, the period from the founding of the First Temple to that of the Second Temple was 480 years (Curtis *ap.* Hastings' *Dictionary of the Bible* I, 403).

[64] 1 Kings, vi. 38–vii. 1, ix. 10.

[65] Ezr. iii. 2 ; v. 2 ; Nehem. xi. 10–11 ; Josephus *Antiquities*, XI. viii. 7, § 347 ; XII, ii. 5, § 43 and iv. 1, § 157 (see Cornill, *op. cit.*, 16–18).

[66] Cf. *Antiquities*, X, viii. 6, §§ 152–3 and XX, x. 2, § 23.

[67] Neubauer, *op. cit.*, II, p. 66, l. 2 (*Sēder 'Ôlām Rabbâ* § 30).

office, whether 35 or even 21 years, is surprisingly high ; and the total figures for the period, if rightly deduced, are both multiples of 7, which also raise suspicions.

The number of years in the middle part of the second group of figures in *Daniel*, namely in 538–171 B.C., as set out above, is wrong ; it is not 434 but 367 and is therefore 67 in excess of the true figure. The desire to obtain a multiple of 7 is the reason for this incorrect figure of 434 (62 × 7) years in keeping with the 49 (7 × 7) years in the first and the simple 7 years in the third group.[68]

The question must then be asked : why has the writer not taken one of the multiples of 7 nearest to the true figure (367), either 364 (52 × 7) or 371 (53 × 7) years ? Why has he made the period 62 instead of 52 or 53 " weeks " of years ? The answer, summarized, is that he has been led or misled into doing so partly by lack of historical and chronological information and partly by the need to bring this figure into harmony with other multiples of 7 in other parts, as well as in the entire length, of the period ; for he is an apocalyptist to whom 7 as an astronomical figure has a mystical importance [69] and as such may be legitimately invoked to make good any deficiencies in his knowledge.

Jewish records for the exile and the Second Commonwealth were seriously defective, especially for the earlier period. Only 4 out of 10 Persian kings were known from the Old Testament [70] and, even if the list of the high-priests was complete, the length of time for which any individual person held office was often unknown ; consequently the historian had few if any direct means of controlling the figures from the end of the kingdom in 586 B.C. to the beginning of the Seleucid era in 312 B.C.[71] In the later period the errors were not so serious, but even in it Jewish historians often found gaps in the records. Strict chronological accuracy was hardly possible before the introduction of the Julian calendar in 46 B.C. in Rome and the publication of the Ptolemaic " Canon of Kings " *c.* A.D. 140 in Egypt ; and, even if the information of the Canon was available in Egypt before Ptolemy's time,[72] it would hardly have been accessible to Jewish writers in

---

[68] See. pp. 62 ff.
[69] See p. 67.
[70] Cornill, *Siebzig Jahrwochen Daniels*, 14–15.
[71] Neubauer, *op. cit.*, p. 66, l. 4 (*Sēder 'Ōlām Rabbâ*, § 30).
[72] Eisler in *Occident and Orient*, 117.

Palestine. Moreover, long after the introduction of these innovations astonishing blunders continued to be made : *e.g.*, Julius Africanus (*c.* A.D. 160–240) fixed the return of the Jews from the captivity in 559 B.C., the year in which Cyrus ascended the Persian throne, by mistake for 538 B.C., that in which he was proclaimed king of Babylon.[73]

The author of *Daniel* too is not alone in his chronological miscalculations.[74] For example, the hellenized Jewish historian Demetrius in the third century B.C. estimated the period from the captivity of the northern tribes (723/22 B.C.) to the accession of Ptolemy IV (222 B.C.) at 573 instead of 500 years, *i.e.*, 73 years too many. Josephus, too, puts the number of years from the return from the exile (538 B.C.) to the accession of King Antiochus V (164 B.C.) at 434 instead of 374 years, *i.e.*, 60 years too many, that from the same event to the accession of the high-priest Aristobulus I (105/04 B.C.) at 481 instead of 433 years, *i.e.* 48 years too many, and that from the foundation of Zerubbabel's temple in the second year of Cyrus (537–36 B.C.) to the destruction of Jerusalem by Titus (A.D. 70) at 639 instead of 607/6 years, *i.e.* 32/3 years too many.[75]

These errors range from 73 to 32 years in excess of the true figure. An error of 67 years therefore in *Daniel* falls well within these margins and may be accepted as conforming reasonably well to the " long chronology " of the period. Further, the error in *Daniel* involved in reckoning 538–171 B.C. at 62 " weeks " of years, namely 434 (*i.e.*, 62 × 7) instead of 367 years is almost the same as that which Josephus makes in reckoning 538–164 B.C. at 434 (*i.e.*, 62 × 7) years instead of 374 years.[76] The former is confessedly using " week " as a round figure for a period of 7 years, while the latter is evidently following the same scheme ; and indeed he once gives a hint, though in a different context, that he is acquainted with *Daniel's* chronology.[77]

The figures for the period under review in the work commonly ascribed to R. Jôsê are also seriously aberrant and reflect a " short chronology," as shown in the following table (where the true figures are added in square brackets) :

---

[73] Eusebius *Praep. Evang.*, x. 10 (488b–c).
[74] Schürer, *Geschichte des Jüdischen Volkes*[3], III, 189–90 and Driver, *Daniel*, 147.
[75] Cf. Destinou, *Chronologie des Josephus*, 30–32.
[76] See. p. 85.
[77] In *Antiquities*, XII, vii. 6, § 322.

(i) Semi-exile (3/4 Jehoiakim–11 Zedekiah, *i.e.* 604–586 B.C. .   .   .   .   18 ⎫
Exile (586–538 B.C.)   .   .   .   .   52 ⎬ years

70 years

(ii) Persian period (538–331 B.C.) .   .   34[207] ⎫
Greek period (331–323 B.C.   6[8] ⎫
Seleucid period (322–166   ⎬   180[165]
B.C.) .   .   .   .   174[157] ⎭   ⎬ years
Hasmonaean age (166–63 B.C.) ⎫   .   103[129]
Roman occupation (63–37 B.C.) ⎭   103[129]
Herodian age (37 B.C.–A.D. 70)   .   103[107] ⎭

420[608] years [78]

Thus the period from the exile to the destruction of Jerusalem
in A.D. 70 is reckoned at 490 (70×7) years and that from the
foundation of Zerubbabel's temple to its destruction in that
year at 420 (60×7) years ; [79] both these numbers are multiples
of 7, and both are wrong.

These results are obtained by the following devices.[80]

The starting point [81] is Daniel's statement that " I understand
by the books the number of the years, whereof the word of the
Lord came to the prophet Jeremiah,[82] for the accomplishing of
the desolations of Jerusalem, even seventy years," [83] combined
with Gabriel's statement that " seventy weeks are decreed upon
thy people and upon thy holy city to finish transgression and to
make an end of sins and to make reconciliation for iniquity [84]
and to bring in everlasting righteousness and to seal up vision
and prophecy and to anoint a most holy place." [85] These
" seventy weeks (*sc.* of years)," *i.e.* (7×70) = 490 years, are made
to extend from the exile to the destruction of the Second Temple

[78] Neubauer, *op. cit.*, II, p. 66, ll. 1–3 (*Seder 'Ôlām Rabbâ* § 30).

[79] *Ibid.*, p. 63, ll. 24–8 (*Sēder 'Ôlām Rabbâ*, § 28), where 420 as a *varia lectio*
for 410 must be preferred.

[80] Cf. Loeb in *Revue des Études Juives*, XVII, 247–54, and XIX, 202–6.

[81] Neubauer, *op. cit.*, p. 64, ll. 24–5 (§ 29).

[82] Jer. xxv. 12, xxix. 10.

[83] Dan. ix. 2.

[84] Cf. Lev. xxvi. 18–24, 2 Chron. xxxvi. 20–21.

[85] Dan. ix. 24.

(586 B.C.–A.D. 70) ; and, if the 70 years of " desolations," *i.e.* of exile, are deducted from them, they leave 420 (60 × 7) years for this temple (538 B.C.–A.D. 70). Both figures are wrong ; the first ought to be 656 and the second 608 years. Gabriel, however, goes on to speak of another " seven weeks," *i.e.* 49 years, as part of the following period [86] ; this figure is significant, since 49/48 rather than 70 years are the true duration of the exile (586–538 B.C.), which R. Jôsê estimates at 52 years.[87] Thus (7 × 3 =) 21 years have fallen out of the account ; but they can be approximately recovered if the exile is calculated from the rebellion in the 3rd or 4th year of Jehoiakim (608–597 B.C.), when Nebuchadrezzar invaded Judah, entered Jerusalem and carried off some of the treasures of the temple.[88] Jehoiakim lived another 8 years, Jehoiakin who succeeded him reigned for only 3 months, and Jerusalem was finally taken and the temple destroyed in his successor Zedekiah's 11th year. Accordingly, the time from the pillaging of the temple in Jehoiakim's 3rd or 4th year to its destruction and the deportation of the king and the principal inhabitants of the city, was approximately 18 years. Thus these 18 years (604–586 B.C.), passed under constant threat of invasion and deportation, seem to have been regarded as a period of semi-exile ; and, if the 52 years of the true exile as calculated by R. Jôsê are added to them, the duration of the " desolations " will come to 70 years.

If the 18 years of semi-exile are raised to 20 as the nearest round figure and these 20 years are deducted from the 430 years assigned to the kings of Judah,[89] the First Temple will have stood for 410 years ; and the addition of the 70 years of " desolations " makes the period from it to the Second Temple 480 years.[90]

R. Jôsê allows only 34 years for the Persian period (538–331 B.C.) in consequence of the lack of any detailed information about it. This number seems to have been obtained by taking the last year of each of the four Persian kings mentioned in the Old Testament and assuming it to be the last of their respective reigns. The figures are the following :

[86] Dan. ix. 25.
[87] Neubauer *op. cit.*, II, p. 64, l. 25–p. 65, l. 1 (*Sēder 'Ôlām Rabbâ*, § 29) and p. 65, ll. 14–15 (*Seder 'Ôlām Rabbâ*, § 30, where 52 as *varia lectio* for 250 as given in the text must be accepted).
[88] 2 Kings xxiv. 1–2 = 2 Chron. xxxvi. 6–7.
[89] See p. 69.
[90] Loeb *ibid.*, XIX, 203–5.

Cyrus, 1st year : [91] number of full years   .   .   0 ⎫
Darius, 4th year : [92] number of full years   .   .   3 ⎪
Ahasuerus (Xerxes), 3rd year : [93] number of full   ⎬ years
years .   .   .   .   2 ⎪
Artaxerxes, 32nd year : [94] number of full years   .   31 ⎭

                                    36   years,

if fractions of years may be left out of the calculation.

The number of these years was then reduced from 36 to 34 and " the six years of the Greek reign in Elam," *i.e.*, those from 330 B.C. (when Darius III was murdered) to 324 B.C. (when Alexander the Great re-entered Babylon), which were generally disregarded by Jewish writers,[95] were added to them so as to make 40 years ; thus once again a round number was obtained. This was required in order to make the combined Greek and Seleucid periods last for 180 years, which were necessary for bringing the duration of the rest of the period to the number of years proper to the preimposed scheme.

Another chronological work attains almost the same result by assigning 12 years to Alexander the Great,[96] *i.e.*, from 335/4 B.C. to 323 B.C., and 175 years to the Seleucid period ; [97] but it produces this result only by adding those from 336 B.C. (when he mounted the Macedonian throne) to 330 B.C. (when he became king of Babylon) and by correspondingly but unduly reducing the length of the Seleucid age.

The Seleucid era was held by the Jews to have begun in 312 B.C.,[98] which is 382 years before A.D. 70. These 382 years, however, were reduced to the nearest round figure, namely 380 years, so that exactly 1000 years could be counted from the departure out of Egypt to the Seleucid era ; for the Exodus was dated in A.M. 2448 and the beginning of the Seleucid era in A.M. 3448.[99] Consequently the destruction of the Temple, being

[91] Ezr. i. 1.
[92] Zech. vii. 1.
[93] Est. i. 2–3.
[94] Nehem. v. 14, xiii. 6.
[95] B. Talmud, '*Abodah Zarah*, 9b–10a.
[96] Neubauer, *op. cit.*, II, p. 71, l. 6 (*Sēder 'Ôlām Zûṭâ* A).
[97] *Ibid.*, l. 13.
[98] See p. 88.
[99] Neubauer, *op. cit.*, (*Sēder 'Ôlām Zûṭâ* A) II, p. 69, ll. 14–15 and p. 71, ll. 3–5, where 3448 is a correct *varia lectio* for 3404.

dated 380 years after this last event, was generally held to have
taken place in A.M. 3828,[100] namely A.D. 68 instead of A.D. 70.[101]

R. Jôsê divides the remaining years, from the end of the
Seleucid rule and the outbreak of the Maccabaean Revolt in
167/6 B.C. to the destruction of Jerusalem in A.D. 68 (70), between
the Hasmonaean and the Herodian ages ; but he reckons them far
otherwise than they are properly counted ; for he assigns 103
instead of 129 to the former and another 103 instead of 107
years to the latter period, thus assigning 206 instead of 236 years
to the combined periods. He obtains this result by taking the
Hasmonaean age from 166 B.C. down to 35 B.C., when the
last Hasmonaean high-priest Aristobulus III was drowned, and
discounting the 26 years of the Roman occupation of Palestine
(63–37 B.C.) ; such an omission, however, is in accord with the
practice of other Oriental historians, who commonly leave out
anything discreditable from their annals. He then counts the
103 years of the Herodian age from that year, namely 35 B.C.,
to A.D. 68, to which he assigns the destruction of Jerusalem by
the Romans, as already explained.[102]

The whole chronology of the exile and the Second Commonwealth is thus explicable on four assumptions : (i) the probable
or possible expectation of life or the length of a generation or of
a man's working life ; (ii) the use of " sacred " numbers derived
ultimately from astronomical observations as round numbers ;
(iii) recourse to similarly based Biblical figures when the records
for the period are defective ; and (iv) occasionally the deliberate
omission of unimportant persons or the suppression of an unfavourable episode.

III

The period during which " the sanctuary and the host (*i.e.*,
the Israelite army) " shall be " trodden underfoot " is said to be
" unto two thousand and three hundred evenings mornings ;
then the sanctuary shall be cleansed."

Elsewhere the persecution is said to be going to last for 3½

---

[100] *Ibid.*, I (*Sēder 'Ôlām Zûṭâ*), p. 170, ll. 18–20, and II (*Sēder 'Ôlām Zûṭâ* B),
p. 75, ll. 11–12.
[101] Loeb, *ibid.*, 205.
[102] See Loeb, *ibid.*, 205–6.

years ; but the number of days in this period will vary according to the calendar used.[103]

Three different years were recognized by ancient chronologists, namely

> the lunar year of   354 days
> the lunisolar year of 360 days
> and the solar year of 364/5 days

(if fractions of days may be omitted).

In the Old Testament some traces of a lunar year can be detected, but the proper Jewish year in it was solar ; and this last is found also in several apocryphal works, notably *I Enoch* and *Jubilees* and in the Scrolls from Qumrân. The lunar year, too, was regarded as something old and sacred and was therefore preserved in pious circles by way of protest against the Hellenistic (*i.e.*, profane) lunisolar year. Correction must have been effected by intercalation, as it was by the Babylonians, but the Old Testament contains no reference (or at any rate no clear reference) to the practice. It is known, however, to have been adopted in the post-Biblical period, when an empirically determined month was intercalated as often as the increasing discrepancy made it necessary ; but nothing is known of its actual incidence.

Several attempts were made in antiquity to rectify the obvious deficiency of the lunar year.[104] In 432 B.C. the astronomer Meton introduced the so-called Metonic cycle ; this was a period of 19 years, of which 8 were called "hollow" as consisting of only 354 days, 4 were called "full" as consisting of 355 days, and 7 called intercalary had each 384 days. This cycle however soon proved itself defective. Callippus therefore in the following century introduced a revised system, known as the Callippic cycle, based on a period of 76 (afterwards increased by Jewish chronographers to 84) years ; of these 31 had 354 and 17 had 355 days, while 26 had 384 and 2 had 383 days, so that 48 were normal and 28 were intercalary years. This was the system current in the Syrian states from the time of Alexander the Great onwards and amongst the Jews in the Maccabaean age.

The normal Jewish year consisted of the following 12 months containing 29 and 30 days in approximate alternation :

[103] Dan. viii 13–14 ; cf. vii. 25, ix. 27, xii. 7.
[104] Cornill, *op. cit.*, 19–20.

Nisan	30	Ab	30	Kislew	30 or 29
Iyar	29	Elul	29	Tebet	29
Siwan	30	Tishri	30	Shebat	30
Tammuz	29	Marcheswan	29 or 30	Adar	29

The intercalary month, called Adar II, contained 30 days and was inserted when needed at the end of the year.

Accordingly the 3½ years in *Daniel* without intercalation would contain the following number of days :

> if lunar, 1239 days ;
> if lunisolar, 1260 days ;
> if solar, 1274 or 1277½ days

(according as the solar year is reckoned at 364 or 365 days).

None of these years amounts to 2300 days, which are nearly twice the number required.

The very plausible suggestion has therefore been made that " two thousand and three hundred evenings, mornings " means not 2300 but 1150 days ; for the burnt or whole offering was sacrificed twice every day, once in the morning and once in the evening, so that suspension for 2300 mornings and evenings would be in fact suspension for 1150 days.[105]

These 1150 days, however, cannot be equated with the number of days in 3½ years, whichever year is taken as the basis of the calculation.

Further, the exact duration of the persecution is known ; for it is stated to have lasted from the desecration of the Temple and the erection of the " abomination of desolation " against the altar on 15 Kislew 168 B.C.[106] to the re-dedication on 25 Kislew 165 B.C.,[107] namely for 3 years and 10 days. As set out below, these dates yield the following number of days :

from 15 Kislew to end of 168 B.C. . . .	103	
one intercalated month (30 days) in 168 B.C. .	30	days
167–166 B.C. (each 354 days)	708	
from beginning to 25 Kislew 165 B.C. . .	261	

$$\text{1102 days.}$$

---

[105] Cornill, *op. cit.*, 22–26 ; cf. Gk. νυχθήμερον, " day-night," for a period of twenty-four hours.
[106] I Macc. i. 41–48.
[107] I Macc. iv. 26.

This figure too cannot be equated with the 1150 days ; for these are 48 days in excess of the required number.

The figures however may be adjusted on the assumption that the *terminus a quo* is not the desecration of the Temple and the altar on 15 Kislew 168 B.C. but rather the date of the edict which Antiochus IV, having entered Jerusalem on a sabbath,[108] issued commanding the Jews to desist from offering the proper burnt offerings but to sacrifice swine and other unclean beasts.[109]

The exact date neither of the king's entry into Jerusalem nor of the edict is known ; but, if this may be assumed to have been issued 1150 days before the re-dedication of the Temple and altar on 25 Kislew 165 B.C., the following figures (calculated backwards) will give the required date :

from 27 Tishri to end of 168 B.C. . . .	151
one intercalated month (30 days) in 168 B.C. .	30
167–166 B.C. (each 354 days)	708
from beginning to 25 Kislew 165 B.C. . .	261

days

1150 days.

In other words, the edict will have been issued on 27 Tishri 168 B.C.

The only objection which has been brought against this solution of the problem is that " how long (shall be) the vision, the daily sacrifice and the transgression of desolation, his giving sanctuary and host to be trampled under foot ? "[110] seems to lay such stress on the cessation of the sacrifice and the defilement of the sanctuary that the date must have been reckoned from those events.[111]

Is this really so ? The vision too is mentioned and is indeed the first thing mentioned, and it must have been seen before the occurrence of the events which are foretold in it and in a way flow from it, and may well have been seen at the time when Antiochus entered Jerusalem, being prompted by the fact that he did so on a sabbath ; and the " trampling down " of the host, *i.e.* the Israelite host, must have been a long process, begun even before his entry into the holy city.[112] The period com-

[108] 1 Macc. ii. 44–49.
[109] Cornill, *op. cit.*, 23.
[110] Dan. viii. 13.
[111] Bevan, *Daniel*, 128–9.
[112] 1 Macc. i. 20–40 and 2 Macc. v. 11–21.

prised in the 1150 days will then have been the whole period of the vision, not merely that of its actual fulfilment.

The $3\frac{1}{2}$ years however still remain unexplained.

In this connexion the numbers also in the statements that (i) " from the time that the daily sacrifice shall be abolished and the abomination of desolation set up shall be a thousand two hundred and ninety days " and (ii) " blessed is he that waiteth and cometh to the thousand and three hundred and five and thirty days " namely " till the end " [113] must be considered.

These 1290 days run from the suspension of the sacrifices on 15 Kislew 168 B.C.[114] to the end, which is generally assumed to have been when Antiochus IV died in 164 B.C. ; [115] the exact date of his death is not recorded but it has been put on the strength of these figures (1290 days after 15 Kislew 165 B.C.) on 6 Siwan 164 B.C.,[116] according to the following calculation :

from 15 Kislew to end of 168 B.C. . . .	103	
one intercalated month of 30 days (in 168 B.C.) .	30	
167–165 B.C. (each of 354 days) . . .	1062	days
one intercalated month of 30 days (in 165 B.C.) .	30	
from beginning of 164 B.C. to 6 Siwan . .	65	

1290   days.

Two months are here assumed to have been intercalated ; for the Jewish practice, at any rate as afterwards known, was to intercalate 3 months in every 8 years.[117] Consequently an additional month might have been intercalated at the end of 168 B.C. and of 165 B.C. ; or alternatively, if 167 B.C. was an intercalary year,[118] the next within the same period of 8 years could have been 165 B.C., inasmuch as only 1 year would intervene between 2 of the 3 intercalary years of the period, although 2 years intervened between the other intercalary years.

These 1290 days are not described as (although they approximately are) $3\frac{1}{2}$ years ; for, if the years were lunar, such an

[113] Dan. xii. 11–12.
[114] 1 Macc. i. 54.
[115] 1 Macc. vi. 16.
[116] Cornill, op. cit., 29–30.
[117] Schürer, op. cit., I, 751–2.
[118] Abel, Livres des Machabées, l.–li. (where no reason is given for making 167 B.C. an intercalary year).

equation would be impossible.[119] Curiously enough, however, they are equivalent to 3½ lunisolar years, if the 1 necessary intercalated month is included, i.e. 360 × 3 = 1080 days (3 years) + 180 days (½ year) + 30 days (1 intercalated month) ; but this equation is probably purely accidental.

Lastly, why are the faithful required to wait for 1335, i.e., another 45, days ?

The only reason for these additional days which has hitherto been suggested is that it is made to allow time for the various events mentioned in the previous verses [120] to take place ; [121] but these seem irrelevant to the date and immaterial in relation to the whole length of the period of the persecution.

May the true reason be that the original 1290 days were fixed in order to equate them with the 3½ years which ran through the author's calculations and that, as or when Antiochus did not in fact die on 6 Siwan, the period was extended by 45 days till the actual day of his death, which then occurred presumably on 29 Tammuz 164 B.C. ?

The words must have been added after the sealing and post eventum ; but whether the author or a glossator [122] may be held responsible for the adjustment will in all probability never be known. In either case the 3½ years, variously described, become the period of the reign of the Antichrist in apocalyptic literature.[123]

A suspicion, however, that these and any other dates as yet based on the figures in Daniel cannot be regarded as certain or definite is raised by the curious point that the difference between 1150 days and 3½ lunar years of 1239 days, namely 89 days, may be reckoned the number of days in 3 consecutive lunar months. This fact, while it may support the conclusion that the author of Daniel is using the lunar calendar, seems to suggest that his figures must not be pressed to give exact dates ; they ought perhaps rather to be treated as approximate or round figures. The dates here proposed therefore for the occasion when Antiochus IV issued the edict of desecration and that when he died must be regarded as provisional until external evidence proves or disproves the one or the other or both. This discussion,

[119] See p. 79.
[120] Dan. xi. 40–45.
[121] Cf. Polybius, Historiae, xxxi. 2, 11, and Appian, Syriaca, 66.
[122] Charles, Daniel, 338–9.
[123] Ascension of Isaiah iv. 12 ; Revelation xi. 2, xiii. 5 (cf. xii. 6, 14).

however, will perhaps have served some useful purpose if, in bringing the problem once again to the fore, it has aroused fresh interest in it and even thrown new light on it.

IV

The murder of Onias III, to which the statement that " after three score and two weeks shall an anointed one, though innocent, be cut off " [124] alludes is known to have taken place in 171 B.C. This event is followed by 1 " week," *i.e.* 7 years ; and " in the midst of the week " the Temple and altar will be desecrated, while the " consummation," *i.e.* the moment when Antiochus IV will die, will be its end.   If then the $3\frac{1}{2}$ years of the former may like those of the latter period be taken as containing 1290 days, this murder will have occurred on 6 Siwan 171 B.C., as shown in the following table :

> from 6 Siwan 171 B.C. to 15 Kislew 168 B.C. . 1290 days ; [125]
> from 15 Kislew 168 B.C. to 6 Siwan 164 B.C. . 1290 days ;
> (including 2 intercalated months of 30 days each)

in other words, the period from the murder of Onias to the death of Antiochus, as originally determined, will have been exactly 1 " week " of years or 7 years.   The correction, extending the period from 1290 to 1335 days [126] does not affect the argument ; and in any case the former and the latter periods can both be regarded as approximately $3\frac{1}{2}$ years.[127]

Thus the " consummation " coincides with the end of the 70 " weeks " of years, as reckoned by the author of this book, from 586 B.C.

These figures look artificial when all the coincidences are considered together.   Other coincidences, almost equally striking, however, have already been noted ; for example, 12 high-priests listed from Aaron to Ahimaaz and 12 from Azariah in the time of Solomon to Jozadak at the restoration, and Onias III ending the 12th generation of high-priests from the destruction of the Temple in 587/6 B.C.   Also, the *gêmāṭr*e*yâ* or numerical value

---

[124] Dan. ix. 26.
[125] Cornill, *op. cit.*, 16–19 (see pp. 9, 11).
[126] See p. 82.
[127] See pp. 81 f.

of the sum of the letters in the Hebrew forms of the names of
" Nebuchadnezzar " and " Antiochus Epiphanes " are the same,
namely 423.[128]   Both methods are combined by the author of
the first Gospel in the first century A.D. ; for by an arbitrary
treatment of the historical facts he divides the genealogy from
Abraham to Jesus into 3 groups each of 14 names,[129] having
apparently derived this number from the *gêmaṭrᵉyâ* of David's
name $(d = 4 + w = 6 + d = 4$ making 14).[130]

To what extent Jewish writers tampered with the details of
their historical records to produce such results will never be
known ; but the existence of such coincidences as those here
listed are a warning against supposing that those in *Daniel* are
" too good to be true."   They may be a consequence of some
manipulation of the records ; but they are in them for all to see
and perhaps not all of them are entirely fictitious.   Truth may
be as strange as fiction.

One important point remains to be noted : if these calculations
might be held to show that the author of *Daniel* was using the
lunar calendar, the reason would be that he wished to avoid
the Hellenistic lunisolar calendar which he regarded as a profane
innovation ; for it was God's privilege, which Antiochus IV had
usurped, " to change the times and the seasons." [131]   Contrariwise,
though in the same spirit, the Covenanters of Qumrân (also
unlike the orthodox leaders of the nation in Jerusalem, who
were heterodox on this as on certain other matters) clung to the
old and sacred solar calendar,[132] which they would have found
in use also in Egypt.[133]

V

This discussion of Jewish chronology has an important bearing on the central problem of the Judaean Scrolls, namely the
identity of the Rightful Teacher ; for the *Zadokite Documents*
apparently determine his date when they say that God sent the
Teacher to His people 390 years after delivering them into the

---

[128] *Ibid.*, 31.
[129] Matt. i. 1–17.
[130] Gfrörer, *Heilige Sage*, II, 9.
[131] Dan. ii. 21, vii. 25.
[132] Cf. Talmon in *Scr. Hierosol*, IV, 162–99.
[133] Cf. Wiedsmann, *Das alte Ägypten*, 403.

power of Nebuchadnezzar, *i.e.*, after the Babylonian captivity in 586 B.C., and that thereafter they were groping like blind men for 20 years.[134]

According to Meyer [135] the Teacher was Onias III who became high-priest *c.* 198–195 B.C., and the 20 years of groping were those of his somewhat ineffective and troubled tenure of office, which came to a sudden end when Antiochus IV deposed him *c.* 175/4 B.C.

The flaw in this reasoning, apart from the impossibility of harmonizing the events of these years with those described in the Scrolls, is that the period from 586 B.C. to 196 B.C. cannot possibly have been reckoned at 390 years by any ancient Jewish historian or chronographer. This fact has indeed long been remarked,[136] but few of those who have noticed it and none who have followed them have taken it into consideration in attempting to determine the Teacher's date by these 390 years.

Two chronologies, a long and a short, are known, as shown above.[137] Josephus, who uniformly adopts a long chronology, has the following figures (followed by the true figures in square brackets) :

first deportation to decree of Cyrus for restoration of Jews to Palestine (597–538/7 B.C.) . . . . . 70 [138] [59] ⎫ years

decree of Cyrus to accession of Antiochus V (538–164 B.C.) . . . . 434 [139] [374] ⎭

504 [433] years

Thus his figure for this period is some 70 years too many ; consequently, he would have counted approximately 460 instead of 390 years for the period at issue. R. Jôsê is equally unfavourable, having the following figures :

[134] Rost, *Damaskusschrift*, i. 5–7.
[135] In *Abhandl. d. Preuss. Akad. d. Wissensch.*, 1919, ix. 13–14.
[136] So already by Schechter, *Documents of Jewish Sectaries*, I, xxii–xxiii. ; cp, Hölscher in *Zeitschr. d. Neutest. Wissensch.*, XXVIII, 40–46.
[137] See pp. 77 ff.
[138] Thiele, *op. cit.* 164–6.
[139] In *Antiquities*, X, vi. 3, §§ 97–8 in connexion with XI, i. 1, § 1 (see Marcus, *Josephus* [Loeb], VI, 210a).

duration of exile (586–538 B.C.)   .   .   52 [140] [48]]
Persian period (538–331 B.C.)   .   .   34 [141] [207]} years
Graeco-Seleucid period (331–166 B.C.) . 180 [142] [165]]

$$\overline{\hspace{3cm}}$$

266   [390]   years

Thus by his short chronology he makes the period 124 years too
few ; he would then assign approximately 265 instead of 390
years to the period here discussed. The only possible conclusion
is that the chaotic state of Jewish chronology for the periods of
the exile and the Second Commonwealth make it in the highest
degree improbable that the author of the Scroll quoted above
can have hit the true figure ; for he cannot be credited with a
knowledge of the chronology established by the aid of Greek and
Roman chronographers.

The figure of 390 years is obviously based on the 390 days of
Israel's guilt according to the Lord's instruction to Ezekiel.[143]
This number, for which the Septuagint have 190 days (*i.e.* 150
years reckoned from the deportation of Israel under Pekah
c. 734/3 B.C. to 594/3 B.C., when Ezekiel may be supposed to have
uttered his prophecy, *plus* 40 years for the iniquity of Judah),[144]
seems to be the result of an arbitrary alteration of the text based
on two principles : a historical calculation reckoning the period
as running from the northern schism *c.* 980 B.C. to the siege of
Jerusalem in 586 B.C., *i.e.* for 394 (or in round numbers 390)
years,[145] and a *gêmāṭrᵉyâ* based on the sum of the numerical
values of the individual Hebrew letters in *ymy mṣr* " days of
siege," *i.e.* ($y = 10 + m = 40 + y = 10 + m = 40 + ṣ = 90 + r = 200 =$)
390, which may have led an ingenious scribe to alter the presumably original figure of the Septuagint into that now found in
the Massoretic text.[146]

A figure so calculated can hardly be precise or absolute, even
in its primary application ; when therefore a secondary use is
made of it to fix the date of an entirely different event, some
latitude must be allowed. At the same time, no author could

---

[140] See p. 75, n. 87.
[141] See pp. 75 f.
[142] See p. 76.
[143] Ezek. iv. 5, 9.
[144] Ezek. iv. 6 ; see Cooke, *Ezekiel*, 52–3.
[145] Cornill, *Ezechiel*, 199–200.
[146] Bertholet. *Hesekiel*, 26.

have put it to such a purpose if it was likely to be wildly mis-leading ; for it would then have had no value. The intention of the author of the Scroll was therefore in all probability to indicate not vaguely hundreds of years but a definite period of time within reasonable margins. Why, however, did he take Ezekiel's 390 years, which on any chronology known to him could not yield the desired result, rather than Jeremiah's 70 years which, treated as they had been by the author of *Daniel*, would have given him approximately what he wanted, if that was the period during which Onias III was high-priest ? The only answer to the question would seem to be that this was not the period which he had in mind ; and another attempt may and indeed must be made to discover what that was.

Although not under the Roman Republic, under the Empire political allusion became so dangerous that writers commonly took refuge behind synonyms. Accordingly, Dr. Roth [147] has suggested that " Nebuchadnezzar " in the passage just quoted from the *Zadokite Documents* [148] is not the Babylonian king of that name but another conqueror or alien ruler of Palestine, *e.g.* Alexander the Great or Seleucus I, and that the 390 years must be reckoned from some event connected with one or other of these two persons. The suggestion is exceedingly plausible ; for the practice of hinting at contemporary persons or events in some such way, which had begun amongst the Jews already in the second century B.C., became usual in the first century A.D. First, the name of the famous conqueror Nebuchadnezzar readily lent itself to this purpose. For example, the " Nebuchadnezzar " of *Daniel* has long been recognized as Antiochus IV Epiphanes ; and *gêmāṭrʿyâ*, if it cannot be held to have prompted, will certainly have lent colour to this identification, inasmuch as the sum of the numerical values of the Hebrew letters in their respective names (Nebuchadnezzar : $n = 50 + b = 2 + w = 6 + k = 20 + d = 4 + n = 50 + ' = 1 + s = 90 + r = 200$; Antiochus Epiphanes : $' = 1 + n = 50 + ṭ = 9 + y = 10 + w = 6 + k = 20 + w = 6 + s = 60$ *plus* $' = 1 + p = 70 + y = 10 + p = 70 + n = 50 + s = 60$) is the same (423).[149] This is a point which no Jewish apocalyptist will have missed and which may partly account for the incorrect spelling of the king's name ; both the New Testament and the Scrolls long afterwards amply

---

[147] In *Historical Background of the Dead Sea Scrolls*, 53–4.
[148] See pp. 84 f.
[149] Cornill, *op. cit.*, 31.

illustrate the practice.[150] Second, in the first century A.D.
" Nabochodonosor king of Babylon " and " Baltasar his son "
(*i.e.*, Belshazzar, who however was not Nebuchadnezzar's son)
are respectively Vespasian and his son Titus, also conquerors of
Jerusalem.[151] Further, the authors of the Jewish *II Esdras* and
of the Christian *Apocalypse of Ezra* both take the destruction of
Jerusalem in 586 B.C. to indicate its destruction in A.D. 70 and
combine it with the prophet Ezekiel's " thirtieth year . . ., as I
was amongst the captives by the canal (called) Kebar " [152] to
indicate the actual years to which they are referring, namely
A.D. 90–100.[153] The method of the author of the Scroll, if the
principle on which his chronology is based is thus rightly
explained, is strikingly parallel to that of these three other
writers who put the same event and the words of the same
prophet to similar purpose ; and on this assumption it must now
be put to the test of its practical application.

Two eras came into use with these two conquerors, the
Alexandrian and the Seleucid. The former, commencing in
333/2 B.C., when Syria and Palestine passed into Alexander's
power, or in 325 B.C., when Babylon was made his capital city,
was employed by some Greek historians and by the city of Acco
(Ptolemais) [154] for dating its coins. The latter began in 312/1 B.C.,
when Seleucus became ruler of the whole East from Babylon to
Jerusalem. This era was adopted throughout the states and
cities of the Middle East with few exceptions and became current
also in Palestine, being employed by Jews in all secular business ; [155] and the author of 1 (if not of 2) Maccabees used it.[156]
The Covenanters of Qumrân, however, who clung to the old
sacred solar calendar in preference to the new Greek lunisolar
calendar,[157] which had already been a subject of protest,[158]
would not be likely to have based their chronology on it. The
famous story, too, of Alexander's visit to Jerusalem in 332 B.C.,

[150] See pp. 68, 83 f.
[151] 1 Bar. i. 11–12 (see Charles, *Apocrypha and Pseudepigrapha of the Old Testament*, I, 574–6, 584).
[152] Ezek. 1. 1.
[153] 2 Esdr. iii. 1, 29 (see Oesterley, *II Esdras*, xliv–xlv. 18) and *Apocalypse of Esra*, i. 1–2 (see Box, *Esra-Apocalypse*, xxviii.–xxix. 8).
[154] Schürer, *op. cit.*, II, 112 (181).
[155] See Neubauer, *op. cit.*, p. 66, l. 4 (*Seder 'Ôlām Rabbā* § 30).
[156] Schürer, *op. cit.*, I, 32–40.
[157] Talmon in *Script. Hierosolym.*, IV, 162–99.
[158] Dan. vii. 25.

including his deferential treatment of the Zadokite high-priest Jaddua and his offering of sacrifice in the Temple under his direction,[159] would further predispose the Covenanters to choose his era rather than the Seleucid, which could be regarded by them as nothing but a heathen innovation.

If, then, 332 B.C. is taken as the starting point of the Scroll's 390 years, what will be the terminal point ? For the Greek and Seleucid periods R. Jôsê's 180 years may be accepted as having already become the established figure of current historiography, but his omission of the 26 years of the Roman occupation of Palestine must be disregarded. These years were said to have been omitted because the Romans then treated the Jews not as subjects but as allies,[160] which could hardly have been the true reason ; this was surely that the period of Roman subjugation was considered a discreditable episode in Jewish history. The Covenanters, however, much as they disliked the Romans and disapproved of Roman rule, would not have omitted these years from their calculations ; for they were, as suggested below, the formative years of their society, when they began to organize themselves as the spear-head of the opposition to Rome, and they were almost within living memory. The figures then will be the following :

Greek and Seleucid periods (332–166 B.C.) .	.	180 ⎫
Hasmonaean period (166–63 B.C.) .	.	103 ⎬ years
Roman period (63–35 B.C.) .	.	28 ⎪
Herodian period (35 B.C.–A.D. 68) .	.	103 ⎭

414 years

Before drawing conclusions from these figures, however, two deviations from the normal dates require explanation. First, the Roman period is taken as ending not in 37 B.C., when Herod obtained possession of the kingdom, but in 35 B.C., because the last Hasmonaean high-priest Aristobulus died in that year ; and, second, the destruction of Jerusalem by the Romans is put in A.D. 68 instead of A.D. 70 for the reason given above.[161] If the difference between these 414 years and the Scroll's 390 years, i.e. 24 years, is now deducted from A.D. 68, the end of these enigmatic 390 years will fall in A.D. 44 ; and, if 390 is a round

[159] Josephus, *Antiquities*, XI. viii. 5, §§ 329–39.
[160] B. Talmud, *Abodah Zarah 8b–9a*.
[161] See pp. 76 f.

F.F.—7

figure for 392 years, the end will have been in A.D. 46, which is
near enough to c. A.D. 46–48, the significant years in the theory,
propounded originally by Mr. H. E. L. Del Medico [162] and Dr.
Vermes [163] and accepted by Dr. Roth, [164] that the Rightful Teacher
of the Scrolls was Manaemus the σοφιστής, i.e., Menahem son of
Judah son of Hezekiah, all three leaders in their time of the
opposition to Rome. Hezekiah raised the original revolt in
47 B.C., his son Judah rebelled in 4 B.C. and A.D. 6, when he was
caught and executed, and Judah's sons Jacob and Simeon
similarly rose but were caught and crucified by the Romans
c. A.D. 46–48 ; and their brother Menahem went into and remained
in hiding in or near the Judaean desert from then for 20 years
until he emerged in A.D. 66 to claim the leadership of the First
Revolt.[165] These 20 years might well be those during which the
Jewish people were " as blind men and as men groping to find a
way " and they are those to which the 390 years of the Scroll
pointed.

Dedicated by the writer to Professor S. H. HOOKE,
once one of his father's students,
who has laughed at the Psalmist's rule of life
שבעים שנה ואם בגבורת שמונים שנה
becoming in turn the teacher of many others,
as a token of gratitude for many years of friendship.
תלמידיך אנו ומימיך אנו שותים

---

[162] In *Deux Manuscrits hébreux de la Mer Morte* (1951), 133–6.
[163] In *Cahiers Sionieus*, 1951.
[164] *Op. cit*, 63–9.
[165] Josephus, *Antiquities*, XIV, ix. 2, § 159 ; and *War*, I, x. 5, § 204 (Hezekiah);
Antiquities, XVII, x. 5, and *War*, II, iv. 1, § 56 (Judah) ; *Antiquities*, XX, v. 1,
§ 102 (Jacob and Simeon) ; and *War*, II, xvii. 8, § 433–9, 448 (Menahem).

INSPIRATION : POETICAL AND DIVINE

By AUSTIN FARRER

Is it infirmity of mind, to think of salvaging some elements of truth from one's indiscretions ? Anyhow the temptation is strong. In a book called *The Glass of Vision* I pressed the comparison between divine revelation and poetic " inspiration." Miss Helen Gardner demolished the literary side of my comparison in her Riddell Lectures, and Professor H. D. Lewis the theological, in *Our Experience of God*.

Much of Professor Lewis's criticism is based on the very reasonable contention, that revelation is fundamentally a personal encounter. Suppose, then, that we adopt this view, and take it as far as we can. By seeing where it begins to fail us, we may find an acceptable place for a supplementary interpretation of revelation in terms of a comparison with the poetic process.

The point I wish to fix attention upon throughout, is the rôle of the imagination. It is a commonplace of philosophy, that we see very little of what we claim to see. It would be an ordinary claim to make, if I said that I saw a matchbox. Now a matchbox is not a matchbox, unless it is a six-sided hollow rectangle, put together in a certain way out of certain materials. But, when I say I see the matchbox, I see only three sides at the most out of the six ; I do not see whether it is hollow or not, nor how it is put together, nor what it is made of. Imagination, acting on the advice of memory, supplies the missing features immediately ; I no sooner see what I see, than I imagine the rest.

We come to a more interesting case of this immediate action of imagination, when human speech or conduct is the subject. I hear you speak—well, what do I hear ? Only a trail of sounds in the air ; yet I immediately supply not only the logical meaning —that could be done by code rules—I supply the attitude and the intention expressed, and the indefinable quality of you, the person who express them. In this case the imaginative build-up is untraceably complex ; the whole of my past history, especially in relation to you, becomes the sounding-board, as it were, for my present hearing of your words. It is the same when you act, and I feel the nerve of your action.

Here, we may well suppose that we come nearer to the case of divine revelation. God in the burning bush speaks to Moses ; and Moses speaks to Aaron. We suppose that the second speaking is somehow in line with the first. And if Aaron understands Moses by all he has previously known of Moses, and indeed, of other Israelites ; does not Moses understand God by all he has previously experienced of him, or heard about other's experiences of him, say Jethro his father-in-law's, or more remotely, those vouchsafed to Abraham, Isaac, Jacob, and Joseph ? Yes, certainly ; apart from such a background of past memory acting through present imagination, it is scarcely conceivable that any event or voice or thought could put itself upon any man as the act or utterance of God.

So far the parallel holds : Moses hears God, and Aaron hears Moses. But, of course, there is an enormous difference. We said that throughout the experiencing of one human person by another, there works the activity of an immediate imagination untraceably complex in its ramifications. Nevertheless, through all this maze, there runs one simple unchanging homespun thread of connexion. All men are men ; their instinctive passions are broadly identical ; the relation of their will or purpose to their tongues and hands is essentially the same everywhere ; and we hold the clue in ourselves, for we too are human, we have the human recipe for action and discourse. Thus it is only in marginal cases that there is any real difficulty in knowing, whether we are up against the expressions of purpose, or not. The most perverse of philosophers will be unable to make our flesh creep with the suggestion, that our fellow beings may all be talking waxworks, or super-subtle robots. We cannot consider the supposition seriously. And there is more than this. Though there are fine shades of intention we may easily miss, and some we can never fix, there are many broad and general directions of attitude and purpose in others, about which it is silly to entertain a doubt.

In the perception of God's interventions, there is nothing like this reassuring certainty. It is not evident by any simple criteria, when we are ever up against signs of his personal communication, or self-manifestation, and when we are not. If revelation takes place, we are, no doubt, subjectively convinced ; for if the act or word of God does not put itself upon us as God's there is not even the appearance of revelation. Yet not all apparent revelation is really such ; and how can we ever be sure, that we are not the dupes of a counterfeit ? We have not the clue in ourselves, for we are not divine, nor do we possess the recipe for acting divinely.

When Moses, or when Jesus himself, sees the hand or hears the word of God, whether in the world without, or in his own mind, he appears to us to be actuated by a human parable about God : and not just *the* human parable in general—that God's ways are thought of as somehow manlike—but human parable of a particular kind. The God of Moses is the divine archetype of a tribal patriarch, the warrior-champion of his people, a stern disciplinarian, a benevolent provider, a wise leader of their march through desert places. The God of Jesus is a compassionate parent, a universal king, a patient redeemer, a righteous judge— it seems trite, or almost blasphemous, for a Christian so glibly to run through the human figures under which the Father's person appears in the thought and speech of Jesus himself ; and indeed, merely to mention these parabolic types is not to do justice to the divine teaching, nor even to touch the substance of it. It is not the mere presentation of the Father under these guises, it is the special twist given to the story in each case, that states for us what Christ has to say.

What is the source, then, of the parabolic form, if we may call it such, in which God's action is seen, and his word understood, whether it be by Jesus, or by Moses ? The source of all parable, in the sense of the quarry from which the materials are digged, is indeed no mystery—all parable draws on the matter of human experience ; if it did not, it would signify nothing. So much for the materials—but what of the form, the story into which they are worked up ? It is something which comes in the mind of the recipients of revelation, and it never is the construction of any single mind alone. Jesus gave a new twist to the parables, but they were already alive in the faith of Israel.

What, then, is the source of the parabolic form ? There can be little doubt of the *locus* in which it takes shape—it is in the imagination of believers ; where else ? And if we were not believers ourselves, there might be little more that needed to be said. But because we are believers, and are convinced by the *content* of revelation, because we find God to have spoken to us through these things, we ask after the source of the parabolic

form, or, let us say, after the control under which it took shape ;
for we cannot suppose it to have taken shape idly or casually.

It is at this point that the analogy of great poetry, or even
some prose fiction which reaches an epical level, appears attractive. For poetry arises in the imagination ; and not under the
direct control of fact, so that it should be the literal transcript
of it. Yet it is not a silly or vain day-dreaming, either ; it is
controlled by realities, but the control is looser or more elastic,
than in the case of literal description. The poet's inventions
respond somehow to the deep nature of human existence, and
give it an expression all the more powerful, because inventive
and free. Moreover the expression is often cast in parabolic, or
symbolic form ; as when Shelley sees the poetical vocation
embodied in the skylark. What is perhaps most significant for
our purpose, is that in poetical composition there is, or anyhow
need be, no conscious attempt to envisage realities in their naked
lineaments, and then to translate them by conscious art. Art is
conscious enough, but not commonly in this way ; the poet
works at his poetry, developing his images ; but the manner in
which his sense of human existence (or whatever is the control)
comes to expression through his inventions, may be largely hidden
from him while he writes ; and perhaps most, where the poetry
is best.

The last thing I want to do is to lay down the law about the
function, or principal aim, of poetry, or even (say) of epic poetry.
I should be horrified if you carried away the impression that I
had made it the business of poets to express the quality of human
existence, or anything of that sort. Poetry seems to me to be
almost stifled nowadays with a sense of its own importance. I
would prefer to say, if I had to say anything, that the business
of poets is to make pleasing inventions ; though I should have
to go on to define the sort of pleasure they rightly give, and the
sort of means they properly employ. And if the poet is to give
the sort of pleasure we look for in epic or in tragedy, his inventions
must not be fantasies ; they must be inventions so made from the
stuff of existence, that they cannot fail to illuminate its character, and to move under its control.

The moral we should wish to draw, is that the parabolic form
through which revelation is received, though it takes shape in
the human imagination, may do so under a similar objective
control. Many unbelievers would agree with us, and say that the

religious picture is precisely this—a racial or cultural poetry, bringing out the deep qualities of human existence. So religion may be healthful ; and yet God need not exist, let alone intervene, or reveal Himself by special action in the world.

It is plain, by way of contrast, that the believer cannot regard the religious parable as just poetry, like any other ; the control must be for him another control ; not the general quality of the life we live, but the special action of a self-revealing God. Now in a sense we can see that the figures of the religious parable are under the control of fact. For those who receive revelation are called upon to live in the parable that is revealed ; and the parable is then tested against the hard reality of facts. Jesus lives in the parable of Messianic Kingdom, and Sonship to omnipotent Mercy ; the parable takes on a strange form, when the facts of history, under the hand of Providence, put down the kingdom and crucify the Son.

We may say, then, that the parabolic form is under the check of fact. Yet to say that facts shape or alter the parable is literally nonsensical. Facts can do no such thing. In face of the facts, the parable needs to be recast ; but to recast it calls for fresh inspiration, it is not done by dead-reckoning. We may compare the absurdity (an absurdity not committed by Marxists) of an exclusively material interpretation of history. It may be, as Marxists hold, that nothing but material necessities will ever set the problems, to which culture finds the answers. The material problems may be inexorable—we must find the answers, or perish ; but it is still human inventiveness which works out the solutions. Not any solution will do ; but whatever solution there is, invention has found it, facts have not dictated it.

To apply the analogy to the matter before us—the death and resurrection of Jesus did not *dictate* the fresh way in which the kingdom of God was seen ; it had to be imagined.

Thus, whatever imaginative overplus there is in divine revelation, cannot be referred simply to the control of facts outside us ; it is in some manner the invention of the human mind.

What shall we say to this conclusion ? Is it scandalous ? Is it an admission of defeat ? Only if we allow ourselves to be lured on to untenable ground, and to conceive our question falsely. When we are seeing the human mind reactive to external facts, we naturally wish to see the reaction as controlled by those facts, if it is to sustain any claim to objective truth ; and so every admission of a subjective element, not capable of external verification, awakens our doubt and our disquiet. And when I think of God as addressing man in revelation, I naturally fall into the same posture, and become the victim of my own parable. If you address me, you are outside me ; so, then, I suppose, is God. But then, on serious reflection, none of us can really maintain this. God is no more outside me, than within ; I am his creation, just as much as you are, or as the physical world is. He has the secret key of entry into all his creatures ; he can conjoin the action of any of them with his will, in such fashion as to reveal himself specially through them. God speaks without, and within ; he reveals himself both through the situation with which he presents the recipients of revelation, and through the imagination, in terms of which he leads them to see and hear the voices and the sights surrounding them. How should it— how could it—be otherwise ? The process is gradual ; God has employed, he has not forced, the action of his creatures ; he teaches us also to discern revelation from revelation and see where the flower and fruit borne by the branching plant of sacred truth are to be found. The occurrence of revelation cannot be guaranteed by the nature of the process, but only by the convincingness of the communication. All we can do about the process is to show what it is, and the relation in which it stands to other processes of the human mind, and especially of the human imagination.

Before we go any further, let us pause, and try to add up the score. We have spoken of the analogy of revelation to poetry on the one hand, and personal encounter on the other. These two analogies, however, are not rivals to one another, nor do they lie in the same plane. It is not as though we should say that jerusalem artichoke tasted something like sweet potato and something like celery-root. The recipients of revelation see themselves to be addressed by God, whether through events, or other persons, or visions, or their own thoughts. And this is nothing like poetical experience, anyhow on the face of it ; it is like personal encounter. When, however, we reflect on such an experience, we see that the God who speaks to them speaks out of a parable ; as though a person in a story came alive and addressed us. The parable, indeed, only speaks, because it has clothed itself with the living world ; it is God's action in some feature of our world, which speaks to us in terms of the parable.

Nevertheless, we must say that the revelation as we receive it is a function of two things equally—partly a function of the divinely-controlled event, and partly a function of the parable in terms of which we personalize, or theologize, the event. Now if we are *believing* enough to accord validity to the revelation, we must be *tough* enough to claim validity for the parable, as well as for the event. We look about for analogies, with which to support our belief ; for though religious faith deals with mysteries which are *sui generis*, because God himself is absolutely unique ; at the same time we expect religious mysteries to bear some analogy with natural realities, because they are revealed in the stuff of our human experience. So it seems that God's encounter with us must be a sort of encounter, analogous to our encounters with men ; and that the parables or symbols through which God teaches us to imagine his action, must be some sort of symbols, parallel, perhaps, to the symbols of valid poetry.

We have been thinking so far of primary revelation ; as when Moses at the burning bush is assured that God has come down to deliver, or as when Peter sees Jesus to be the Anointed of God. In such cases, attention is fixed on the moment of action. What is seen is seen in the parable ; but the parable is taken for granted. If the symbolism undergoes development then and there, the Moses or the Peter is hardly aware of it ; nothing appears to happen in his mind, like the free growth of poetry in the invention of a poet.

But we can think of a more reflective occasion, when the seer is inspired to explore the mysteries, so that he may know all that God has to show him about them. In such a case, the facts may be taken as fixed ; it is the symbolism investing them, that will move and grow. The Messiah *was* crucified ; he *did* rise again and manifest himself alive ; he sent the apostolic mission. So much for the facts. But, in the supernatural dimension, what does all this mean ? What was the heavenly counterpart of these earthly events ? To ask these questions is to invite symbols to grow in the mind.

Now if the seer sat down and worked it out, if he simply constructed and elaborated, his experience would not have to himself a revelatory character. If it is to seem to him that God is opening the mysteries to him, the images must impose themselves. There is, of course, no psychological mystery about images getting out of hand, and seeming to dictate to us ; and it would be puerile to suggest, that wherever this happens, there is special revelation. We are reasoning the other way round. Supposing that our Creator wishes to speak to us in the mode of revelation, will it not be our imaginative faculty that he employs, because of its capacity of presenting to us a seemingly independent object ?

Because, in this sort of experience, the revealing image imposes itself, it presents itself as a symbol, not as an allegory. The seer sees the imaged object ; it comes as something charged with divine significance ; what significance, and how much, he does not at first know. He may read several allegories off it, and still not exhaust it.

Although the Scripture abounds with passages in which imagery or symbol is seen to grow, impose itself, and suggest applications or decipherings, the most continuous and concentrated example of such writing or thinking (for these men thought with their pens in their hands) is the Revelation of St. John the Divine.

St. John's task is, in broad outline, comparable to that undertaken by many poets. Virgil sets out to see, and fill out, and bring alive the bare bones of a tradition about the origins of Rome. So St. John has the naked shape of things to come in the prophecy Christ uttered on the Mount of Olives, with its background in the Old Testament Prophecies. He is called upon to experience these future mysteries through living symbols ; and the starting-point is a returning to him of the Christ who formerly prophesied, to open the secrets he had then adumbrated. Let us follow the growth of images in St. John's mind from the beginning of his vision. He is himself an apostolic minister, carrying the Seven Churches of Asia in his heart, and he is, for the present, a suffering witness, or martyr, for the word of God and the witness of Jesus. Jesus is the supreme witness, or martyr, but now in heaven—" the Faithful Witness in heaven," says the Psalmist speaking evidently of the Sun (Ps. lxxxix.). But Jesus is the Sun—anyhow, the Sun's day is the Lord's Day ; and it is on this day that St. John has his rapture, and sees the Lord of Sunday, the Christ of the Resurrection ; and he sees him with a countenance that shines like the sun at midday. St. John falls before him as though dead, and himself receives a resurrection from his touch : " Fear not," he says, " I am the First

and the Last, the Living that was dead, and lo, am alive for
evermore, and have the keys of Death and Hell." He is the
First and the Last in the Great Week of the World's ages ;
his is the Sunday of Creation and, when the week of history
has run through, his, in his Advent, is the Sunday of universal
regeneration. So too, in the little week of days which gives
shape to Christian life, running from Sunday to Sunday, he is
the first and the last, embracing in his grasp the days of the
seven planets (for it is after these seven that the weekdays are
named). And so St. John sees him whose face shines as the sun,
holding the seven planets in his right hand.

St. John sees Jesus in vision, and St. John is a prophet :
what more natural, than that he should see through the eyes of a
former prophet, Zechariah, who had seen in vision a former
Jesus, God's High-Priest, under the solar name of Dayspring,
and manifested as a type of the Resurrection, " as a brand
plucked from the burning." The vision in which Zechariah saw
him was paired with a vision of worshipping Israel, which he
saw under the form of a sevenfold candlestick ; and what can
the seven flames mean to St. John, but the seven worshipping
congregations of Christ's new Israel in the Province of Asia, the
subjects of his own pastoral care ? Seven flaming wicks in the
Seven Churches, seven shining stars in the grasp of Christ, seven
earthly and seven heavenly fires, how are they related ? Stars
are gods to the heathen, to Israel they are angels : the Churches'
candles shine on earth, their angels in the heavenly grasp of Jesus.
In Zechariah's vision, the seven lamps were in one lampstand,
which was Israel ; the lampstand held the centre of the scene,
while like heraldic supporters on either side stood the two oil-
trees, the two anointed stocks of principality and priesthood,
feeding the lamps from the oil of their anointing. In St. John's
vision, the pattern cannot be the same. The two anointed stocks
are united in one and fuse at the centre of the scene ; Christ is
Zorobabel as well as Jesus, he is as much prince as high-priest.
Moreover the seven lamps are not combined in one lampstand ;
the congregations of God, that is, are no longer contained in one
city or one temple as formerly : they are planted out upon the
earth in several cities. Their union lies in this, that their life is
hid with Christ in God—their angels are stars clustering in the
hand of Glory.

The lineaments of Glory are seen by St. John in the feature

scriptural vision, such as showed to Daniel, Isaiah, or Ezekiel either the figure of God, or the angel-figure representative of him. It would take us into too much detail to trace the web of allusion, or the pattern of meaning it makes for the seer. Let us continue to follow the development of the symbols we have already brought into play.

There are the candles, or to speak more exactly, the lamps of the Churches, planted round Christ's feet ; and there are the stars, their Churches' angels, in the keeping of his hand. In the world of the image, someone is responsible for the burning of the lamp, as in Christ's parable of the wise and foolish virgins—it burns brightly, only if the wick is trimmed, and if it is supplied with oil. A lamp does not perform these services for itself. So the lamps of the vision can only stand for the objective fact or phenomenon of the Churches' worship, or witness ; the admonitions which Christ metes out according to merit must go to the address of the angels ; just as it is the virgins of the parable, not their lamps, that are foolish or wise. And so St. John feels the divine dictation—" To the angel of the Church in Ephesus, write. . . . I will remove thy lampstand out of its place, except thou repent. . . ." The several messages are addressed, indeed, to the Churches ; but in their invisible, spiritual, and (as it were) angelic aspect ; in respect of that life which they have in Christ, and indeed, in heaven. For, either motived by that very development of images we have just been following, or by a prior conviction with which the imagery wonderfully chimes, St. John is henceforth consistent in maintaining that Christians, *qua* Christians, have their existence in heaven : the description " dwellers upon earth " is pejorative, and refers to those alone whose spirits know no better habitation.

We may notice, in retrospect, that whereas the seven planets owe their place in the hand of Christ to the symbolism of the sacred week, in which Jesus, the Lord of Sunday, being the first and the last, is master of time, the developed application of the image is in another direction. It is controlled by the significance of the sevenfold lamplight as expressing a sevenfold Israel ; and by the parallel between seven lamps and seven stars, as between earthly and heavenly fires. Yet if the weekday significance of the seven is pushed aside, it is only for the present ; it comes back with full force in the sequel.

St. John has seen the countenance of Glory on earth, presented in the person of Jesus Christ. His next vision translates him to heaven, to see Glory enthroned in the person of the Father. As in the previous vision, seven lamps of fire burn before the divine figure, and a sevenfold cluster is in the grasp of his right hand. But not a cluster of stars this time, a cluster of seals, securing the scroll of a book. What is the sealed book in the right hand of the Almighty ? It is the book of his purpose, the book of prophecy, or of destiny. As the seven seals are broken one by one, the destiny of the world will begin to unroll in seven successive acts : like the seven days of action by which God in the beginning both created the world, and appointed the Sabbath, and with it the sacred week imposed on Israelite observance, and transformed in Christian experience.

In the former vision, the series of seven messages to seven Churches arose out of a relation between the sevenfold cluster in the divine hand, and the seven lamps before the divine feet ; and in the second vision a similarly dynamic relation obtains. The seven lamps are the seven powers of the Holy Ghost ; and how is it conceivable that the sevenfold seal upon the mystery of God should be broken by any interpreter, but one on whom the sevenfold power of Spirit has descended ? An angelic herald issues the challenge ; who is worthy to open the book and to break the seven seals thereof ? None is found able to open the book, or to scan it : until there appears the figure of a Lamb, his head crowned with seven horns and ringed with seven eyes, declared to be the seven powers of the Holy Ghost, which range the world—manifested here as horns of strength, to take and open the book, and eyes of vision, to scan its pages. So the Lamb endowed with the sevenfold plenitude of spirit breaks one by one the seven seals of the book, and as he breaks them a series of seven events, a " week " of divine judgements unrolls ; the first of three such weeks, which taken together give shape to the Apocalypse, and carry it forward to its destined consummation.

For convenience of exposition, one takes a single strand of imagery, and follows it through. But to do this, as we have perfunctorily done, is to give no idea of the complexity of the total imaginative process. There are so many such strands, and none of them is dominant ; the miracle is, that concrete images of vision, briefly and simply presented, conform at once to so many principles of symbolical sequence. In the more interesting visions, the interweaving of sequential themes is subtle and self-concealing. In the more perfunctory passages, it is mechanical and obvious. For example in the trumpet-visions. The blowing of the seven trumpets expresses a piece of directly preceding liturgy, the scattering of coals from an angelic censer, after the incense has been offered. This means that the acceptance of the prayers of the saints (the incense) draws, as its consequence, coals of fire on the heads of their persecutors. So now the trumpets of advent blow ; and every blast brings a different sort of fiery thing—a falling star, a comet, lightning—down from the sky to the earth. But now each of these fiery agents falls upon a distinct element of nature, taken in order—on land, on sea, on freshwaters. By so doing it produces one of the plagues of Egypt, as recorded in Exodus ; and it must be a plague appropriate to the smiting of that particular element, by that particular fiery agent.

Here, then, St. John in the most deliberate manner has felt moved to impose *a priori* a threefold bondage on his inspiration : each little vision, each trumpet-plague must be so conceived as to meet three distinct requirements. Not that any of these is arbitrary ; all arise from the general movement of the Apocalypse. We have seen why the judgements are " coals of fire " ; their smiting of the elements in order shows that nature turns all her constituent forces against God's enemies ; the echoing of Egyptian plagues shows the continuity of judgement through recorded history into a prophesied future. The threefold chain is meaningful ; yet when St. John lets himself be tied by it, he is not only conforming to requirements of meaning, he is adopting a technique of inspiration. For to be so bound is, in fact, no bondage, but a liberation to the creative faculty. The setting of the conditions challenges, directs, and supports the act of the imagination.

The comparison here with the procedure of poets is obvious. Since we mentioned Shelley and his skylark, we may as well return to that example. Before he has written the poem, he does not know, at least in any detail, what he is going to say. By the time he has projected the first stanza, he has laid down the following rules for every succeeding sentence until the end. (*a*) It must fill its place in the metrical stanza ; (*b*) it must supply the rhyme-words demanded by the scheme ; (*c*) it must continue the address to the skylark ; (*d*) it must so speak to, and about the skylark as to make what is said appropriate in a treatment of her as no bird, but a " blithe spirit "—in fact, as a poeticals oul.

Now all poets have groaned, from time to time, under the bondage of the formal conditions they accept ; the metre, for example, and the rhyme. It may often happen that the poet discovers what he wants to say and projects it in a formulation which he is sorry to sacrifice, and then hacks it into the required stanza or couplet. Such is, almost chronically, the condition of verse-translators, because what they have to express already exists in a complete verbal formulation, though in another language : and the translator will show almost superhuman restraint, if he keeps himself from rendering his French or his Latin into a literal English prose equivalent, before he tries to knock it into English verse. And so the requirements of rhyme and metre seem to be there for the express purpose of stopping his saying just what he wants to say. But the poet composing freely in his own language need not be in so painful a fix. He may allow the rhyme and metre to help him discover what he wants to say ; as Hudibras has it :

> For rhymes the rudders are of verses
> Whereby like ships, they steer their courses.

For the poet is not trying to make a prose communication, under wantonly unfavourable conditions ; he is trying to create a piece of verbal music, in which sound and sense have each their part to play. No doubt one of the elements in the compound will often take the lead, and require to be checked by the others ; but taking it all in all, the total set of formal requirements challenge a writer's invention to the harmonious satisfaction of them all together.

Now it is evident, by contrast, that the inspired writer such as St. John is not set to create a pleasing, or even a noble, piece of verbal music ; he is the mouthpiece of the Spirit in revealing mysteries and it would be incongruous that rhymes should be the rudders of his verses. It is true indeed that the prophets of the Old Testament spoke in verse, but a form of verse so adapted to the rhythm of their language, and with so elastic a pattern, that it was as easy to extemporize as the measure of Longfellow's *Hiawatha*. It added something no doubt, but very little, to the requirements which supported their inspiration. One can hardly think of a prophet prophesying in sonnet-form. Anyhow, we are talking of St. John, who writes no kind of verse, but at the most (like the author of the *Imitatio Christi*) a rhythmical prose :

$$Καὶ\ ἀνέβη\ ὁ\ καπνὸς\ τῶν\ θυμιαμάτων$$
$$ταῖς\ προσευχαῖς\ τῶν\ ἁγίων$$
$$ἐκ\ χειρὸς\ τοῦ\ ἀγγέλου$$
$$ἐνώπιον\ τοῦ\ θεοῦ.$$

So, then, if he is to set himself a complex of formal requirements, comparable in the stringency of their demands with those accepted by a poet, he must multiply sense-requirements, to compensate for the diminution of sound-requirements. And this, anyhow, we see him to do ; he is always at any point under the combined control of so many trains of significance ; always plaiting so many strands of allusion into his rope.

The Apocalypse of St. John is an extreme example of its kind ; but an extreme example will suffice to overthrow a universal negative. If St. John could seek and gain inspiration by such means, it cannot be universally true, that spiritual and Christian writers of the first age could never have received inspiration through such means. Yet it is this universal negative with which we are met, when we timidly suggest (say) that St. Matthew has written the beginning of his gospel in antitype to a train of events running through Genesis into Exodus. " Nonsense," it is said : " how could he ? He gives us a narrative which develops by its own logic, and a narrative which does justice (we presume) to the traditions about Christ which the writer had received. How could he have made it a continuous antitype to Old Testament narratives, without the whole structure's creaking at the joints ? People just do not write in this way, keeping (like jugglers) half a dozen balls in the air at once." To which we can only reply : " Don't they, though ? Don't they just ! " and shew them a few of the obvious examples. Nor do we need to be content simply with exhibiting the examples. We can call attention to the psychology of poetical composition, and the way in which a multiple control may liberate, not fetter the pen.

We have fallen from the universal to the particular. From the most general considerations about poetry and divinity, we have slipped into the consideration of one particular proceeding which inspired writers and poets have in common. And even here it is most necessary to emphasize the limitations attaching to the parallel. Religious seers and secular poets may be led to seek inspiration in these similar ways ; but the fact casts no light whatever on the fundamental mystery of divine inspiration. Shelley uses certain methods to set his imagination acting ; and this gives his imagination scope to act. St. John uses similar methods ; and this gives the Holy Ghost scope to move his imagination. Looking into a crystal or into the embers of a glowing fire, gives the imagination of the clairvoyant the opportunity to project its images ; what comes, comes from within the crystal-gazer, it does not come out of the crystal. It comes from within ; and Shelley is within himself ; St. John is also within himself, but so (in his belief, which we share) is the Spirit of God. Belief in inspiration is a metaphysical belief ; it is the belief that the Creator everywhere underlies the creature, with the added faith, that at certain points he acts in, as, and through the creature's mind. We have argued that if this really happens, a part will be played by imagination. Imagination, in such an employment, will be suppled, and made responsive, or creative ; there will surely be an analogy here to the workings of the poetic mind. But that which obtains expression in the two sorts of case will be widely different ; and so will be the significance of the product.

THE ARABIC BACKGROUND OF THE BOOK OF JOB

By A. GUILLAUME

THE Book of Job is shrouded in mystery. Despite the many studies that have been devoted to it nothing certain has been predicated of its provenance, its date, and its author. Now, in the light shed by recent discoveries of what was happening in Arabia in the middle of the sixth century B.C., it is permissible to reopen the question and to consider whether the book can be brought into closer relation with Arabia proper.[1]

In 1956 Professor D. S. Rice discovered in Harran inscriptions of Nabonidus in which he described his ten years' sojourn in Arabia round about the year 550 B.C. He took the road to Tema, Dedan, Fadak, Khaybar, Yadî' and Yathrib (i.e., Medina), making Tema his temporary capital. In all these places he established garrisons composed of Babylonians and levies from the west. These oases lie within a few days. camel journey of Medina. As would be expected, foreign occupation was not effected without fighting and a recently discovered Thamudian inscription records an engagement with " the king of Babel."

It is a most significant fact that at the time of Muhammad large Jewish settlements were established in four of the five places named above (Yadî' is known only by its name in Arab geographers), and the question as to how long they had been there at once arises. Hebrews may have fled there after the fall of Samaria, or Jews after the fall of Jerusalem. But, as Professor Gadd says [2] : " at least a presumptive occasion is found for a widespread Jewish occupation of the northern Ḥijāz, an occupation identified with those places which are both exclusively and exhaustively named. . . . Short of actually naming the Jews, its implication could scarcely be stronger." He goes on to cite a fragment of an Aramaic manuscript from Qumrān which

---

[1] I have drawn deeply on Prof. C. J. Gadd's erudite article " The Harran Inscriptions of Nabonidus " in *Anatolian Studies*, 1958, 35 ff.

[2] *Ibid.*, 87.

mentions a Jewish diviner who gave advice to Nabonidus while he was at Tema.

It is likely that Job vi. 18 f. relates to this occupation : " caravans changed their path. They went up into the void and were lost. The caravans of Tema looked. The companies of Sheba waited for them. They were disappointed because they had hoped.³ They came on them and were abashed." It looks as though the caravaners, hearing that Tema was in the possession of the Babylonians, *went up* into the Nafud. There must have been some compelling reason for their forsaking a well-marked route that had been taken by their predecessors for centuries. After waiting in vain the merchants of Tema went in search of them and found them dead or dying of thirst.

Another pointer to a Hebrew settlement in Arabia is the mention of *priests* in xii. 17. Two priestly tribes in Medina were known to the Arabs as the Kāhinayn. They formed the hard kernel of the Hebrew tribes of Nadîr and Qurayẓa.

Again, the raid which the *Chaldaeans* made on Job's camels and servants (i. 12 f.) may well have occurred during Nabonidus's wars and skirmishes with the local Arabs. At any rate this is the one and only time, so far as we know, that the Chaldaeans were warring in this area. Further, Eliphaz's words in xv. 19 imply that foreigners had but recently arrived in the land.⁴

Furthermore, when Job longs for the quiet of the grave he says (iii. 14) that there he would be with kings who *rebuilt* ruined sites for themselves. Though it is the constant boast of Accadian rulers that they rebuilt ancient ruins, it is significant that it was the opposition of priests and people to Nabonidus when he planned to restore the temple of Sin in Harran that led to his self-imposed exile in Arabia. On his return one of his first acts was to rebuild this temple, and at the same time he rebuilt and enlarged Harran as the god had commanded. Job's contemporary, the Second Isaiah, prophesies of Jehovah restoring the ruins of Jerusalem (xliv. 26, xlix. 19, and cf. li. 3).

---

³ Or, perhaps, " were safe." The meaning would then be that the caravan traffic was allowed to proceed unmolested, and therefore the caravaners had nothing to fear.

⁴ It is probable that Eliphaz the Temanite hailed from Tema, rather than from Teman. Eusebius said that " Thamon " was fifteen Roman miles (Jerome, five miles) from Petra. The form Teymānî would in Arabic be the man of Teymâ'u, cf. Ṣan'ânî from Ṣan'â'u (Brockelmann, *VG*, I, 399). Tema is spelt without *yôdh* in Job vi. 19, but LXX has Thaiman. Remains of the old Jewish town there are still extant. See *Handbook of Arabia*, I, 118.

In addition to these historical pointers it may confidently be affirmed that no Hebrew writing comparable with the majestic flow of Job's verse has come down to us since the sixth century. The difference between exilic and post-exilic writing, apart from the Second Isaiah, is as palpable as it is notorious.

Medina was the centre of Jewish Arabian fusion. In later days Jews vied with Arabs in writing verse. Arab proselytes were numerous and educated Jews were masters of both languages. For these reasons Job may be regarded not as an Edomite, but as a Hebrew (I prefer to write Hebrew rather than Jew because the possibility that Job's grandparents came from Samaria cannot be ruled out) settled in what is now known as the Ḥijāz, and his acquaintance with the Old Testament writings which from time to time emerges is what one would naturally expect. If we add to these considerations the use of a peculiarity in Ḥijāzi Arabic, noted below,[5] the cumulative evidence for a sixth-century date and a Hebrew-Arabian author is impressive.

Though it has always been recognized that Job is an Arabian figure, the paramount importance of the Arabian language in the book has received less than justice. To begin with, the *mise en scène* is Arabian. Three poets, later to be joined by a fourth, meet together to deal with a given theme in verse of surpassing beauty, just as the old Arabs did when tribal poets engaged in poetic contests at the annual fairs, a custom which still survives to the present day in Syria. The first readers of this book would have understood at once what the circumstances were and would have followed the language as well as the arguments with the eyes of literary critics. They were left to form their own judgement on the first point, but the second was removed from their province. In place of the human umpires whose office it was to pronounce on the artistic merits of the protagonists the inspired writer enthroned Jehovah, the Lord of the worlds, whose verdict was concerned with His government of the universe.

Inasmuch as the text of Job has been subject to "emendation," *i.e.*, deliberate falsification of the evidence, to an appalling degree, and inasmuch as the integrity of the book has been called in question I determined to read it as though it were an Arabic work with the hope of throwing light on passages which have never been satisfactorily explained; deciding whether the language of Elihu and the poem on Wisdom differ philologically

[5] On xxvii. 8.

from the rest of the book ; and whether any part of it is
" strongly marked by Aramaisms." [6] To save space Arabic
parallels cannot be given, but it may be said that Aramaisms in
Job [7] are very rare indeed, and that the Elihu and Wisdom
chapters contain words and forms familiar in Arabic but unknown
in Biblical Hebrew.   One of these is too beautiful to be passed
over : " out of the north cometh golden splendour " (xxxvii. 22).
Here *zahabh = dhihbah*, falling rain shot through by the rays of
the sun.   Pompous and didactic as Elihu is depicted, his creator
allows him his inspired moments.

So skilfully and convincingly has the inspired writer clothed
the speakers with personality that we lose sight of the possibility
that they may never have existed outside his imagination.   Job's
friends are not only champions of an untenable theology : they
are rivals in a poetic contest, a fact which the rhetorical figure of
taurīya explained in the notes on iii. 22 brings clearly to the fore.
Thus when in xviii. 2 Bildad says : " *How long* will you [8] lay
traps for words ? " he is expressing his irritation at this habit of
Job, who replies (xix. 2) : " *How long* will you pain my soul and
make me sick with (or, about) words and never answer my
charges ? "

Before any discussion of the contribution of Arabic to the
interpretation of Job it must needs be said that Arabic is a
language of far greater content than " classical " Arabic which is
based on the language of the poets of Najd.   Arabic includes the
dialects of all the tribes in all areas of the peninsula : consequently it is legitimate to cite dialectical forms that are
known [9] and forms that have arisen through metathesis or the
interchange of consonants.   Philologically the Book of Job is a
valuable source of information about old Arabic, for the Arabic
words that it contains and its rhetorical devices are not to be
found until they appear in Arabic literature nearly two thousand
years later.

The following study is confined to texts which seem to me to

---

[6] *Century Bible*, 24.
[7] They are cited in *ICC*, xlvi. f.   " *Roqebh* in xiii. 29, if it meant wine-skin,
would also be an Aramaism."   It would not, as an Arabic lexicon would show.
[8] The 2nd p. plural is a mark of Arab politeness which a speaker begins with.
He generally falls back on the 2nd p. singular as his discourse continues. I have
noticed this habit in my Arab correspondents.
[9] See C. Rabin, *Ancient West-Arabian* (London, 1951), and my " Arabic and
Hebrew Lexicography " in *Abr-Nahrain*, 1961, 3 f.

be wrongly translated in the Revised Version and to those which commentators have abandoned or mutilated :

iii. 22

Which rejoice exceedingly (marg.: unto exultation),
And are glad, when they can find the grave.

hassemēḥîm 'elê gîl
yāsîsû kî yimṣe'û qebher

Commentators, seeing that parallelism is lacking, would read *gal* with one MS. Against this there is no evidence for the use of *gal* as a heap of stones over a grave; but there is an Arabic word *gâl* which means the interior side of a grave. Thus the verse should be rendered :

Who are glad when they come to the grave,
Who rejoice when they find the tomb.

Here there is the first of many examples of the use of a metonym, a rhetorical figure which the Arabs call *taurīya*. The Koran—lv. 4, *al-šamsu wal-qamaru biḥusbâni, wal-najmu wal-šajaru yasjudâni,* " the sun and the moon (run their course) by a reckoning, and the herbs and the trees bow in worship " [10]— provides a classic example of this figure. The ambiguity lies in *najm* which means star as well as herbs. One would expect the mention of stars to follow sun and moon, but then one would be left with stars and trees, unlikely companions, so that one is forced to conclude that the less common meaning of " herbs " is to be understood. Similarly *gîl*, " rejoicing," is the natural sequent of *simḥāh*, but the context requires the mention of a grave.

v. 5

Whose harvest the hungry eateth up,
And taketh it even out of the thorns,
And the snare gapeth for their substance.

'asher qeṣîrô ra'ēbh yōkēl
we'el-miṣṣinnîm yiqqāḥēhû
wešā'af ṣammîm ḥeylām.

Translators ancient and modern have made heavy work of

[10] Cited by A. F. Mehren, *Die Rhetorik der Araber* (Copenhagen, 1853), 177 f.

this verse, but read in its Arabian setting the text is faultless, though the pointing sadly errs. What the writer said was :

> Whose harvest the hungry eat,
> And take it to the(ir) famished ones.
> The starving are eager for their substance.

Obviously, as the *maqqēf* indicates, the *miṣṣinnîm* are the people to whom the food is taken. The word should be pointed *moṣnîm*, a *hofal* participle of *ṣānāh* = Ar. *ḍaniya,* " was emaciated," *aḍnā,* " made ill by hunger." Those who are eager for the stolen food are the *ṣāmîm,* not the *ṣammîm* ! In BH *ṣām* always means " fasted," but in Arabic it has a wider meaning, " went without food," as when it is used of a horse. The variant *ḥelqām* in one MS. is attractive : the starving are eager for their *share.*

xi. 12

> But an empty man will get understanding
> When a wild ass's colt is born a man. (marg.)
>
> *we'îš nābhûb yillābhēbh*
> *we'îr pere' 'ādhām yiwwalēdh.*

Though there is no doubt that the old Jewish commentators were right in explaining the verse thus, and though the rhetorical antithesis between that which is hollow and that which has a heart is obvious, the full force of the words is to be felt only in Arabic. Thus an *unbūb* is a hollow pipe or tube, while the *lubb* is the heart, pith, or kernel of a tree or nut. The rendering of RVm. stands.

xii. 21

> He poureth contempt upon princes,
> And looseth the belt of the strong.
>
> *šōfēk būz ʿal-nedhîbhîm*
> *umeziaḥ 'afîqîm rippāh.*

There is nothing " dubious " about this verse. *BDB* gives the correct Arabic parallel, *afiqa,* " excelled," but overlooks the parallel of *nādhîbh,* " noble in mind and character," with *'ufuq* and *âfiq,* " excelling in mind and generosity." Thus the categories are the noble and the generous and the translation should be altered accordingly.

xiii. 12

Your memorable sayings are proverbs of ashes,
Your defences are defences of clay.

zikhroneykhem mišley 'efer
legabbey-ḥomer gabbeykhem.

Neither " defences " (*ICC*), nor Stevenson's seemingly
attractive suggestion of " cisterns " is appropriate here, for it is
Job the speaker who is on the defence, not his " comforters " ;
and to compare their arguments to earthen cisterns which after
all normally hold their water has not much point. As Job is
saying that the maxims of which his friends remind him are as
dry as dust and their answers to his complaint against God are
no better, we need a word that will supply a " dusty answer."
This is supplied by the Ar. *jâba* of which on the analogy of *ḥâja*,
pl. *ḥâj*, would be *jâb*, the third radical being sharpened in
Hebrew.   There is no need to insist on translating *ḥomer* by
" clay."   In xxx. 19 it is parallel with *'efer* as here and means
no more than dust or dirt.   Thus the verse may be rendered :

Your reminders are proverbs of ashes,
Your replies are dusty answers.

(Note the asseverative *le-* here.)

xvi. 5

But I would strengthen you with my mouth,
And the solace of my lips should assuage *your grief.*

a'ammiṣekhem bemô-pî
wenîd sefāthay yaḥsok

The next verse is connected by discourse and paronomasia with
its predecessor :

Though I speak, my grief is not assuaged :
And though I forbear, what am I eased ?

'im-adhabberah lō'-yēḥāsek k'ēbhî
we'aḥdelāh mah-minnî yahalōk.

The meaning of *ḥāsak* in the two verses is not the same.   Failure
to see this has led to mistranslation in ancient times and to
mutilation more recently.   In Arabic *ḥašaka* is used of a full
flow of milk, of copious rain, and as an adjective *ḥāšik* means

" continuous," " consecutive." *Nîd* should be taken literally with LXX (κίνησιν). In *v.* 6 *ḥāsak* bears its normal Hebrew meaning. Its concrete embodiment is Ar. *ḥišāk*, a little piece of wood put into the mouth of a kid to restrain it from sucking its dam.[11] The two verses then read :

> I could strengthen you with my mouth,
> And the movement of my lips would not stop.
> Were I to speak, my pain would not be kept back,
> And were I to stop talking, how should I be eased ?

Again we have a *taurīya.*

xvii. 15

> Where then is my hope ?
> And as for my hope, who shall see it ?
>
> *we'ayyeh 'ēfô tiqwāthî*
> *wetiqwāthî mî yešurennāh*

The same phenomenon again. Targ. and Vulg. agree in giving the meaning *patientia*, and LXX prosperity, to the second *tiqwāh*. But as Job is still persisting in maintaining his innocence and complaining of God's injustice in reducing him to such a state that he is tempted to long for death, one would expect that he would be lamenting that his godly reputation and his hope of vindication would be lost in the grave. This expectation is realized if we interpret the word in the sense of Ar. *taqwā*, " godly fear." *Two* nouns are required as the subject of *tēradnah* in the following verse, and no alteration in the text can be tolerated. The second hemistich should be rendered :

> And who will see my steadfast piety ?

This word *tiqwāh* occurs in another *taurīya* in vii. 6 where Job says : " My days are swifter than a shuttle, they come to an end without hope." Ibn Ezra noted that *tiqwāh* here could mean " thread."

xviii. 12

> His strength shall be hungerbitten,
> And calamity shall be ready for his halting.
>
> *yehî-rā'ēbh 'onô*
> *we'ēydh nākhôn leṣal'ô*

---

[11] So Albright in *BASOR*, 83, 24.

The difficulty felt by commentators in this verse disappears when *rā'ēbh* is given its Arabic meaning of " weak and cowardly." Thus the first hemistich should run :

His strength becomes weak.

xix. 2

How long will ye vex my soul,
And break me in pieces with words ?

*'adh-'ānāh toghiyûn nafšî
uthedakke'ûnanî bhemillîm*

Ar. *wajiya* means " felt pain " and *dukka* means " was ill." This is clearly the meaning of *nidhkeythî* in Ps. xxxviii. 11. See p. 109 above.

xix. 8

He hath fenced up my way that I cannot pass,
And hath set darkness in my paths.

*'orḥî ghādar welo' 'e'ebhôr
we'al nethîbôthay ḥošek yāsîm*

To put *darkness* on a path is a strange and unnatural expression, and if the path was walled up darkness would make very little difference to the traveller in a place where further progress was impossible. Parallelism requires an obstacle, in this case a hedge of thorns, known to the Arabs as *ḥasak*. Doughty [12] saw a Bedu and his wife dragging away large boughs of the *ṭalḥ* tree, which has large curved thorns, to form a sheep-pen. Probably the word here should be pointed *ḥāšāk*. The second hemistich should run :

And has put a thorn hedge on my paths.

xx. 6

Though his excellency mount up to the heavens,
And his head reach unto the clouds.

'im-ya'aleh laššāmayim sî'ô

Obviously a parallel to " head " is needed here. This is supplied by the Ar. cognate, *šawā*, which means the head or skull of a

[12] *Arabia Deserta*, II, 220.

human being. A literal rendering would be " topknot," but as
this would be intolerable here it would be best to invert the
order of the synonyms and translate :

> Though his head mount up . . .
> And his crown reach . . .

xx. 25

> Terrors are upon him.
> *yahalok 'aläyw 'ēmîm*

Here vocabulary and syntax are Arabic. *Halaka* means " fell,"
and when the predicate is separated from its subject it is
normally written in the 3rd p. sing. masculine. The text therefore
is correct.

xxii. 30

> He shall deliver *even* him that is not innocent ;
> Yea, he shall be delivered through the cleanness of his hands.
>
> > *yemallēṭ 'iy-naqi*
> > *wenimlaṭ bebhor kappeykha*

Again no alteration of the text is tolerable : *'i* is the Ar. form
'ayya, " whomsoever." Some Vss. understood this, and they
cannot be quoted in support of the footnotes in Kittel's *BH*.
The pointing *nimlaṭṭa* (Hoffman) is undoubtedly correct. The
verse should be translated :

> He will deliver whomsoever is innocent,
> And thou wilt be delivered through the cleanness of thy hands.

xxiii. 9

> On the left hand, when he doth work, but I cannot behold him :
> He hideth himself on the right hand, that I cannot see him.
>
> > *sem'ôl ba'asothô welō' 'āḥaz*
> > *ya'aṭof yāmîn welo' 'er'eh*

Here *'āsāh* is not the common Hebrew verb, but the Ar. *ghaša*,
" he came to," and the verse should be translated :

> When he goes to the left I cannot behold him ;
> When he turns to the right I cannot see him.

There is no need to follow Syr. and Vulg. in reading " When *I* turn," as the context plainly shows that when Job seeks God He seems to have removed Himself. Though omnipresent, God cannot be apprehended.

xxiv. 5

Behold, as wild asses in the desert
They go forth to their work, seeking diligently for meat.

mešaḥarey laṭṭāref ʿarābhâh lô leḥem lanneʿārîm

ICC errs in asserting that the text is corrupt and " admits of no rhythmical articulation." Obviously the metre requires three beats in each half of the verse, and so the colon must come after *ʿarābhāh*. It is the word *lô* that has caused difficulty to commentators, some of whom would strike it out altogether and others would alter it to the negative particle. But the text is perfectly sound : all that is needed is to punctuate *lû* [13] and the verse would then read :

They go early to the steppe for meat,
(To see) if there be food for the(ir) children.

xxiv. 6

And they glean the vintage of the wicked.

wekherem rāšāʿ yēlaqqēšû

The Vss. agree with RV ; but most moderns, objecting to the importation of the ethical character of the vineowners as irrelevant, wrongly alter *rāšāʿ* to *ʿāšîr*. But the word is correct. In Arabic *rassagha* means " he provided handsomely for his family," and *ʿayš rasîgh* means " ample means of subsistence." Almost certainly *rich* is what the writer meant.

xxiv. 19

Drought and heat consume the snow waters ;
So *doth* Sheol *those which* have sinned.

ṣîyyāh gam-hom yigzelû meymey šeleg
šeʾôl ḥāṭāʾu.

ICC brands this verse as " unrhythmical, awkwardly expressed, and no doubt corrupt." But if the colon is put in the right

---

[13] See Reckendorff's *Arabische Syntax*, 497, and Wright's *Arabic Grammar*, II, 348.

place there is nothing wrong with the metre, and read as Hebraeo-Arabic verse a straightforward meaning is forthcoming :

> When drought and heat are great
> The snow waters fail to flow.

In Arabic *jazala* means " was large " and *jazl* "much of anything." *Še'ôl* could be the equivalent of *sāla*, " flowed," while *ḥāṭā'* means " missed," as in Pr. xix. 2, etc. Alternatively *še'ôl* might conceal *sayl*, " watercourse " or " torrent," *sā'il*, " fluid," etc. Thus it is possible that the second hemistich should run " the snow waters miss the watercourse." The snow that had fallen on the high ground and should have flowed down the wadi to water the land parched by the summer heat, had melted immediately where it lay and sunk into the ground, and so failed to reach the torrent-bed to bring fertility to the land below. This would happen if rain did not dissolve the snow and bring it with it to its accustomed channel. But on the whole the rendering adopted above seems preferable.

xxvii. 8

> When God taketh away his soul.
> *kî yēšel 'elôah nafšô*

It has been suggested that *yēšel* is a by-form of *šālal*, as of course it could be if such a verb existed in Hebrew ! Many moderns advocate altering the text to *yiš'al*, " When God demandeth his life," an idiom found in Luke xii. 20. The idea is right, but the method wrong. It is unnecessary to tamper with the text, for in Arabic *yisal* is often written for *yis'al*,[14] and *the elision of hamza is a characteristic of Ḥijāzî Arabic.*[15] Departures from the strict orthography of " classical " Arabic are much older than is commonly supposed if we accept the evidence of Job here and elsewhere.

xxviii. 4

> He breaketh open a shaft away from where men sojourn ;
> They are forgotten of the foot *that passeth by* ;
> They hang afar from men, they swing to and fro.
> *pāraṣ naḥal mē'im-gār*
> *hanniškaḥîm minnî-rāgel*
> *dallū mē'enôš nā'û*

---

[14] Wright, *op. cit.*, I, 77.   [15] Rabin, *op. cit.*, 131.

Every word in the first line has been regarded with suspicion, but once it is read as Arabic its obscurity dissolves. To begin with, *ICC* rightly points out that *pāraṣ* elsewhere in the Old Testament does not bear the meaning it must have here. But Arabic *faraṣa* means " cut, slit, pierced," and so is aptly used of cutting a shaft. *Naḥal*, a noun to which no Arabic cognate is assigned in *BDB*, is akin to *khalla*, " hole," and *khalal*, " gap, interstice," and so the meaning " shaft " is established. *Mēʿim gār* was rendered ἀπὸ κονίας by the LXX, so that they must have read *mēʿim gēr*, meaning chalk, gypsum, or lime. The word is used by Isaiah in xxvii. 9.[16] *BDB* questions the reading *mēʿim*, to which it assigns the meaning " away from, far from," but as the preposition *ʿim* was not written by the author the point is irrelevant. The word should be pointed with a *pathaḥ* and referred to Ar. *ghamma*, " covered," and so the meaning is " from the covering of chalk." *Hanniškāḥîm*, translated as it must be " *they that are* " something, leaves us without a predicate! But there must be one and it is there. The verb *šakhaḥ* has already been shown by Eitan [17] to be subject to methathesis in Ps. cxxxvii. 5, where it means " let my right hand be paralysed " on the strength of Ar. *kasiḥa* (i) " crippled." Here almost the same thing has happened, but in this case the form of the Arabic verb is *kasaḥa* (a), " swept away." [18] With *dallû* the predicate begins, and without any alteration or additions to the text the verse says :

> He cuts a shaft through the covering of chalk ;
> Those who are swept off their feet
> Hang suspended far from men, they swing to and fro.

Mr. Tom Hirst, one of London's consultant geologists, kindly tells me that " shafts sunk through chalk and limestone for working mineral deposits are common throughout the world. Iron ores are commonly found in limestones, and veins containing gold, silver, and copper ores could occur, as well as lead and zinc. Most of the world's silver is obtained from lead ore, galena, and most galena deposits are found in limestones." Mr. Hirst has listed precisely the minerals of which the author speaks, adding

[16] It is permissible to question whether Fränkel was right in including this among the words alleged to have been borrowed by the Arabs from their Aramaic-speaking neighbours.

[17] *JRAS*, 1944, 34.

[18] Lane, *Arabic-English Lexicon*, 2610a.

zinc for good measure. Thus there can be no doubt that the sacred writer is describing mining sites which he had actually seen and which he could assume that his readers would know of. The mention of gold in *v.* 1 suggests a site in the Ḥijāz where ancient gold-mines have been discovered and reopened.[19]

xxix. 10

The voice of the nobles was hushed.

qôl nedhîbhîm neḥbā'û

Here the RV is right and the marg. is wrong, because the verb is cognate with Ar. *khabi'a*, " (the fire) died out." The same word is used in *v.* 8 in the sense of " hid themselves." The homonym has not been recognized by commentators.

xxx. 6

In holes of the earth and of the rocks.

ḥôrey 'āfār wekēfîm

Unless we acquiesce in the importation of an Aramaic word here, which is highly improbable, the meaning is not " rocks," but " mountain-tops." Arabic has no word *kēf*, but *'akâfîf* means " the tops of mountains." Jeremiah (iv. 29) said : " they *go up* into the mountain-tops " (*kēfîm*), fleeing from the invader.

xxx. 13

Even men that have no helper.

lô' 'ozēr lāmô

Read as Arabic this would be an imprecation, " May they have no helper," and the text needs no alteration.

xxx. 14

As through a wide breach they come :
In the midst of the ruin they roll themselves *upon me*.

keferes rāḥābh ye'ethāyû
taḥath šo'āh hithgalgālû

---

[19] K. S. Twitchell, *Saudi Arabia* (Princeton, 1947), index under " gold " and " Mahad Dhahab."

Rolling is hardly appropriate here, and parallels to " breach " and " come " are needed.   In Arabic *ṭā'a* means " bored a hole," and *tajaljala* means " moved, set in motion."   Thus we could render :

> As through a wide breach they come,
> Where the gap is made they advance.

xxx. 18, 19

> By the great force *of my disease* is my garment disfigured ;
> It bindeth me about as the collar of my coat.
>
> *berobh-koaḥ yithḥappēs lebhûśî*
> *kefî khuttontî ya'azrēnî*

The key to the meaning of this verse is to be found in *koaḥ* which in Arabic, where Q and K frequently interchange, means " pus " (*qayḥ*), so that the answer to Peake's pertinent question, " Does it mean that the discharge from his ulcers saturated his clothes, so that they stuck to him ? " is Yes.   *Yithḥappēs*, which commonly means disguising oneself by a change of clothes, here is to be explained by Ar. *ḥafaša*, " the water ran, the clouds brought violent rain."   Thus the verse should be read :

> My clothing is saturated with much suppuration ;
> It sticks to me like my undergarment.

The now familiar device of *taurîya*, latent in *ḥāfas*, is carried on in *v.* 19 which begins *horanî laḥomer*, " he hath thrown me into the dirt," for Ar. *waryun* is a synonym of *qayḥ*.   Incidentally by its reference to ii. 8 where Job is sitting in ashes, this verse should dissolve any lingering doubt that the prologue is an integral part of the book.

xxxi. 29

> If I rejoiced at the destruction of him that hated me,
> Or lifted up myself when evil found him.
>
> *wehith'ararî kî meṣā'ô rā'*

Parallelism calls for the meaning " was glad."   To obtain this sense which was apparent to the Targumist many would alter the text to *hithro'a'tî* as in Ps. lx. 10, lxv. 14, as though metathesis had never been heard of.   It is worth noting that neither *BDB* nor *KB* do justice to the $\sqrt{r\hat{u}^{\epsilon}}$ which in Arabic is a denominative from *rû'un*, " heart." *Râ'a* means " his heart was affected with fear " or (with the opposite meaning with which the Arabs delight to complicate their language), " . . . with joy." This ambiguity resides in Hebrew also, for *hērî'a*, as *BDB* shows, can mean " shout in triumph," " cry in distress," etc. Render :

> Or was glad when evil befell him.

xxxiii. 7

> Neither shall my pressure be heavy upon thee.
>
> *we'akpî 'āleykha lō' yikhbādh*

This is not an Aramaism. The concrete meaning is clearly that of Ar. *ikâf*, pack-saddle, as in *BDB*, so that the meaning must be weight or burden.

xxxiii. 19

> He is chastened also with pain upon his bed,
> And with continual strife in his bones.
>
> *werîbh 'aṣāmāyw 'ēthān*

It may be asked what is meant by the *Qerē rôbh*. If this is to be referred to Ar. *râba*, churned, the meaning would be the *tumult* in his bones.

xxxiii. 24

> Deliver him from going down to the pit.
>
> *pedā'ēhû mēredheth šaḥath*

The " emendation " *perā'ēhû* (supported by 2 MSS.) is unsatisfactory for the reason given in *ICC*. If we read this as Arabic we get the required meaning, treating the *peh* as the conjunction with the imperative of *wada'a*, " he allowed, let him off exempted." The speaker says : " Do not let him go down to the pit." The use of *fā'* with the imperative is very common.[20]

---

[20] Reckendorff, *op. cit.*, 318 f. The Arabic conjunction was irrepressible. It is to be found in Aramaic, Nabataean, and Palmyrene inscriptions. See Cooke, *NSI*, 165, etc.

xxxiii. 27

He singeth before men and saith . . .

yāšor ʿal-ʾanašîm wayyomer

Here RV is implicitly altering the punctuation ; but it is correct. The verb is Ar. *sarra*, rejoiced, and so the verse should be rendered :

He says joyfully to men . . . he hath redeemed my soul.

The man is rejoicing at his restoration to health and happiness.

xxxiv. 29

When he giveth quietness, who then can condemn ?

wehû yašqîṭ ûmî yaršiʿ

One MS. has *yišqôṭ*, and the meaning would then be " if God by remaining quiet and not interfering, fails to condemn a man what right has anyone to do so ? " Nevertheless it is tempting to regard the verb as a metathetical form of *yaqšîṭ* (see Prov. xxii. 21 for the noun and cf. Ar. *qasaṭa*, " he acted justly ") and translate :

If *He* declares a man just, who then can condemn him ?

At any rate only thus can the latent antithesis be clearly brought out.

xxxvi. 17

But thou art full of the judgement of the wicked
Judgement and justice take hold *on thee.*

wedîn-rāšāʿ mālēthā
dîn ûmišpāṭ yithmōkhû

Here again there is an obvious *taurîya*. The first *dîn* = Ar. *zuwân*, " food," and so follows naturally the reference to the riches of Job's table in the preceding verse. The first hemistich should be translated :

Thou art full of a wicked man's food.

xxxvi. 31

By these he judgeth the peoples ;
He giveth meat in abundance.

ki bhām yādhîn ʿammîm

As the last note shows the verse should be rendered

By these he feedeth the peoples.

D interchanged with Z in the dialect of the Ṭayyi'. The form is
not Aramaic.

xxxviii. 10

And I prescribed for it my decree (marg. : boundary).

wā'ešbōr ʿalayw ḥuqqî

No authority recognized in *šābhar* the meaning " broke." The
Vss. have " fixed," " made," " decided," " encompassed " :
all guesses. *Ḥōq* is translated " boundaries," " decree," " my
decree," " my boundaries." What seems to be needed is a verb
that implies measuring, and this must be the Ar. *šabara*,
" measured by span." [21] Lane quotes *man laka an tašbura
l-basîṭata*, " Who will guarantee for thee that thou wilt measure
the earth with thy span ? " This sentence and Isa. xl. 12, " Who
hath measured the waters of the sea [22] in the hollow of his hand,
and meted out the heavens with a span ? (*zereth*)," admirably
illustrate the thought of this verse. With Targ. render " my
decree " and the verse runs :

I measured it by span by my decree.

xxxviii. 17

Have the gates of death been revealed unto thee ?
Or hast thou seen the gates of the shadow of death ?

*haniglû lekha šaʿarey-māweth
wešaʿarey ṣalmāweth tir'eh*

Here is another example of homonym noted in xvii. 15 above.

[21] The view that Hebrew *shîn* must = Ar. *sîn* and *vice versa* is antiquated and
untenable. See my notes in *Abr-Nahrain*, 5 *et passim*.
[22] The reading of *DSIsᵃ*.

The second *ša'r* is to be compared with Ar. *ṭaghr*, " boundary," and so we should render :

> Have the gates of death been revealed to thee ?
> And hast thou seen the confines of darkness ?

xxxviii. 22

> Hast thou entered the treasuries of the snow ?
> Or hast thou seen the treasuries of the hail ?
>
> *habhâthâ el-'oṣerôth šeleg*
> *we'ôṣeroth bārādh tir'eh*

Again the same phenomenon. The second *'ôṣerôth* is to be explained by Ar. *wadrā* or *wadrā'u*, " large rock." The meaning then is

> Hast thou seen the huge hailstones ?

Cf. Josh. x. 11, " The Lord cast upon them *great stones* from heaven." Hebrew shuns initial *waw* and either changes it to *yôdh* or prefixes an *aleph*. In Arabic the interchange of *alif* and *waw* is common.

xxxviii. 24

> By what way is the light parted,
> Or the east wind scattered upon the earth ?
>
> *ēy-zeh hadderek yēḥāleq 'ôr*
> *yāfēṣ qādîm 'aley-āreṣ.*

The text is perfectly clear and no alteration can be tolerated. Here *'ôr* does not mean " light," but " heat," as in Arabic where *'uwâr* means " the heat of a fire " (cf. Isa. l. 11, etc. ; there the pointing is *'ûr*) ; *yāfēṣ* introduces a relative clause, and the verse runs :

> Which is the way to where the heat is distributed,
> Which the sirocco scatters over the earth ?

xxxix. 4

> Their young ones are in good liking ;
> They grow up in the open field.
>
> *yaḥlemû bheneyhem yirbû bhabbār*

Bār is not an Aramaism. All the words in this hemistich would bear the same meaning in Arabic with but trifling adjustments. *Taḥallama* means " grew fat," and so the verse could begin :

> Their young put on flesh as they grow up in the open.

xxxix. 13

The wing of the ostrich rejoiceth ;
But are her pinions and feathers kindly ?

> *kenaf-renānîm ne'elāsāh*
> *'im-'ebhrah ḥasîdhah wenoṣāh*

Here we have no less than three homonyms : (i) the letters *'-b-r-h* could mean " pinion," or is " strong " ; (ii) *ḥasîdhāh*, " kindly " or " stork " ; (iii) *n-s-h*, " feathers " or " hawk." Now, as in the Arabic examples quoted in the notes on iii. 22, the reader is " conditioned " to accept the impossible : the mention of pinions and feathers after wings would seem to be natural and inevitable, but they are a trap for the unwary. In each case we must adopt the second alternative and the meaning then becomes clear. The *stork* has large and *powerful* wings, and the wings of a *hawk* which enable him to hover over his prey are stronger than those of most birds. The Massoretic punctuators must be counted among the writer's victims, for *'-b-r-h* could be pointed *'ābherāh*, and *n-s-h* should be *niṣṣāh*, a *nomen unitatis* of *nēṣ* in *v*. 26. Lastly *'alas* here has nothing to do with rejoicing but = Ar. *'alaza*, " was weak " ; and so the verse reads :

> Is the wing of the ostrich weak,
> Or is it strong like that of the stork and hawk ?[23]

This verse is of extraordinary interest because it indicates that the poetry of Job is a literary composition. Had it been recited, or, like the poetry of the prophets, been proclaimed in the ears of the people, the homonyms would have vanished into thin air. The author must have written his book for a highly cultured and sophisticated society.[24]

---

[23] The construction is the *comparatio decurtata*, *GK*, 118*r* and N2.
[24] For the *written jinās* see Mehren, *op. cit.*, 156 f.

xl. 23

Behold, if a river overflow, he trembleth not :
He is confident, though Jordan swell even to his mouth.

hēn ya'ašōq nāhār lō' yaḥpôz
yibhṭaḥ kî-yāghiakh yardēn 'el-pîhû

hēn = Ar. *'in*, " if " ; *'āšaq* = Ar. *'afaqa*, " came and went " ; [25] *bāṭaḥ* = Ar. *inbaṭaha*, " lay extended " (as in *BDB*) ; and *yarden*, " flowing water," as in Mandaean, with no reference to the Jordan. Thus the verse runs :

Though the river rise and fall, he is not alarmed :
He lies outstretched though the flood swell.

Metre requires that *'el-pîhû* should be transferred to the next verse.

xl. 24

Shall any take him while he is on the watch,
Or pierce through his nose with a snare ?

be'ēnāyw yiqqāḥennû
bemôqešîm yinqabh-'āf.

Môqešîm here are amphibians ; cf. *maqasa*, " he vied in diving with," while *naqab* is to be explained as a by-form of Ar. *qabba*, " was dry." The verse may be rendered :

Into his mouth with open eyes he receives it ;
(Alone) among the river animals his snout is dry.

The great beast lies unperturbed with his snout above the water.

xli. 22

His underparts are *like* sharp potsherds ;
He spreadeth *as it were* a threshing wain upon the mire.

yirpadh ḥāruṣ 'aley-ṭîṭ

Rafadh = Ar. *arthada*, " dug down to wet ground," [26] so the hemistich should be rendered :

He leaves imprints on the mud like a threshing sledge.

---

[25] See my note in *BSOAS*, 1954, 8. Ar. *ghasaqa*, suggested by Prof. Driver in *Studies in Old Testament Prophecy* (Edinburgh, 1950), 60, is applied only to tears, pus, or light rain.

[26] See my note in *Abr-Nahrain*, 1961, 15 and 34.

It will have become plain that much of the text of Job is unintelligible without recourse to Arabic,[27] and everything points to the author having lived in an oasis in the Ḥijāz. For example his hero possessed land which was ploughed by cows, and round him lay the desert and the salt land. A knowledge of local agricultural practice would have saved critics from questioning and then altering the statement " the cows were ploughing " in i. 14. *In this area cows and not oxen were put to the yoke.* Doughty [28] saw " small humped kine " at work ploughing at Tema and al-ʿUlā (Dedan). Furthermore salt ground lay outside the old Jewish settlement at Khaybar.

As it would be all but impossible for a foreigner coming with Nabonidus's occupation force to acquire the wide knowledge of Arabic that the author possessed, it would not be too much to infer that the tradition that the Hebrew occupation of the oases dated from the fall of Jerusalem may well be founded on fact ; while the hypothesis that he was a contemporary of the Second Isaiah is strengthened by the fact that the writer preserved the ancient purity and beauty of the poetry of the prophets influenced only by a vocabulary richer, so far as we know, than that of Israel.

It is a joy to me to offer this modest tribute of affection and gratitude to Professor Hooke, whose inspiring teaching, more than fifty years ago, put my feet on the ladder whose top reaches to heaven.

[27] Syntax and accidence are often Arabic. For lack of space details cannot be given.

[28] *Arabia Deserta*, I, 151 f. and 286.

THE OLD TESTAMENT AND SOME ASPECTS OF NEW TESTAMENT CHRISTOLOGY [1]

By A. J. B. HIGGINS

JESUS believed himself to be the fulfilment and embodiment of all the messianic hopes of his people. The New Testament writers bear eloquent witness to the early church's acceptance of this claim, especially in the appeal to scriptural testimonies to his being the Christ. More important than individual passages, however, is the correspondence of *ideas* in the Old Testament and the New Testament. In Christian retrospect it may even be permissible to speak of Old Testament " Christology." But the drawing up of parallels is always hazardous, and can become misleading and even perverse. The one sure safeguard is the principle of promise and fulfilment. History is rich in illustrations of how this principle works out in practice. Often the fulfilment of what was long expected turned out to be something more than fulfilment—a fresh phenomenon with features entirely new. Of no history is this so true as it is of salvation history. The one who was to come, the Christ, was such that when he came he was not recognized but was rejected at large by his own people. The new community he founded, on the other hand, claimed that its own understanding of the Jewish scriptures proved that Jesus Christ its crucified and risen Lord was foretold in them. This use of the scriptures, however, vital though it was felt to be, was really only secondary, for the belief of the early church in the " messiahship " of Jesus in its various aspects stemmed from his own claims. These claims in their turn were not based on but supported by scripture. The beginning of Christology is to be found ultimately in Jesus' own thought about himself and his mission. What follows touches upon a few aspects of this problem.

This study is an examination of the origin of what may be

[1] A revised form of an article first published in the *Canadian Journal of Theology*, VI (1960), No. 3, pp. 200 ff.

called the " Son Christologies " in the New Testament—Son of
David, Son of God, the Son—as seen against the background of
the Old Testament.   These Christologies are of the greater
interest in that they are held by some to have originated in the
mind of the founder of Christianity himself.   How far this may
be true, and in what sense, it is the purpose of this paper to
re-examine.   The Son of Man, while not the subject of special
and separate study here, belongs to another category of what
may be called " intercessory " or " sacrificial " Christologies—
the Servant of the Lord, the High-Priest—and it serves as the
focus of the Christologies to be discussed in this paper.

Son of David

Although the title Son of David does not itself appear in the
Old Testament, there are many passages which testify to Jewish
belief that the Messiah would be of Davidic descent,[2] an expectation which was in full vigour shortly before and at the time of
the rise of Christianity.[3]   It is true that of the Synoptic Gospels
it is in Matthew that the term is commonest.[4]   Otherwise it is
used only in the Bartimaeus story (Mk. x. 47 f., cf. Matt. xx. 30 f.,
Luke xviii. 38 f.).   But the tradition of Davidic descent is not
confined to such references.   More important than Acts xiii. 22 f.
(" of this man's [David's] seed God has brought to Israel according to his promise a saviour, Jesus ") are Rom. i. 3 f. :

> concerning his Son, who was born of the seed of David according to
> the flesh, declared Son of God in power according to the spirit of
> holiness through his resurrection from the dead, Jesus Christ

and 2 Tim ii. 8 :

> Remember Jesus Christ risen from the dead, of the seed of David.

Both these passages read like adaptations of an early creed.
The tradition of Jesus' Davidic descent was current, then, before
Paul wrote to the Roman church in the fifties.   Although not
prominent, it survived until the end of the first century, not only
in 2 Tim. ii. 8, but in the Jewish Christian elaborations of the

---

[2] Ps. lxxxix. 3 f., cxxxii. 11 f. ; Isa. ix. 6 f., xi. 1 ; Jer. xxiii. 5, xxxiii. 15, 17 ;
Hos. iii. 5 ; Amos ix. 11 f.
[3] Cf. Pss. Sol. xvii. 23 ; Jn. vii. 42 (Mic. v. 2).
[4] Matt. i. 1, ix. 27, xii. 23, xv. 22, xxi. 9, 15.

idea of Davidic sonship in the Apocalypse (iii. 7, v. 5, xxii. 16), and beyond.[5]

It is very difficult to accept the view that the passage about to be discussed was the creation of the Hellenistic church.[6] Whether the Son of David Christology is the creation of the Palestinian community or of Jesus himself is the real question, the answer to which depends on the view adopted of Mk. xii. 35–37 (cf. Matt. xxii. 41–45 ; Luke xx. 41–44) :

> And Jesus answered and said, as he taught in the temple, How do the scribes say that the Messiah is the son of David ? David himself said in the Holy Spirit,
>> The Lord said to my Lord, Sit at my right hand
>> Until I put thine enemies under thy feet.
> David himself calls him Lord, and how is he his son ?

Even if this passage records an actual historical incident, in which Jesus points out that Messiahship depends on higher considerations than Davidic ancestry,[7] it does not follow that Davidic ancestry is being denied, though it is certainly not being asserted. The real difficulty often urged against this passage as being anything else than a community formation is the use of Ps. cx. 1. That this verse of the psalm was widely used in the early church is clear both from the quotations of it in Acts ii. 34 f. and Heb. i. 13, and from allusions to it in Mk. xvi. 19 ; Acts vii. 56 ; Rom. viii. 34 ; 1 Cor. xv. 25 ; Eph. i. 20 ; Col. iii. 1 ; Heb. i. 3, viii. 1, x. 12, xii. 2 ; 1 Pet. iii. 22. A recent writer [8] has asked whether, in the pericope with which we are concerned, Jesus, on the view that he took care to conceal his Messiahship from all but his closest followers, would have ventured to defend it openly against Jewish opponents. This is an acute observation. But it is difficult to take him seriously when he later remarks [9] that the passage appears to be a defence of Jesus' Messiahship on the part of the church, based on a common acknowledgment of his non-Davidic descent. It must, therefore, it is argued, be earlier than Paul's assertion of Jesus' Davidic descent in Rom. i. 3. When may this hypothetical *volte-face*, from conviction of non-

---

[5] Barn. xii. 10 ; Ign. *Eph.* xviii. 2, xx. 2 ; *Rom.* vii. 3 ; *Smyrn.* i. 1 ; *Trall.* ix. 1.

[6] According to this view the purpose of Mk. xii. 35–7 would be to demonstrate that Jesus was not so much Son of David as Son of God, R. Bultmann, *Die Geschichte der synoptischen Tradition* (4th edn., 1958), p. 146.

[7] T. W. Manson, *The Teaching of Jesus* (2nd edn., 1935), p. 266, n. 2.

[8] J. Knox, *The Death of Christ* (1959), p. 41.

[9] *Ibid.*, p. 49.

Davidic lineage to the strongly-attested belief in Davidic descent, be conjectured to have taken place ?   There is a strange reluctance in some quarters to allow the possibility that not only the primitive Christian community but its founder may occasionally have quoted the Jewish scriptures.   The allusive nature of the saying, if it expresses the doctrinal belief of the church, is in striking contrast to the unmistakable clarity of early preaching and teaching, while it is in accord with the idiom of Jesus himself (cf. Luke vii. 22 f.).[10]   The conclusion up to this point is that the citation of the psalm is here rightly attributed to Jesus, and that the wide use of it in the community tradition was first suggested by this fact.

It is not, I think, irrelevant here to call attention to the reply of Jesus to the high-priest's question whether he was the Messiah. " I am, and you shall see the Son of Man sitting at the right hand of power and coming with the clouds of heaven " (Mk. xiv. 62).[11] Since this answer combines Dan. vii. 13 and Ps. cx. 1, the Messiah's session at God's right hand in Ps. cx. 1 is described in terms of the Son of Man.   The Son of Man intrudes itself into another Messianic concept.   Is not the same intrusion to be assumed in Mk. xii. 35–7 ?   In Mk. xiv. 62 Jesus apparently declares that it is as the Son of Man, and not as the [Son of David-] Messiah, that he will fulfil Ps. cx. 1.   The upshot is that if the authenticity of Mk. xiv. 62 is accepted, that of Mk. xii. 35–7 must also be accepted. That he is Son of David Jesus does not deny, but he implies that the psalm will find its fulfilment in him as in some sense the Son of Man.[12]

[10] V. Taylor, *The Gospel according to St. Mark* (1955), p. 493 ;   O. Cullmann, *The Christology of the New Testament* (E.T., 1959), p. 131 f.

[11] We are not here concerned with the strongly attested variant " Thou sayest that I am."

[12] It is significant that the Lukan parallel (xxii. 69) retains the fusion of the two concepts, while omitting the coming with the clouds.   This omission is characteristic of the third evangelist's tendency to tone down apocalyptic ideas ; he reports the session, but not the descent of the Son of Man.   That it *is* a matter of descent and not of ascent, as it is now fashionable to believe (*e.g.*, T. F. Glasson, *The Second Advent* [1945], pp. 63–8 ;   J. A. T. Robinson, *Jesus and His Coming* [1957], p. 45), is confirmed by the fact that the coming with the clouds, omitted by Luke, is subsequent to the sitting at God's right hand ;   so rightly G. R. Beasley-Murray, *Jesus and the Future* (1954), p. 259 ;   *A Commentary on Mark Thirteen* (1957), pp. 90 f.

Bultmann, *op. cit.*, p. 145, concedes the possibility " dass der in Mk. xii. 35–37 vorschwebende Gegensatz zum ' Davidsohn ' in der Tat der ' Menschen-sohn ' ist."   Jesus could then have uttered these words, but of course, in Bult-mann's view, with no reference to *himself* as Son of Man ; cf. E. Lohmeyer, *Das Evangelium des Markus* (1954), pp. 262 f.

Son of God

A Hellenistic origin is unlikely because of the early appearance of this Christology in the Pauline epistles. The most important instances are 1 Thess. i. 10 (very early fifties) and Rom. i. 4 (from a pre-Pauline liturgical formula). Is the Son of God Christology a creation of the early Palestinian church, or is it derived from its founder ? Can a decision be reached on the basis of the Old Testament background ? In the Old Testament, apart from angels as sons of God (Gen. vi. 2 ; Job i. 6, xxxviii. 7), both Israel (Ex. iv. 22 f. ; Isa. i. 2 ; Hos. xi. 1), and the king are called God's son (2 Sam. vii. 14 ; Ps. ii. 7, lxxxix. 26 f.). The question at first sight virtually amounts to a decision as to whether Ps. ii. 7 was first regarded by Jesus as expressing his filial consciousness. If so, it would be natural to explain the Son of God Christology as derived ultimately from him. The alternative would be that the Palestinian church seized upon the psalm and from it, or with its help, evolved the Christology, for there appears to be no certain example of the use of Son of God as a Messianic title in pre-Christian Judaism which might have lain ready to hand.[13] Yet it might have been expected that the Messiah, like the king, should occasionally be so called, in view of the fact that the Messianic hope arose out of the expectation of the fulfilment of the unrealized ideals of kingship.[14]

Right in the forefront, therefore, as a point of departure, stands Ps. ii. 7 : " Thou art my son, today I have begotten thee." Like Ps. cx. 1, it was current in early Christian use, for it is quoted in Acts xiii. 33 ; Heb. i. 5, v. 5. Nor was this the only part of the psalm to be quoted. In Acts iv. 25 f. its first two verses are quoted as fulfilled in the hostility of Gentiles and Jews and of Herod and Pilate against Jesus, and in Rev. xii. 5 and xix. 15 its ninth verse is utilized in the manner of the Psalms of Solomon to illustrate the vengeance which the Messiah will wreak upon his enemies. Whether this Christian use of Psalm ii is due entirely to the creativity of the church or to the known use of its seventh verse by Jesus himself, may turn out to be not

---

[13] Cf. G. Dalman, *The Words of Jesus* (1902), pp. 272, 275 ; C. H. Dodd, *The Interpretation of the Fourth Gospel* (1953), p. 253 ; S. Mowinckel, *He That Cometh* (1956), pp. 293 f., 368 ; O. Cullmann, *op. cit.*, pp. 274 ff.

[14] Cf. R. Bultmann, *Theology of the New Testament*, I (1952), p. 50.

the vital question as regards the genesis of the Son of God Christology. There is no evidence that he made any use of the psalm apart from *v. 7*, and even this is uncertain.

The voice at the baptism, " Thou art my beloved Son, in thee I am well pleased " (Mk. i. 11 ; cf. Matt. iii. 17 ; Luke iii. 22), is customarily regarded as containing allusions to both Ps. ii. 7 and Isa. xlii. 1 (" Behold my servant, whom I uphold, my chosen, in whom my soul delights "). The view, however, has been advanced, that only the latter passage is echoed, that υἱός μου in Mk. i. 11 represents παῖς μου in Isa. xlii. 1, and that this clarification of the Hebrew took place on Hellenistic soil before Mark took over the tradition. This transition, it is urged, might indeed have been facilitated by reminiscence of Ps. ii. 7, the second stage being the explicit quotation of the LXX version of this verse of the psalm in the " Western " text of Luke iii. 22 (" Thou art my Son, this day have I begotten thee ").[15] According to this view, Ps. ii. 7 is an excellent illustration of the creative rôle of the Old Testament in the development of New Testament Christology.[16] This view, however, labours under the disadvantage of removing from Palestinian to Hellenistic soil the possible influence of Ps. ii. 7 as a factor in the emergence of the Son of God Christology. It is difficult, if not impossible, to reconcile this with the early appearance of this Christology in Paul.

The view that Isa. xlii. 1 alone is at the basis of Mk. i. 11 would gain some support if the original reading in John i. 34 were ὁ ἐκλεκτός ; but it is by no means certain, despite its age, that this is the original text.[17] It seems far more likely that the evangelist, who concludes his Gospel by stating that its purpose was to inspire belief in Jesus as the Son of God (xx. 31), should in its opening scenes record the forerunner John the Baptist as testifying to the Son of God. There is, therefore, much to be said in favour of the opinion that the usual text of John i. 34 independently

---

[15] W. Zimmerli and J. Jeremias, *The Servant of God* (1957), p. 81.

[16] Cf. also the conclusions drawn from acceptance of the variant reading ἐκλεκτός (for υἱός) in Jn. i. 34, which is attested by Papyrus 5, Codex Sinaiticus (*prima manu*), the Curetonian and Sinaitic Syriac, an Old Latin MS (e), and St. Ambrose ; see the discussion of J. Jeremias, *op. cit.*, p. 61, n. 261, and p. 82 ; and O. Cullmann, *op. cit.*, p. 66, n. 3.

[17] It may be remarked that the substitution of υἱός for ἐκλεκτός, even if the latter is accepted as the true text, may not be anything more than a mere scribal alteration, all too easy for a copyist familiar with the Son of God title in the Fourth Gospel.

confirms the Son of God Christology in Mk. i. 11, expressed in terms of Ps. ii. 7.

It is widely (though not unanimously) held that Son of Man was the self-designation of Jesus ; but Son of God can hardly have been a self-designation at all. Even if the voice he heard at his baptism reflects his consciousness of sonship, this affords no more proof that he spoke of himself as the Son of God than does the temptation narrative in Q (Matt. iv. 3, 6 ; Luke iv. 3, 9). It is not in the Synoptics (apart from Matt. xxvii. 43) but in the Fourth Gospel that Jesus calls himself the Son of God, implicitly in v. 25, ix. 35 (variant reading), xi. 4, and explicitly only in x. 36. But it is as " the Son " that the Johannine Jesus is characteristically depicted as referring to himself.[18] There is no doubt that in the Fourth Gospel " the Son " is entirely interpretative. The same is true of the few Synoptic occurrences of this term. Mark has only one example : " But of that day or hour no one knows, not even the angels in heaven nor the Son, but the Father " (xiii. 32, cf. Matt. xxiv. 36). It can be conceded that, so far as limitation of Jesus' knowledge of the end is concerned, there can be little or no doubt of the genuineness of this logion. But this admission of ignorance on the part of Jesus has been reframed in an interpretative manner so as to represent him as calling himself the Son,[19] quite in the Johannine style. This means that the interpretative use of " the Son " in the Johannine Gospel (16 times) and Epistles (8 times) already lay ready to hand in earlier tradition. This is confirmed by the Q logion in Matt. xi. 27 (cf. Luke x. 22) : " All things have been delivered to me by my Father, and no one knows the Son except the Father, nor does any one know the Father except the Son and any one to whom the Son wishes to reveal him." It is hackneyed to call this saying, in the words of K. A. von Hase, " a meteor from the Johannine heaven " (cf. John iii. 35, xvii. 2).[20] There is no need to doubt its substantial genuineness,[21] but as with Mk. xiii. 32, the Son Christology has determined its form in the tradition. Both sayings prove the pre-Johannine

---

[18] iii. 17, 35 f. ; v. 19, 20, 21, 22, 23, 26 ; vi. 40 ; viii. 36 ; xiv. 13 ; xvii. 1.

[19] It is, therefore, unnecessary to suppose, with the editors of *The Beginnings of Christianity*, I (1920), p. 396, and R. P. Casey (" The Earliest Christologies," *JTS*, n.s., IX [1958], p. 267), that " the Son " here stands for " the Son of Man."

[20] Quoted by Cullmann, *op. cit.*, p. 286, n. 2.

[21] As is done by, among others, Dibelius, Bultmann, and Bousset ; see V. Taylor, *The Names of Jesus* (1953), p. 63.

existence of this interpretative Christological title. The factor
which has operated on the formulation of these Synoptic logia
is the same one which produced the numerous instances of " the
Son " in the Johannine circle, namely, the movement towards
a Trinitarian theology which is expressed in the formula in
Matt. xxviii. 19, where the nations are to be baptized in
the three-fold name of the Father, the Son, and the Holy
Spirit.

Son of Man, whichever view is adopted as to its use by Jesus
as a self-designation, at least already existed and lay ready to
hand as a title in apocalyptic circles. The same cannot be said
of " the Son." It has been noted already that the pre-Christian
use of Son of God as a Messianic name is open to doubt. When
it comes to " the Son " the doubts become formidable indeed,
for there is obviously no pre-New Testament precedent at all
for its employment as a self-designation. I therefore find it
impossible to agree with Dr. Vincent Taylor when he calls " the
Son " Jesus' self-designation.[22] Elsewhere he writes that " it
is clear that, according to our earliest sources, Q and Mark, Jesus
spoke of Himself as ' the Son ' (Mk. i. 11, xiii. 32 ; Luke x. 22 =
Matt. xi. 27) . . . It is a fact of importance that, if the genuineness
of these sayings is accepted, Sonship has a dominical basis." [23]
But important though these sayings are, they are not the real
evidence for Sonship. Having dealt with Mk. xiii. 32 and the
Q logion, we are left with the quotation of Ps. ii. 7 in Mk. i. 11,
which displays a Son of God Christology associated with the
quotation. To say that the Son of God Christology here exhibited
is a creation of the Palestinian church is not tantamount to
calling it a *creatio ex nihilo*. The dominical basis of the Son of
God Christology does not rest on the authenticity of Mk. xiii. 32,
or of Matt. xi. 27, or even of Mk. i. 11. The genesis of the
Christology does not depend on supposed self-descriptions of
Jesus as Son of God, much less as " the Son," for which the
evidence is tenuous in the extreme. The root is his consciousness
of a special relationship to God as Abba, Father [24] (Mk. xiv. 36).
It was this which led the Palestinian community to call their

[22] *Ibid.*, p. 57.
[23] *The Person of Christ in New Testament Teaching* (1958), p. 149.
[24] On " Abba," see T. W. Manson, *The Sayings of Jesus* (1949), p. 168 ;
J. Jeremias in *Synoptische Studien* (Festschrift A. Wikenhauser, 1953), pp. 86–9 ;
V. Taylor, *The Person of Christ in New Testament Teaching* (1958), pp. 176–80 ;
cf. O. Cullmann, *op. cit.*, p. 289.

Lord the Son of God and the Son.[25] Ps. ii. 7, as used in the baptism narrative (and also in that of the transfiguration, Mk. ix. 7, and parallels), was a potent, if secondary, factor in this process. And I certainly believe that both these narratives and that of the temptation reflect Jesus' filial consciousness.

We have noted an intrusion of the Son of Man concept into that of the Davidic Messiah in the thought of Jesus. There appears to be a similar intrusion of this concept into that of the Son of God in the mind of the author of Hebrews in the catena of Old Testament quotations in the first two chapters. That " intrusion " is again the correct term is justified by the prominence in Hebrews of the Son of God Christology (i. 8, iv. 14, vi. 6, vii. 3, x. 29). Ps. ii. 7 is quoted twice, in i. 5 (followed by 2 Sam. vii. 14) and in v. 5. The former quotation is introduced by the question, " To which of the angels did he ever say ? " In ii. 5 f. we read :

> For it was not to angels that God subjected the world to come, of which we speak. But someone testified somewhere,
>> What is man that thou art mindful of him,
>> or the son of man that thou visitest him ?

The following verses make it clear that the author, in quoting Psalm viii., has in mind a Son of Man Christology, for the promise of sovereignty held out to man has been fulfilled in Jesus as the Son of Man. The second quotation is followed at once by Ps. cx. 4 :

> So also Christ did not glorify himself to be made a high priest, but it was he who said to him,
>> Thou art my Son, to-day I have begotten thee,
> as he says also in another place,
>> Thou art a priest for ever after the order of Melchizedek.

The result is, on the one hand, the intrusion of the Son of Man into the Son of God concept ; on the other, the association of the idea of the Son of God with that of the High-Priest. The importance of this association for our present purpose lies in the close affinities between the ideas of the Son of Man and the

[25] R. P. Casey, *op. cit.*, p. 267, concludes that the expression " Son of God " must be " a product of early Gentile Christian usage," on the ground that in Aramaic-speaking circles " *bara* [the Son] by itself would convey no meaning at all and *bar alaha* [the Son of God] would suggest an angel." But given the Christology, the Palestinian community was surely not incapable of expressing it by attaching new and deeper meanings to familiar terms.

High-Priest, and the possible source of the application to Jesus of Ps. cx. 4.

In later Judaism certain figures, whose relationship to the apocalyptic Son of Man is somewhat obscure and need not concern us here, perform priestly functions. Enoch in Jub. iv. 25 " burnt the incense of the sanctuary " ; [26] in 2 Enoch he performs mediatorial functions ; in 3 Enoch the figure (Enoch-)Metatron occupies a throne of his own as " the Prince of the Presence " (xlviiiC 7), and in the Talmud intercedes in heaven for Israel.[27] The idea of a heavenly intercessor would not, therefore, appear novel or revolutionary to Jews. Is this, perhaps, partly the explanation of the sudden introduction, with no preamble, of the notion of the Christian Messiah as " a merciful and faithful high priest " in Heb. ii. 17 ? On the other hand, Ps. cx. 4 is not applied in Judaism to the Messiah.[28] The New Testament conception of the Priest-Messiah is radically different from, and basically independent of, any Jewish parallels which may be adduced from the problematical *Testaments of the Twelve Patriarchs* and from Qumrân. It is, therefore, not enough simply to say that the writer of Hebrews was familiar with a (Jewish) idea, and desired to apply it to Jesus.

At what point are we to seek Christian origination ? C. H. Dodd holds that the author of Hebrews himself is an innovator in his use of Ps. cx. 4 (Heb. v. 6, vi. 20, vii. 17, 21), though " his argument rests upon secure grounds if he could count upon the general acceptance of the hundred-and-tenth psalm as being, in its entirety, a testimony to Christ." [29] But other New Testament books seem to reflect the same belief, though without recourse to this psalm. In John xvii. 19 Jesus " sanctifies " himself as both priest and sacrifice. Other possible allusions to the idea are Rom. v. 2 ; Eph. ii. 18, v. 2 ; 1 Pet. ii. 24, iii. 18 ; 1 John ii. 1. The possibility of a Johannine origin for the conception [30] remains open, as does the suggestion of T. W. Manson that Hebrews, so far from being original, is anticipated by Rom. iii. 21-6.[31] W. Manson went so far as to suggest that

---

[26] See H. Odeberg, 'Ενωχ, *TWNT*, II (1935), p. 554.
[27] Bab. T., *Chagiga*, 15a.
[28] Cf. my article " Priest and Messiah," *VT*, III (1953), pp. 324 f.
[29] *According to the Scriptures* (1952), p. 104.
[30] Cf. O. Cullmann, *op. cit.*, p. 105, on Spicq's suggestion to this effect.
[31] " ΙΛΑΣΤΗΡΙΟΝ," *JTS*, XLVI (1945), pp. 1-10 ; *Ministry and Priesthood* (1958), p. 48, n. 16.

Ps. cx. 4, " Thou art a priest for ever," belonged to a primitive confession.[32] Without regarding this as anything more than a guess, the suddenness with which Jesus is called " a merciful and faithful high priest " in Heb. ii. 17 at least gives the impression that the conception was not unfamiliar in Christian circles. The observation that other places in the New Testament outside Hebrews appear to reflect the same idea without using the term priest or high-priest suggests that it was not based on Ps. cx. 4. The author of Hebrews elaborates for the purpose of his argument a belief which was taken for granted, that the declaration in this verse did in fact refer to Jesus, since the psalm as a whole, and particularly *v.* 1, was held to do so. But can we go back further than this ? If the doctrine of the high priesthood of Jesus is traceable independently of Psalm cx., what is its ultimate source ?

I have elsewhere stated the opinion that the origin of this Christology is to be found " in speculations set in motion by the belief in the exaltation of [Jesus as] the risen Messiah to the heavenly world." [33] I should now wish to modify that opinion, and the nature of the modification is best indicated by the substitution of " Son of Man " for " risen Messiah."

In discussing the Son of David and the Son of God we have seen that Christologies which might appear at first sight to have arisen from Christian interpretation of passages from the psalms, turn out on closer examination to go back to Jesus himself. But the results are not exactly the same. The conclusion was reached, on the one hand, that Son of David in Christian use is due to Jesus' own borrowing from Ps. cx. 1 and to the fact of his Davidic descent ; on the other, that the Christologies expressed in the related titles Son of God and the Son, although community creations hastened by Messianic application of Ps. ii. 7, are fully justified by, and gain impulse from, the special relationship which Jesus believed he enjoyed with God as Father.

The question of the origin of the High-Priest Christology has, as we have seen, received varying answers. To these must be added Cullmann's argument [34] from the use by Jesus of Ps. cx. 1 in Mk. xiv. 62, that he may have viewed his own mission as a fulfilment of the true priesthood. Cullmann's thesis is as follows.

---

[32] *The Epistle to the Hebrews* (1951), pp. 54, 108.
[33] " Priest and Messiah," *VT*, III (1953), p. 336.
[34] *Op. cit.*, p. 88.

In Mk. xiv. 62, Jesus links together the Son of Man of Dan. vii. and the Messiah's session at God's right hand in Ps. cx. 1. " Sitting at the right hand " is inseparably connected with the thought of the priest-king " after the order of Melchizedek." To the Jewish High-Priest before him Jesus replies that he will be not an earthly Messiah, but the heavenly Son of Man, not an earthly but the heavenly High-Priest.   Just as before the earthly ruler Pontius Pilate he declares that his kingdom is not of this world (John xviii. 36), so before the earthly High-Priest he shows that his priesthood is of an entirely different order.   This is an ingenious but unconvincing case as stated by Cullmann.   Nevertheless, although Cullmann lays the main emphasis on the close connexion between the sitting at God's right hand and the Melchizedekian priesthood, he does also equate the ideas of the Son of Man and the High-Priest, and it is *here* that we may seek a solution, but in the sense that Jesus viewed the rôle of the Son of Man as that of an *intercessor* rather than specifically as that of a priest.   There is no Synoptic evidence that Jesus viewed the work of the Son of Man as in any way priestly.   When he is reported as associating Dan. vii. 13 with another passage, it is with the *first* verse of Ps. cx. that the association is made (Mk. xiv. 62 ; Matt. xix. 28, xxv. 31), not with the fourth. Although the author of Hebrews was to do so,[35] Jesus did not, so far as we know, associate these two parts of the psalm. Cullmann, therefore, reads into Mk. xiv. 62 what is not there.

Although it is not very prominent, evidence is not lacking that Jesus viewed the rôle of the Son of Man as that of an intercessor or mediator.   " Every one who confesses me before men, the Son of Man also will confess before the angels of God " (Luke xii. 8 ; cf. Matt. x. 32).   Would not intercession have been included by him among the functions of the Son of Man ?   In the *Similitudes of Enoch* the Son of Man is the judge of the wicked and the champion of the righteous.   To him is given " the sum of judgement " (lxix. 27 ; cf. John v. 22, 27), and this includes an assessment of righteousness (lxii. 3) ; the Elect One " shall choose the righteous and holy " from among the resurrected ones (li. 2).   The Son of Man exercises all the prerogatives of the Lord of Spirits in condemnation and acquittal.   For condemnation by the Son of Man see Mk. viii. 38 ; Luke xii. 9 (cf. Matt. x. 33),

---

[35] This is at its clearest in Heb. viii. 1 ; it is as High Priest that Jesus sits " at the right hand of the throne of the Majesty in heaven."

and for the Son of Man as judge the sayings on the Son of Man
as the sign of Jonah (Luke xi. 29 f.) and the day of the Son of
Man (Luke xvii. 24). But as regards intercession, if the view be
correct that the Son of Man beheld by the protomartyr Stephen
was standing at God's right hand as his advocate (Acts vii. 56),
the passage provides further evidence of the intercessory (but
not necessarily priestly) rôle of the Son of Man and probably
testifies to primitive doctrine.

The early church, therefore, had every justification for
regarding its Messiah as an intercessor at God's right hand—
" Christ Jesus . . . who is at the right hand of God, who also
makes intercession on our behalf " (Rom. viii. 34).[36] In 1 John
ii. 1 f.—" We have an advocate with the Father, Jesus Christ
the righteous ; and he is the expiation for our sins "—the term
Son of Man is not used ; but the passage represents, in ἱλασμός
(" expiation "), a transition from intercession or advocacy
(παράκλητος—" advocate ") to *priestly* intercession and self-sac-
rifice, as in Heb. vii. 25 f., ix. 24–6. More striking is 1 Tim. ii. 5 :
" There is one Mediator of God and men, (*the*) *Man* Christ Jesus,
who gave himself a ransom for all " (ἀντίλυτρον ὑπὲρ πάντων).
This is a Hellenistic rewriting of the original Semitic form in Mk.
x. 45, *viz.*, " *The Son of Man* came not to be served but to serve,
and to give his life a ransom for many " (λύτρον ἀντὶ πολλῶν).
In the former passage the association of mediation and ransom is
explicit. The Mediator is the *Man*. This comparatively late
passage thus interprets a logion concerning the Son of Man, in
which mediation or intercession is only implicit, by borrowing
μεσίτης (" mediator ") from popular Greek speech. Moreover,
" mediator of God and men " (μεσίτης θεοῦ καὶ ἀνθρώπων) is
the precise description of Michael as intercessor and high-priest
in the *Testament of Dan* vi. 2. We are here very near to the
thought in Hebrews of the High-Priest who intercedes for men,
having offered himself as a sacrifice (Heb. vii. 25–7). If Mk. x. 45
is (at least in substance) authentic, the source of this kind of
thought is clear. But there is nowhere any hint that Jesus
thought of the intercessory activity of the Son of Man as priestly,
nor that he made any use of Ps. cx. 4. It was the primitive com-

[36] That this statement is in all probability not Paul's own, but is derived from
an earlier credal formulation, is strongly suggested by the sequence : Christ's
death, resurrection, and heavenly session. For the idea of intercession in Judaism
and in Christianity, cf. N. Johansson, *Parakletoi* (1940).

munity which did this. That the High-Priest Christology was not actually based on Ps. cx. 4 is shown by the appearance elsewhere in the New Testament of the same Christology, with no reference to the psalm ; but the use of the verse was encouraged by the Christological use of the first verse of the psalm. The conclusion, therefore, would be that Ps. cx. 4 did indeed encourage and support the belief in Jesus as a High-Priest, but the idea itself arose from the teaching of Jesus about the Son of Man and his heavenly intercession, interpreted by the church as a priestly function.

I have spoken of the intrusion of the Son of Man concept into that of the Davidic Messiah in the thought of Jesus, and into that of the Son of God in the mind of the author of Hebrews. It may be suggested that the explanation is the use by Jesus of the term Son of Man. Although it was not customarily used by the church as a title for that very reason, yet its influence could not be avoided. This is clearest in the case of the High-Priest idea. It is not without significance that the strongly Jewish Apocalypse actually describes the Son of Man in priestly language : " one like a son of man, clothed with a long robe and with a golden girdle round his breast. "[37]

<hr/>

[37] Rev. i. 13.

KINGSHIP AS COMMUNICATION AND ACCOMMODATION

By N. Q. KING

I

In the Judaeo-Christian world of thought Kingship is a dangerous symbol of communication, yet it is one which hardly can be avoided. It is useful, ancient and deeply embedded in the human mind. Some accommodation has to be made with it, an acceptance of part and a positive rejection of part.[1] It is the purpose of this essay to examine against this background of communication and accommodation a few of the effects of calling God King, the use of certain ideas of divine Kingship and ruler-cult, the promise contained therein and its fulfilment. We shall now briefly consider these matters in certain parts of the Bible, in early Byzantine times and in some districts of Africa in modern times.

The advantages to the religion of the Hebrews of communicating ideas about God in terms of Kingship are too obvious to mention in detail. Here was a concept which had already long been in use in connexion with the divine, it was readily understood by most people ; here was a method of glorifying their God, who was the King above all gods, a means of directing their King in the right path, for, since he was in special relation towards God, he had to show forth God's ways. So we see ideas of human Kingship being reflected up to teach us about God, and we find the sacral ruler in some sense representing God and in myth and ritual acting in his person or on his behalf.[2] But

---

[1] " Communication " is used of the attempt to " get across " certain ideas so as to influence the thinking of others. " Accommodation " is taken from the literature of the theology of mission which discusses, for instance, the methods of de Nobili in India and Ricci in China. It indicates the attempt to present a religion in the thought-forms of the culture being addressed and in the process to admit the higher elements of those thought-forms into the heart of the religion being presented.

[2] Since this essay has been put together from notes and memory during a period of extensive travelling in various parts of tropical Africa, which included

it was the very antiquity and widespread nature of Kingship ideas which made Kingship a most dangerous symbol of communication regarding the God of Israel. Let us illustrate this danger. A cursory glance at the use of the root *m-l-k* in the Hebrew Bible reveals that Yahweh was not the only divine being who used the title. With other vowels (perhaps taken by later hands from *bōsheth*, that word of shame) we get Molech, and we know something of his ways. Children were passed through the fire to this divine King.[3] Anyone who has stood in the *Tophet* at Carthage or seen the engraving in the *Bardo* at Tunis showing the priest or god with the baby on his arm ready for the fire, can hardly say that associating Yahweh with the term was without danger. Again, anyone who has seen Kingship before it has been greatly modified, realizes how closely it is bound up with fertility. A King demands at least one Queen. We get only a few hints of the struggle the reformers of Israel had in this matter ; they seem here to have attempted little accommodation ; it was left for the Church to refine and spiritualize and accommodate.[4]

In the matter of the connexion of Yahweh with child-sacrifice, the reformers in Israel had no small difficulty in condemning it and dissociating Yahweh from it.[5] But even out of this horror of accommodation, some good came, for they learnt that the King who did not require man's children to pass through the fire, demanded man's dedication and complete self-giving. Christians would add that out of the transcending of this corpus of ideas men were enabled to grasp the Kingship of one who not

---

the loss of papers and luggage in Ethiopia, it is hoped that the reader will forgive the lack of detailed examples and bibliographical material at a number of points.

[3] 2 Kings xxiii. 10, Jer. xxxii. 35, Lev. xviii. 21, xx. 2–5, etc. On Molech, see also Amos v. 26 ; cf. Acts vii. 43. Milcom of the Ammonites (*e.g.*, 1 Kings xi. 5 and 2 Kings xxiii. 13) was another god whose name included the consonants. There is some relationship to Baal-Melqart of Tyre, to *Muluk* of the Mari texts, and to *Malik* in the Akkadian. (See W. F. Albright, *Archaeology and the Religion of Israel*, Baltimore, 1946, pp. 162 ff., and J. A. Thompson, *s.v. Molech* in Douglas's *New Bible Dictionary*, which will undoubtedly be a boon to many an unfortunate far from a specialist library.)

[4] *Malkah* is innocuous enough but what of *mᵉlekheth haśśamayim* (Jer. vii. 18, xliv. 17 ; cf. the personal name Hammolecheth in 1 Chron. vii. 18) ? The lady may be connected with Ishtar or Anath (Yau's wife at Yeb and perhaps Mizpah), or Ashtoreth. Albright (*op. cit.*, pp. 74 ff.) on Astarte (Ashtaroth), Anath and Asherah says : " Sex was their primary function . . . they were both mother-goddesses and divine courtesans."

[5] Lev. xviii. 21, xx. 2–5 ; 2 Kings xvii. 17, xxiii. 10. Cf. Jer. vii. 31, xix. 4 f. ; Ezek. xvi. 20 f., xx. 26, xxiii. 37. The story of the sacrifice of Isaac (Gen. xxii) may be part of this campaign.

only did not demand other people's sons, but did not spare his own.[6]

So far as one can see at the moment, no voice was raised in Israel against calling God King. An accommodation was made with the concept. But besides the somewhat disreputable divinities associated with the title King, the Bible abounds in examples of exceedingly nasty human characters who were Kings and who did credit neither to the idea of Kingship nor to the divine monarchy they were supposed to reflect. Human Kings were known for their tyranny, their arbitrary whimsicality with tragic consequences, their all-consuming and insatiable desires and uncontrollable moods. In regard to human Kingship the Biblical writers did contemplate complete rejection. One stratum of I Samuel states the objection to Kingship in Israel in no uncertain terms. The children of Israel want a King so that they can be like all the nations.[7] It is a continuation of their apostasy since they left Egypt, to leave Yahweh and serve other gods. It is accommodation to the ways of the heathen. To have a human King is to reject the Kingship of God. The " Manner of the King " is then described, his use of their children and resources.[8]

Hosea speaks on the subject in similar terms. Israel asked for a King but he is unable to save them. God gives a King in his anger and takes him away in his wrath. A king then is a mere helpless puppet thrown to a foolish nation to stop its whining and taken away again (xiii. 10 f.). At another point he includes the setting up of kings who are not from God, of princes whom he did not know, together with idolatry, as a casting off of that which is good (viii. 2 ff.). Earlier the prophet described how the Lord told him to love an adulteress (iii. 1 ff.). He bought her and told her to sit alone for him and not go after men, and he would not come to her. That is, she was to sit completely alone. The analogy between the prophet's treatment

[6] How much the " African " (i.e., Roman African Patristic) doctrine of the Atonement owed to a memory of the rites of human sacrifice known to Tertullian to have taken place as recently as the reign of Tiberius and still continued by substitution, may one day be made clearer. It was " Yahweh " Simpson of Oriel who often declared that a religious idea never dies. It is transmuted. On the African side and the " MOL'K " sacrifices, see J. Carcopino, " Survivances des sacrifices d'enfants par substitution," Revue de l'histoire des relig., CVI (1932), pp. 592–9, and C. Picard, Carthage (Paris, 1951), pp. 20 ff.

[7] I Sam. viii. 5, kᵉkhol haggoyim. The phrase is repeated at v. 20. It is not without contempt.

[8] I Sam. viii. 8, 7, 11–18.

of his wife and Yahweh's intended treatment of Israel is clear, and Hosea proceeds to say that for many days the children of Israel shall sit alone bereft of King, prince, sacrifice, ephod and teraphim. The meaning is not without ambiguity but it is at least possible to suggest that King, prince, sacrifice and so on are the lovers and false husbands Israel has awhored after.[9] It is of course possible to interpret this passage in a manner more favourable to Kingship, especially because at another point Hosea causes the rebellious people to say : " We have no King, for we do not fear Yahweh ; and the King, what can he do for us ? " (x. 3). This seems to imply that at times in the writer's mind to deny the King and his power was to cease to fear the Lord. Hosea was dealing with an actual living situation ; the Kings of the Northern Kingdom had brought their people tottering to the brink of ruin. Their only real claim to their position was that Kingship appeared to be a necessity if the nation was to survive the attacks of its enemies, whereas in fact it was the very Kings who made it vulnerable and who destroyed it. Perhaps the objection was not so much to Kingship as to its exponents. Whether they liked it or not, Kingship could not be rejected in the circumstances. It was Kingship or chaos.

We now turn to some other passages to see how the Biblical writers grappled more constructively with this problem of the poor human exemplars of Kingship. Probably none of the Biblical Kings equalled a Nero or some of the great oriental sovereigns of those days in lust and cruelty. The stories of David's treatment of Uriah or Ahab's of Naboth stand out because of the context of prophetic Yahwism in which they are set. Because they should have known better their crime is great. Otherwise, they and Manasseh and Jehoiakim and the other " bad " Kings of the Hebrew people were mere petty delinquents as compared with the ethnocides and perverts the Gentiles produced. The writers of the Books of Kings divide up the Kings into good and bad not on a basis of whether they were successful or not but on whether they followed the Lord.[10]

---

[9] In iii. 5 we are told that Israel will return to God and David their King in the latter days. This view belongs more with the matter of the Davidic Kingship which is treated below.

[10] The authors of *1066 and All That* rightly divide up history into a succession of good and bad kings. Unfortunately they did not realize that the authors of these books of the Bible and not that man from Halicarnassus were the " Fathers of History."

There begins to emerge the idea of the " godly prince." The writer of the Book of Deuteronomy also turned his attention to the problem (xvii. 14–20). He considers it inevitable that when his people enter Canaan they will want a King " like all the nations around them." Clearly Kingship is a concession, an accommodation to surrounding custom 'and Israel may have it, but with safeguards. The King must be from amongst themselves, he must not increase his horses at the expense of men sold into slavery nor have too many women nor too much riches. Above all, he should study and keep the Law. The two princes who most lived up to this ideal, Hezekiah and Josiah, were both of the House of David. It is but a short step forward to the ideal of Davidic Kingship where the King is not divine but owes his position to his obedience to God. If he did wrongly he was subject to correction like other men ; at the same time, if he wanted to do right, there was a pattern to follow. He is to be a King closely under the protection of God and God's special representative, but he is not himself divine nor can he be above the priest, the Law and the prophet.[11]

The great shepherd chapter in Ezekiel can naturally end, after the Prophet has described the evil ways of leaders who only exploit and ill-treat the flock, by telling of the one Shepherd, David. Yahweh will be their God and his servant David the Prince. This in its own way is the culminating point in the evolving concept of ideal human Kingship in the Old Testament, and it leads forward to the hope of one who is to come, for the old Israel was never again to have a Davidic King who bore worldly political rule.[12] It is at once a fulfilment and a promise.

[11] David came in as conqueror to Jerusalem where there seems to have been already established a group of kingly priests whose antecedents may go back to Melchizedek and whose descendants go forward to the Zadokites and the men who as High-Priests ruled in the absence of a Davidic king. They had their privileges and it is insisted upon that the Davidic king is not to sacrifice (2 Chron. xxvi. 16 ff.). We may find a remote analogy in the position of the *ten'dana* in parts of Northern Ghana. Formerly he ruled as priest and King, when over-run by a military Kingship he has become more priestly and struggles to maintain his position against the King who has usurped his political power. More is said of him below.

[12] Ezek. xxxiv. One is led to wonder whether a son of David was prevented from regaining the throne by the foreigners or rather by native Jewish influences some of which were hostile to human Kingship, while others militated against the Davidic intruders in favour of Jerusalemite Priest-Kings.

II

By New Testament times the King of the Biblical world was the Roman Emperor. His representative had put the Lord of the Christians to death. In the sixties in the person of Nero the Emperor himself was putting Christians to death, at a time when by no means all the New Testament had been committed to writing. Yet, far from abandoning the imagery of Kingship the Christians used it extensively to convey their own ideas and, in accommodating it, transformed in part both the imagery and their own ideas. This could be illustrated from most strata of the New Testament, but let us glance briefly at parts of the Gospel according to St. John and of the Apocalypse, especially because at first sight these writings appear to be hostile to Kingship ideas.

The βασιλεία, βασιλεύς, βασιλεύειν complex of words is little used in the Gospel of St. John. The phrase " Kingdom of God " so common in the Synoptists is used only twice, both times in the conversation with Nicodemus (iii. 3, 5). Βασιλεία is used twice in the conversation of Jesus with Pilate to insist each time that his Kingship is not of this world or " hence " (xviii. 36). The verb " to reign " is not found in the Gospel, but the use of the noun βασιλεύς is most significant. Nathanael, that Israelite indeed, recognizes Jesus as the Son of God and the King of Israel. Twice in the " royal " welcome given with palm branches as Jesus comes to his own City in an impromptu *Felix Adventus*, the people call him King, he is hailed as King of Israel and as the King whom Zion was to expect (Zech. ix. 9 ; John xii. 13 ff.). In these cases the evangelist has employed the word in a context where something of the true nature of Jesus' Kingship was understood by its users. In the remaining cases the sinister connotations of the word are more apparent. Jesus after the feeding of the five thousand is hailed by ἄνθρωποι (presumably the men fed, but with Johannine double intention probably including men in general). Then Jesus, knowing that they would come and grab him by force so that they should make a King, withdrew into the mountain alone (vi. 15). There summed up is the tragedy of the use of Kingship in connexion with Jesus ; men understood it immediately, they want to make out of him a King, their sort of King. His own people not having understood,

Jesus rather despairingly struggles to explain to Pilate, the Gentile. " You, are you the King of the Jews ? " says the Roman with contempt, probably as much for that race as for the bedraggled specimen of it before him (xviii. 33 ff.). Jesus asks whether this is his own idea or whether someone else told him about him. That is, he owns that he is a King. Soon afterwards he tries to explain that his Kingship is of another sort. Pilate says, " Are you not therefore a King ? " All he can grasp is that the poor mad fellow claims to be a King of some kind. Jesus tries again : " You say that I am a King. For this was I born and for this I came into the world, that I should witness to the truth . . ." Pilate hears the word " truth " and his attention goes off onto that. It is possible to suggest that Jesus had not turned from Kingship to truth, but was trying to explain the truth of his Kingship. Pilate on his part cannot resist the fun of taunt-ing the Jews with their King (*v.* 39). He accepts the title for Jesus, " King of the Jews." The evangelist in Nathanael has accepted it ; ironically, the Gentile in his mockery has also found the truth.

In the next chapter (xix.), the play on this title continues. The soldiers crown him as King and give him the purple robe of royalty.[13]   When Pilate hesitates the Jews cry out that everyone who makes himself the King (" the Emperor " is a possible translation of the Greek), contradicts (the Kingship of) Caesar (*v.* 12). Pilate shows them their King and asks whether he should crucify their King. Then an appalling blasphemy on behalf of the people of God is put in the mouth of the High-Priests : " We have no King but Caesar." This is where the Kingship of Yahweh and the theocracy has ended up. Pilate puts " King of the Jews " as a title on the cross in the three official languages for all to read, and when the High-Priests ask that rather the title should say that Jesus *said* he was such, he refuses (*vv.* 19, 21). So this is where Jesus' use of the idea of Kingship as a method of communication landed him. It looks like an accommodation-method that failed. But we are bound to look further. Jesus' mind usually turned things upside down. He chose an ass instead of a stallion for his *Felix Adventus*. It is part of the same thing that his crown should be of thorns and that his reigning should be from a seat on a cross invented

---

[13] The purple reminds us a king is also a victim. As a true King, Jesus goes out to die for his people, whether they care or recognize does not matter. To some the ancient ritual of the humiliation of the King finds here its fulfilment.

to prolong the torture of malefactors. He had found the true meaning of Kingship.

We see here then that St. John employs Kingship as one of the means of communicating the unimaginable truth about the unique Logos, who has become flesh. Even if he had wanted to avoid using it, it is too deeply embedded in the tradition. So far as the religious courts were concerned Jesus died for blasphemy. So far as the Romans of St. John's Gospel are concerned, they were crucifying a man who claimed to be a King. St. John explains what kind of King, and presumably this is the highest and the lowest point Kingship ever reached.

In the Book of Revelation, despite the writer's virulent hatred of the Roman power, extensive use is made of imperial imagery. God sits enthroned in a style not only reminiscent of the throne scenes of Isaiah, of Ezekiel and Daniel, but of the iconography of cosmic Kingship of the Ancient East which lies behind them (iv. 2). But we may pick out other features which point forward to the more developed Roman Emperor-cult of later days and perhaps reflect the actual cult of the writer's time.[14] In the hippodrome the King in the royal box surrounded by his chief courtiers and officials beheld the games. It is easy enough to evisage great parts of the Apocalypse as being that which is seen from God's royal box of the adventures of the Christians below, as they face the beasts and other tormentors. There is here a new cult of victory, only it is the defeated who are the victors.[15] It was part of the liturgy of the hippodrome that at certain points a litany of praise of the Emperor would be sung, sometimes with music, and the great officials would fall down in *proskynesis*. This ceremonial takes place in Revelation before God no less than five times.[16]

[14] The Emperor-cult has received careful study in (for instance) some of the works of H. P. L'Orange, R. Delbrück, A. Alföldi, and E. Stauffer. (Detailed references will be found in the writer's *There's such Divinity doth hedge a King* [London, 1960], pp. 26 ff.) One must be cautious to avoid anachronisms and importing the cultus of Constantine Porphyrogenitus into the first century ; also it is impossible in Revelation to trace down the antecedents of any given set of thought-forms to one particular source. The Apocalyptist may be drawing on what he has seen of contemporary Kingship, he may be well versed in ancient Middle-Eastern Kingly lore, certainly his mind is soaked with Biblical imagery. By this time Kingship imagery was so much a part of the heritage of the human race, it was inevitable that it should take certain shapes whatever was a man's immediate cultural background.

[15] Rev. vii. 9, iii. 21, xv. 2.

[16] Rev. iv. 10, v. 14, vii. 11, xi. 16, xv. 2 ff., xix. 4. Other imperial themes such as *Dominus legem dat* and the setting of thrones for judgement with the

Besides Almighty God, the Father, there are a number of other divine and super-human royal figures in this Book. The Logos too is a King. He is the ruler of the Kings of the earth. He has many diadems on his head and bears the name " King of Kings and Lord of Lords."[17]

Perhaps in the Lady in the heaven clothed with the sun, the moon at her feet, about her head a crown of twelve stars, herself pregnant, we have the ultimate refinement of the Queen of Heaven theme (xii. 1 ff.). Over against her is a false Queen clad in purple, scarlet, and gold ; the Kings of the earth fornicate with her. She is the great city which has dominion over the Kings of the earth.[18] The idea of the demonic parody or diabolical imitation emerges. God and those on his side are not the only ones to have the trappings of royalty. His opponents in the cosmic battle also wear diadems and crowns. Satan, too, has a throne. The Beast has images and an imperial cult with *proskynesis*.[19] As for the Kings of the earth they are but minor dependent figures. If they follow the Beast they do evil and perish with him, or they follow the Lord and share his victory.[20] In the heavenly Jerusalem, as in Israel of old, God himself is King, the Kings of the earth bring their glory into her (a procession of Kings or Durbar) and the redeemed reign as Kings with God.[21]

The Apocalyptist then uses the language of Kingship extensively to communicate his ideas. His method of accommodation is to make God the paradigm of all that is good and great in it. Satan or the beast are made the exemplars of all that is evil

decision and will of the King contained in a book or scroll which is opened, also appear in Revelation.

[17] Rev. i. 5 f., xvii. 14, xix.16. In xiv. 14 one like a Son of Man has a crown, and a sharp sickle. These are both considered emblems of royalty.

[18] Rev. xvii. 1 ff., xviii. 2 ff. Perhaps we have here the original of the two *civitates* which fascinated the thought of St. Augustine and his Donatist predecessor.

[19] Rev. ix. 7, 20, xii. 3, xiii. 1, ii. 13, xiv. 9, xv. 2, xvi. 2, xix. 20. We may compare Justin Martyr's idea that pagan sacraments were demonic parodies of the Christian (*Apologeticus*, i. 66).

[20] On the one side : xvi. 14, xvii. 1 f., 10, 12, xviii. 3, 9, xix. 19. On the other i. 5, xv. 3 (reading ἐθνῶν), xxi. 24.

[21] Rev. xxii. 1–3, 5, xxi. 24. It is through the Kingship of the Logos and his victory that we become a Kingdom of priests and reign with him (i. 5 f., xvii. 14b, xx. 4–6, iii. 21). This " democratization " of Kingship is typical of the eventual out-working of many great religious ideas. We may compare life after death. Whether it is their culminating point of development or their final collapse in ridiculous disintegration is not for us to say.

and bad in it. Earthly Kings can copy either, the jungle of Kingship is neutral. Neither the Apocalypse nor the Gospel has to deal with a Roman Emperor who himself inclines towards Christianity, but there are principles here full of promise. As long as Christians do not forget that Christ's Kingship is not of this world and that the earthly should be a reflection of the true Heavenly Kingship, Kingship can be confidently admitted into the system. The test came in the fourth century and we shall see what happened in the event.

III

It was not till Constantine turned towards Christianity that the Church fully faced the new situation in Kingship presented by a Roman Emperor who claimed to be a believer. Yet her reaction to the challenge was quick and intellectually brilliant. Soon she was going further than usual in her use of Kingship symbolism to convey her message and had found a theory of accommodation. This whole way of thinking is presented to us in a pure form in the work attributed to Eusebius of Caesarea known as *de laudibus oratio Constantini in eius tricennalibus habita*.[22]

For Eusebius, God himself is the great King, his throne is the arch of heaven, the earth the footstool of his feet. The heavenly host and the powers above the world recognize him as Master, Lord, and King. Angels, archangels, and companies of hallowed spirits derive from him their radiance. Hymns of praise ascend to God the Great King also from the human race in its hierarchy, ranging from the Emperor and the Caesars, the army, the government, the citizens down to other men and the natural world (Col. 1320). The Emperor receives his power from above, he is God's friend. God gives him power to overcome his enemies, and he uses his power to bring men to God. Formerly Emperors gave thanks for a long reign by sacrifices to demons, now the Emperor offers first the sacrifice of himself, then of his people (1328 f.).

The Emperor reflects the Kingship of God, he is arrayed with the image of the heavenly Kingdom and looking upwards, he directs things below according to the archetypal idea of those

22 Migne's *Patrologia Graeca*, XX, columns 1316 ff.

things that are above.[23] Equally and conversely, the heavenly
monarchy is made to reflect the earthly. For a long time we
have known heaven to have its armies, but Eusebius makes the
great luminaries into torch-bearers and gives God's Court a dark-
blue curtain (1320B). Above all, the position of Christ the Logos
is continually explained as being that of a kind of Caesar to an
Augustus (after Diocletian's reform) or of a high official to the
Emperor.[24]

It is true that Eusebius, in his likening of the Emperor's
Kingdom to God's, logically implies that subjects should give
him full obedience such as they give to God. But in saying this
he takes the opportunity to remind the Emperor of the need of
god-like qualities and to instruct him in the faith (1373 f., 1376 ff.).
The long and slow process of baptizing all amenable features of
Roman Imperial Kingship is resolutely begun. The Emperor
was "Victor" and the cult of victory surrounding him was
carried on *ad nauseam*, on the coins, in the court, in the hippodrome. Eusebius hails the Emperor as Victor over his passions
(1336 f.). Constantine's treatment of Fausta and Crispus, Theodosius's of Thessalonica, show us these men had need of such
victory.

Over against the true King, Eusebius sets the "anti-King,"
the tyrant as against the Basileus (1336). The one's vices balance
the other's virtues. This is not only the old contrast of Greek
political science, but it is theological too. As Constantine reflects
the true God, Licinius and his ilk had reflected the false gods they
served. Eusebius expressly looks to Scripture to speak to us
not only of that paradigm of the royal which is with us but also
of its abominable caricature.[25]

[23] Κἄπειτα τῆς οὐρανίου βασιλείας εἰκόνι κεκοσμημένος, ἄνω βλέπων, κατὰ τὴν ἀρχέτυπον
ἰδέαν τοὺς κάτω διακυβερνῶν ἰθύνει (1329B). On some of the coins we find Constantine
with his head and eyes raised, the heavenward-looking ruler. In others we find
him with his right hand raised, greeting and commanding men with heavenly
authority behind him. Dr. C. H. V. Sutherland of the Heberden Coin Room
kindly writes to say that volume VII of *The Roman Imperial Coinage* dealing
with the period 313–337 is in MSS. but these themes can be illustrated from
J. Maurice : *La numismatique constantinienne*. For instance, vol. I, pl. ix. 3
(r. hand raised), 4 (head and eyes raised) ; or again, vol. III, pl. iii. 5 (r. hand
raised), 10 (head and eyes raised).

[24] For instance it is said of the Logos (1332B) : οἷά τις μεγάλου βασιλέως
ὕπαρχος. Alongside this, Eusebius's more famous remark that the Constantinian
regime is a fulfilment of the saying that the Saints of the Most High shall take
the Kingdom (1329A, Dan. vii. 18) is harmless enough.

[25] Λογίων δὲ χρησμοί, οὐκ ἐκ μαντείας μᾶλλον ἢ μανίας παράφρονος, φωτὸς δ' ἐπιπνοίαις
ἐνθέου προσπεφωνημένοι, τῶν τελείων ἡμῖν γενέσθωσαν διδάσκαλοι, ἀμφὶ βασιλείας αὐτῆς,

The antecedents of Eusebius's way of thought on Kingship
have been sought in Hellenistic thinking going back at least as
far as the successors of Alexander the Great, and parallels may
be found in the panegyrical literature of the time. But not a
little arises from the Bishop's own study of the Bible. He states
explicitly in the Prologue that the divine oracles obtained not
by divination but by divine illumination are to be our teachers
concerning Kingship itself, of the King Most High.[26] He interpreted his Bible in the traditions of his day, he took it that the
earthly was a shadow of the heavenly and that the heavenly was
in some sense like the earthly.

An attempt to outline some of the effects of the thinking on
Kingship of men like Eusebius in the fourth century can be
made, without, we hope, going too far astray.[27] God was
presented in the likeness of a Roman Emperor. A great deal
was immediately and readily known about him, and at least so
far as the theory of fourth-century Kingship was concerned, it
was not altogether unworthy. Yet, if he is a God of Love, such
presentation of him must be inadequate, to say the least of it.
On the other side, the Roman Emperor was presented as someone
close to God, someone endowed with more than ordinary access
to God's will, someone whose duty it was to see that his will
was done in earth as a reflection of heaven. Clearly in the end,
pagans, Jews, and heretics, since they did not believe as the
Emperor believed, would have to be assisted to the will of God
as understood by the Emperor, by such methods as the Emperor
held at his disposal. A little use of violence, of deportation, of
imprisonment without trial, of rewards to individuals and towns
if they fell into line, were all indicated, for after all, God had
put these things at the disposal of his earthly regent.[28]

Yet in accepting the " Eusebian " notions of Kingship, the
Roman Emperor ultimately, though not immediately and not in

ἀμφί τε βασιλέως τοῦ ἀνωτάτου, δορυφορίας τε θείας ἀμφὶ τὸν πάντων βασιλέα, τοῦ τε καθ'
ἡμᾶς βασιλικοῦ παραδείγματος, καὶ τοῦ τὸ χάραγμα κεκιβδηλευμένου, τῶν θ' ἑκατέρῳ
συνομαρτούντων τάγματι (1317C). It is hoped " abominable caricature " or "forgery"
conveys part of the meaning of Eusebius's lovely expression. There may here
be an echo of the Abomination of Desolation, though Eusebius was no lover of
the apocalyptic outlook.
26 Ibid., 1317C (quoted in n. 25).
27 For an account of it in some relics of early Byzantine Art and in some of
the Fathers see the author's There's such Divinity doth hedge a King, pp. 17 ff.
28 For these ideas put into logical effect later in the century, see the writer's
Theodosius and the Establishment of Christianity (London, 1961).
P.F.—11

Constantine's day, abdicated his own position as a god in his own right and as Pontifex Maximus. This teaching on Kingship must have brought many to true religion during at least the subsequent millennium, but the consequences of it in distortion of the truth and in agony for many honest men were as long-lasting. This way of thinking with its effects for good and ill was taken into the Byzantine system, which lasted till the fifteenth century, and was partly adopted into the Carolingian system. It may even have affected the thinking of some of the Anglican divines of the sixteenth and seventeenth centuries.[29] Whatever we may think of Eusebius's ideas on Kingship, there is no doubt that they represent one of the greatest adventures the Church has ever made in communication and accommodation. It is easy for critics in the modern world, which is in this matter somewhat naïvely pre-" abominable-caricature," though it fancies itself cynically post-Constantinian, to doubt the wisdom of such attempts, but in the glad dawn of Christian Kingship, there was boundless promise and the subsequent centuries were not without glorious fulfilment.

IV

We may now turn our attention to some aspects of Kingship as accommodation and communication in Ghana in the last century.[30]

Kingship amongst the Akan of Ghana is not only highly developed and vigorous but it is amongst the best documented in Africa.[31] A study of these writings, of some of the ceremonies

[29] See the " Prayer for the King's Majesty," meant to be said at Morning and Evening Prayer daily. Procter and Frere (*A New History of the Book of Common Prayer* [London, 1949], pp. 397 ff.) trace its earliest form to the end of the reign of Henry VIII. If not by Cranmer, it was at least congenial to his spirit.

[30] Professor Hooke spent a term in Ghana in 1958 as visiting Professor to the University College there, rendering as usual the service of three ordinary men. He was much struck by the liveliness of sacral ruler-cult and some of the rest of his favourite themes in Ghana. On his birthday, being now well on in his eighties, at Labadi beach near Accra, he was tripped up by a fishing-net when swimming and was washed out through the breakers by the tide. Another Professor went after him and was also washed away. They were brought in by the life-guards. It is said that when he had brought up a fair amount of sea water and got his breath, Professor Hooke remarked : " I suppose this will start a myth and ritual of a miraculous draught of Professors."

[31] See Captain R. S. Rattray, *Ashanti* (Oxford, 1923) ; *Religion and Art in Ashanti* (Oxford, 1927) ; *Ashanti Law and Constitution* (Oxford, 1929). (Amongst other things this trilogy contains some of the best passages of English descriptive prose written during the twenties.) Cf. also Kofi Busia, *The Position of the Chief*

therein described, as well as conversations with Akans learned in the lore of their people, ranging from the Ashantehene downwards, suggests that " the divinity which hedges " Akan kingship is not so much connected with Onyame, the supreme God, or with any of the " gods," but more with the spirits of the ancestors.[32] The King owes his position to his relationship to these ancestors. In the rites of enstoolment, in the sacrifices and remembrances connected with the blackened stools of departed Kings, in the state ceremonies, the King acts as the link between human and divine, or better, between the tribe alive as human beings and the tribe alive as ancestors. The King is himself given the title " Nana," literally " grandfather," which is also the title given to the ancestors in libations and prayers. In the great traditional praise-songs of the drums the drummer will again and again hail the reigning King for the feats of his ancestors. The reigning Ashantehene will be credited with the victories of Osei Tutu. In a sense the King *is* his ancestors ; he is not an incarnation of them or of the divine, but in him they are.[33] At the same time the Ashanti has a clear notion of *Onyame*, the supreme God. It is true that he sometimes is said to be far away ; the well-known myth says he was close to man until, being so often hit by the pestle of a woman pounding *fufu*, he went far off. Yet, he has not withdrawn completely, as the proverb says : " No one shows a child *Onyame*." [34] There was

---

in the Modern Political System of Ashanti (London, 1951) ; B. S. Akuffo, *Ahemfi Adesua* (Exeter, 1945) ; E. L. R. Meyerowitz, *The Sacred State of the Akan* (London, 1951) ; *Akan Traditions of Origin* (London, 1952) ; *The Akan of Ghana* (London, 1958) ; *The Divine Kingship in Ghana and Ancient Egypt* (London, 1960).

[32] On such categories as " Supreme God " and " gods " see Geoffrey Parrinder, *West African Religion* (London, 1961). Dr. Bolaji Idowu's *Oludumare* (London, 1962) is a study of the Yoruba supreme God. It is possible that the categorization will eventually be modified and we will be shown that God and the ancestors are differing manifestations of the same living force and power. At least one seems to be on the verge of this in some of the thinking of J. B. Danquah, see especially his *Gold Coast Akan* (London, 1945).

[33] Professor J. H. Nketia has numerous publications on the language and poetry of the drums. The point made here is especially plain in a sketch for broadcasting on Asantehene Osei Tutu where the Professor drew on songs which are still in current use. Cf. recent thinking in the West on *Vergegenwärtigung*.

[34] " Obi nkyerε Abofra Nyame." This story and proverb brings out the ambiguity of the word. Christaller (the missionary " father " of the Twi language) writes *s.v.* in his *Dictionary of the Asante and Fante Language* (Basel, 1933) :

  " Onyame : 1. heaven, sky, prob. called so from its *splendour* or *brightness*, *cf*. nyam and the root *div* in Sanskritic languages.
  2. The Supreme Being, the Deity, God."

also firmly embedded in the indigenous religion the idea that
Onyame is a King.[35]

When therefore the Christian pioneers came up, the position
must have looked promising. They took over the name *Onyame*
and said their religion was *onyamesom*, the pure form of *Onyame*-
worship. They said their God was a King and were readily
understood. The difficulty is that to an Akan a King, like *Onyame*,
is someone far off ; he cannot be approached directly and simply.
There are the proper channels and formalities. Every King has
his *okyeame*, " spokesman," " linguist," through whom he must
speak and be spoken to. If they readily grasped that Jesus
Christ was mediator, the Word of God, they could not so easily
be expected to realize he was himself God and King. If they
were told he was the Son of the King, this did not help in a
society with matrilineal, uncle-nephew succession. Again, *Onyame*
had " children," the River Tano, Lake Bosomtwe, Opo the
Ocean, but they are *abosom*, spirits, " godlings."

The same promise seemed to be before them when it came to
the matter of baptizing Kingship. In a close-knit tribal society,
if the King were converted, the whole group could be Christianized
together. It is surprising, but true, that though these pioneers
were of a Protestant and individual-salvation kind of background, they did not at the beginning shrink from the methods
used by the catholic missionary of the " Dark " Ages. They
went to the King first and longed for his conversion. When
Andreas Riis, the Basel Mission pioneer, at last broke through
the coastal curtain, he made Akropong his centre. From here
education and Christianity (later joined by the cocoa plant) went
out conquering and to conquer. It was the seat of the Paramount
Chief of Akwapim. The same kind of story might be told of the
Basel men at Odumase Krobo or Kibi, the seats of two other
of the outstanding Kingdoms of Southern Ghana. The same
can even be said of the greatest of the Kings of Ghana, the
Ashantehene. Nana Prempeh I became Christian during his
exile in the Seychelles and his nephew and successor regularly
attends Church.[36] Great efforts were made to convert the King ;

[35] The writer has this on the authority of Mr. A. A. Y. Kyerematen, Director
of the Ghana Cultural Centre, who is deeply versed in the old Ashanti religion,
as well as from Dr. Patrick Akoi whose thesis on *The Spiritual Kingdom of the
Akan God Onyame* has not yet been published.
[36] The Konorship of Manya Krobo from Odumase is not of course an Akan
Kingship. It belongs to the Ga Adangbe group where inheritance is patrilineal

without his benevolence little would have been possible. Members of the chiefly families became Christians, but whenever a Christian was called to the stool, in most cases, sooner or later, he felt it necessary to forsake the fulness of his Christian ways. He might even still attend Church, but could not be admitted to Communion. This was probably because the next steps in the accommodation of Christianity and African culture were not taken. It is also said that this was not so much because the Chief could not give up his sacrifices in connexion with the ancestors, but because he could not detach Chieftaincy from polygamy in the structure of African society of those days. But that is another subject.

The attitude of the later missionaries towards African institutions seems to have been different from that of the pioneers. Perhaps they were infected by something of the spirit of their imperialist brothers who had now overrun Africa ; more probably things were moving very fast, their African fellow-workers seemed not to care, so Kingship came to be ignored. Whilst the British colonialists tried to use Chiefs in indirect rule (and they lumped Kings and Chiefs together), the work of the missionary and the merchant tended to put education and riches with their resultant power into other hands. The African Christian came too often to be the person who accepted Kingly and tribal authority only when and if it suited him. " The Palace " came to be more and more ignored. This is the gist of one of the chief complaints of Nana Ofori Atta I of Akyem Abuakwa in his Memorandum to the Synod of the Presbyterian Church of the Gold Coast, meeting at Kibi in 1948.[37]

So then in Southern Ghana there had been promise of communication and accommodation in the matter of Kingship but more disappointment than fulfilment. Let us turn to review briefly the situation in the North.

Amongst the tribes of Northern Ghana, sacral Kingship is

and the Chief retains some remnants of the position of Priest-King. This merits separate treatment. For the moment it is possible to include the Manya Krobo Konorship as an example of a Kingship which nearly, but not quite, became Christian.

[37] The Memorandum was printed and distributed and then withdrawn from circulation by the *Omanhene*. A reply entitled *The Church in the State* was published at Accra by the Synod in 1942, and an Address of Welcome by Nana Ofori Atta II at Kibi in 1954. All these documents bear on our subject and show how much hard thinking had already gone into it in the Gold Coast before Independence.

well understood. Broadly speaking, most of their Kings belong to one of three types. There are those who have been " created by the white man." [38] That is, when the British and Germans came up at the beginning of this century they did not understand the vastly complicated structure of authority in existence among the people they were attempting to rule. Quite often they gave power into the hands of people who did not possess it by native custom ; the bold, the impudent, the rich, would come forward while the real rulers would hang back until too late. By the time the country became independent again, these men had deeply entrenched themselves. Secondly, there are Kings who are descendants of a conquering military aristocracy who sub-jugated the people they now rule before the European came, but not so long before as to have coalesced with them. Thirdly, there is the class of royal and priestly person whom Rattray refers to as " *Ten'dana* or *Tegatu* or *Tinteintina* (or whatever was the local dialectical form) or Priest-King." [39] Perhaps " Priest-King " is a dangerous term here because of the associa-tions it imports from the connotations of that term in Comparative Religion, and a literal translation, " Lord of the Land," is better. The *Ten'dana* nearly always belongs to that tribal group in a particular place which can best claim to be autochthonous. Where he has no overlord superimposed by conquest or by government, he has much of the power of a King as we know it in other parts of Africa, but where he has lost political power we find he still bears some form of rule over those who are strictly his own people and he still exercises priestly powers connected with the land even where his own people do not actually occupy it now. He appeases and placates the spirits of the land and offers sacrifice. Through his connexion with them, he is con-concerned with ownership of the land, with its use for farming or burial, with its fertility and the avoidance of drought and locusts.

[38] See R. S. Rattray, *The tribes of the Ashanti Hinterland* (Oxford, 1932), pp. xi, xiv, xv f., 487 f. That great anthropologist's opinions and findings were amply borne out by conversations with old men and chiefs in different parts of the country between 1956 and 1962.

[39] *Ibid.*, xi. Nearly always educated informants happily used as an alterna-tive the Twi term *Asasewura*, " master or lord of the land." But the writer has also heard illiterate informants use the Twi word *ɔbosomfo* of him. (Christaller translates this " fetishman," synonymous with *ɔkɔmfo*, " priest." " Fetish " is today a bad word, so " priest of the indigenous religion " may indicate the mean-ing.) This may show merely their ignorance or a better understanding of his priestliness.

The first type of Chief, the creation of the government, hardly concerns our present purposes. We may now discuss one example of the second type of King, the leader of a military aristocracy which has superimposed itself on subject people. We take as example certain aspects of Kingship amongst the Gonjas.[40] The Gonjas invaded the country they now occupy about the Black and White Voltas from Bole to Salaga probably in the sixteenth or seventeenth century. They were led by Sumaila Ndewura Jakpa, who conquered the land and settled his " sons " as Kings to rule the subject people who in many cases retained their own Kings under the Gonjas. Jakpa was slain, it is said by no ordinary bullet, when fighting the Ashantis. He was to have been buried at Gbiniwurape where the great royal mausoleum is, but his body was too far gone and he was buried at Buipe. The Buipewura, who is one of the great Gonja Kings, seems to owe some of his considerable religious authority to his guardianship of Jakpa's tomb. He it is who sends a representative to " enskin " or " enrobe " the eldest son of Jakpa, that is, the Yabumwura, the Paramount Chief of the Gonjas, whose seat is now at Damongo.

Christian work among the Gonjas is fairly recent.[41] So far as describing God as a King is concerned, the people seem to welcome and understand it, and it entails no unavoidable misrepresentations. So far as baptizing Gonja Kingship, there are optimists who think this would be a way of bringing in a people amongst whom Kings still wield tremendous power. If one listens to one of the great Gonja Kings explaining the part he plays in the religious life of his people, one perceives that he is a great sacral figure but that already he has become detached from much of the actual religious ceremonial, partly by handing it over to a Muslim *Liman* or by leaving it in the hands of a " Lord of the Land " belonging to the *Nyamasi* (people of the

[40] Besides informants in Gonja country, notably Rev. Christian Natoma, himself of Kingly family, and Rev. Otto Rytz who has worked there since 1949, the writer is here drawing on a collection of unprinted MSS. mainly written by British political officers in the 1930s and preserved at the Government Agent's office at Damongo. Tribute must be paid to those lonely young men who loved the people they ruled and in trying to understand their ways, noted down their customs. Printed accounts of the legends of origin may be found for instance in E. F. Tamakloe, *A Brief History of the Dagbamba People* (Accra, 1931), pp. 21 ff., or D. St. John-Parsons, *Legends of Northern Ghana* (Longmans, 1958).

[41] The Assemblies of God and the World-wide Evangelization Crusade, the Roman Catholic Church, the Presbyterian and Methodist Churches of Ghana are all represented.

land), or by employing a deputy. The majority of informants felt the difficulty in the way of a King becoming or remaining a Christian would not be in the rites repugnant to Christianity he would have to fulfil, but in the hostility of the Muslim section of his people.[42]

It would seem then that in connexion with this type of Kingship, both communication and accommodation would be comparatively easy. But with regard to the *Ten'dana*, the " Lord of the Land " type of King, it is agreed the task would be more difficult. The concept perhaps in basis has more to do with Baal than Yahweh. It has to be demonstrated that we do not get increase of crops and fertility from the spirits of the land but from the one God. Again, those of these " Lords of the Land " who have come over to Christianity, have found it necessary to abandon every connexion with their former rôle, and at the same time their families have considered it essential that someone else should take it up.

But the cult of the ruler who has divine associations cannot be left here. Busia in 1955 said at a Conference : " I think it is true to suggest that for the Akan, the Stool is the symbol, *par excellence*, of his culture. This is why I threw the challenge, which I throw again, that the question of the place of chieftaincy in the Christian Church of the Gold Coast is important and urgent, if Christianity is to touch the whole of our group life." [43] He was right. The nation demands a *Herrscherkultus* and one has developed. Osagyefo Dr. Kwame Nkrumah, the President of the Republic, is without question a great charismatic leader. Dancing takes place before his statue and it is garlanded on certain occasions. There has been a fully reported discussion in Parliament about the sense in which he is divine. The Ghana Young Pioneers, meeting all over the country in the open air, hold a ceremony for all to hear, called " The Institutionalization of Osagyefo the President," in which litanies are chanted which bring out the eternity and inerrancy of Dr. Nkrumah. The

[42] It is not easy to be precise about the extent and purity of Islam amongst the Gonja. The Lord Jakpa is said to have made an agreement with the Mallam who helped him, Fati Morukpe, that the latter's descendants would have special rights. But some of the important Muslim families, for instance at Salaga and Larabanga, do not seem connected with Fati Morukpe. Also the Gonja Kings themselves do not appear to be too greatly influenced by Islam, and they certainly keep up close ties with the pagan elements amongst their people.

[43] *Christianity and African Culture* (published by the Christian Council at Accra in 1955), p. 22.

leading article almost any day of the *Ghana Evening News* will provide material of this kind.

At the same time the Churches of Ghana have not been without constructive treatment of Kingship ideas. In the Fante-speaking section of the Methodist Church a tradition has been established of taking songs from the old African culture and using them in Church. We may give as an example, the lyric " Ɔyɛ Ɔhen " :

> He is King.
> *Onyame* is King.
> The Warrior (Ɔsabarimba) is King.
> My father 'Nyame is King.[44]

It is said that the new edition of *Christian Asɔre Ndwom* (" Christian Church Songs ") will contain a larger number of lyrics with this theme, enshrining such ideas as : " God is a great King, he does what he says " (a reference to a well-recognized trait of Akan Kingship), " Speak, o mighty King, speak with the storm and rain," " Give glory to God, the Great King." [45]

A group of Ghanaian Christian scholars who love and value their own culture has turned its attention to this matter over a period of years. Their thinking may be summed up somewhat as follows.[46] They realize how much of their native culture is bound up with Kingship. They see its faults of the past, its connexion long ago with human sacrifice, then with pagan offerings, with uneducated and ignorant incumbents, with allegedly necessary polygamy. But time has removed much of

---

[44] Given as Lyric i by my late colleague Dr. S. G. Williamson, " The Lyric in the Fante Methodist Church," *Africa*, XXVIII (1958), pp. 126 ff.

[45] Personal communication from Rev. Kwesi Ellis of Anomabu.

[46] Typical of this group are Dr. C. A. Akrofi, and Rev. R. O. Danso. The latter's book *Yen Ahemfo*, published by Oxford in 1949, followed by five impressions and then a second edition in 1955, partly summarized previous discussion and stimulated new. The writer thanks Mr. E. Amoah, his secretary, for his verbal running translation and commentary upon it as well as for typing this essay and other help. He is also indebted to Mrs. Evelyn King for much patient research assistance, and discussions which have assisted clearer thinking. He is also indebted to the University of Ghana for their yearly travel grant which made the necessary field work possible. The University and these helpers are not responsible for any views expressed in this essay. The writer regrets he was unable to get access to G. E. F. Laing, *A King for Africa* (Lutterworth, 1946), though he had the benefit of a number of conversations with the late Provost of Accra before his sudden death and has tried to incorporate something of his wisdom on the accommodation of Christianity and African culture. He is also grateful to Rev. L. H. Ossae-Addo for comments and advice.

this and Christianity can reject some and baptize other features of what is left. This would still be essential African Kingship, containing the best in the old system but also modelling itself on Biblical Kingship. They now await a generation of well-educated Christian Kings who with courage and resolution will put these ideas into practice.

In conclusion, we may say that though we have only examined Kingship in parts of the country, probably these are not untypical of the whole of Ghana, nor Ghana of Africa. Kingship, the demand for *Herrscherkultus* and the response of the Church and the Bible to them are living and burning issues of the greatest importance. In the new Africa here is one of the places where the Church must set her watch, not to destroy, but to communicate, to accommodate, and to fulfil.

THE PENTATEUCH AND THE TRIENNIAL LECTIONARY CYCLE : AN EXAMINATION OF A RECENT THEORY

By J. R. PORTER

No one in this country has done more than S. H. Hooke to show how many sections of the Pentateuch have been shaped originally by cultic and liturgical considerations. The purpose of this small tribute of admiration for his genius and gratitude for his friendship is to examine a recent theory that the existing arrangement of the Pentateuch is the result of the material it contains having been adapted to fit a triennial synagogue lectionary cycle not later than the fourth century B.C. This is the view most persuasively propounded by Professor Aileen Guilding in her book *The Fourth Gospel in Jewish Worship* (Oxford, 1960). It is not the purpose of this article to discuss the main thesis of her work concerning the relationship of the Fourth Gospel to the lectionary cycle nor even to consider her opinion that the Psalter also owes its present form to this same cycle. Nor will it be possible to review the evidence for the existence of a triennial lectionary cycle nor, other than incidentally, for the probable date of its emergence. The question is simply this : assuming the existence of a triennial lectionary cycle, can it be shown that the existing arrangement of the material in the Pentateuch has been devised to fit it ?

Professor Guilding states her position succinctly : " the triennial cycle was not superimposed on the Pentateuch, but the Pentateuch was adapted to suit the cycle." [1] In support of this theory, leaving aside the question of the arrangement of the Psalter, four other arguments are adduced,[2] and perhaps we may begin by some general remarks about the third of these, *viz.*, the indications in the Pentateuch of two different cycles, one beginning in Nisan and the other in Tishri. It is difficult to

---

[1] *Op. cit.*, p. 26.
[2] *Op. cit.*, pp. 26-7.

see how the mere fact, if such it be, of *two* distinct lectionary cycles can be used to support the contention that the existing Pentateuch has been adapted to fit a *single* cycle, and indeed it rather suggests the opposite. For the existence of two cycles, on Professor Guilding's argument, would imply the existence at some date of two different arrangements of the Pentateuchal material appropriate to each, and the fact that these arrangements have now been combined into a single complex strongly indicates that the final pattern of the Torah was not determined by lectionary considerations, since, had it been, it is clear that the indications held to prove the existence of one cycle would not fit the scheme of the other. Thus, for example, the dates at Ex. xl. 17 and Deut. i. 3 are right for a Tishri cycle but not for a Nisan one.[3] It may seem curious that redactors who, on Professor Guilding's view, indulged, in the interests of liturgical use, in the addition of many dates and whole paragraphs as well as in a considerable rearrangement of the Pentateuchal material, should have left these and other incongruities, if liturgical use was in fact their overriding concern.

At least a partial answer to this objection, though *The Fourth Gospel and Jewish Worship* does not state it explicitly, might be found in Professor Guilding's contention that in the existing Pentateuch, considered as reflecting a triennial lectionary system, we find similar themes sometimes being repeated at six-monthly intervals and that the explanation of this phenomenon is a combination of two cycles, so that, for instance, the passages appropriate for and read during Shebat in a Tishri cycle would be read during Ab in the Nisan cycle to which the present Pentateuch is supposed to conform. At first sight, the evidence adduced to support this view appears impressive, but on closer examination of its details doubts begin to arise. Thus, the argument about the Day of Atonement on pp. 36 f. of Professor Guilding's book rests on the sudden introduction of a cycle beginning on the 15th Shebat, for which there is really no evidence at all. Again, on p. 38, much is made of the correspondence between Lev. xxiv. 1 f. and Ex. xxvii. 20 f. as the sedarim for

---

[3] Assuming, of course, that even with a Tishri cycle Nisan was still reckoned as the first month. Professor Guilding is inconsistent on the point, for, commenting on p. 15 on the date in Ex. xl. 17, she writes : " this would be correct on the basis of a triennial cycle beginning in Tishri." This is not the only instance which will have to be noted of Professor Guilding's desire to both have her cake and eat it.

Hanukkah in the second year of the Nisan and Tishri cycles respectively. Can it reasonably be claimed, however, that Lev. xxiv. in a Nisan cycle would ever fall to be read at Hanukkah in such a cycle ? Hanukkah is celebrated on the 25th Kislev for eight days. But according to the calendar constructed by Professor Guilding on p. 234 of her book, Lev. xxiv. would not be read until the second sabbath of Tebeth, while according to that on pp. 13 f. it would apparently fall later still. Even if this particular seder did fall occasionally within the eight-day Hanukkah period, the occurrence would be too infrequent to support the contention that its position in the Pentateuch was deliberately fixed so that it would be read at this time. Again, the alleged correspondence on p. 30 of the themes of the lections for Shebat in a Nisan and a Tishri cycle respectively is not as marked as a first glance might suggest. So Deut. xxxiii–xxxiv. would be read with a Nisan cycle in Shebat only if Büchler's theory of the arrangement of the lectionary were correct, and though Professor Guilding appears to accept this when it suits her purpose (*e.g.*, *op. cit.*, p. 27), she elsewhere gives lengthy and convincing arguments for rejecting it (*op. cit.*, pp. 236 f.). Nor would Gen. xlix.–l. fall to Shebat every year,[4] and, if this is so, the argument that the content of these chapters would be particularly appropriate to Shebat is seriously weakened. In any case, the argument drawn from the character of these chapters is in danger of seeming somewhat subjective, as may be seen from the fact that whereas on pp. 31 f. it is contended that Gen. xlix. and Deut. xxxiii. are especially suitable for Shebat because of their association with mourning and death, yet on p. 29 it is maintained that these very chapters are liturgical additions to make the books in which they now occur end with " an oracle of good omen." Further examples along these lines could easily be given, but perhaps a more general point may be adduced to conclude this part of the discussion. The very fact that at least by the time of the compilation of the Mishnah special lessons, outside the regular sequence, were provided for the Jewish Festivals is weighty evidence against the view that the readings which would fall to these Festivals in the lectionary, whether a Nisan or a Tishri one, were specially appropriate : for had they been, it is hard to see why it would have been necessary to replace them.

[4] *E.g.*, they would be read in Tebeth according to the calendar *op. cit.*, p. 234.

We may now turn to the other arguments used to support
the theory under consideration, and consider first the claims
made for the Pentateuchal dates. Professor Guilding contends
that " most of the Pentateuchal dates fit a triennial cycle beginning in Nisan," [5] though at least two of them, Ex. xl. 17 and
Deut. i. 3, have to be accounted for on the assumption of a cycle
beginning in Tishri. It so happens that dates occur in the
Pentateuch most frequently in the Book of Numbers—although
they are not very frequent even there—and several of these,
namely Num. i. 1, 18 ; xx. 1 ; xxxiii. 3, will not fit either with a
Nisan or a Tishri cycle. It is true that Professor Guilding states
that in Numbers " a new set of dates to suit a triennial cycle
has clearly been superimposed on a more ancient system of
dating," [6] but such an assumption would only be justified if her
theory were conclusively proved on other grounds, and no reason
is given for holding, *e.g.*, that the date at Num. xxxiii. 38 is later
than the dates listed above. But even some of the dates adduced
in support of the theory under review require some rather curious
juggling to make them fit. For example, in order to bring
Num. x. into the second month, sedarim beginning at Num. vii. 48
and ix. 1 have to be postulated (*op. cit.*, p. 27). No evidence is
given for the existence of these and they are ignored in the
scheme on p. 234 which, following the Massoretic sedarim, puts
Num. x. in the *first* month, which is inconsistent with *v.* 11 of
that chapter.[7] In addition, in order to have Num. x. 11 read on
or about the 20th Iyyar, the date mentioned in the verse, it is
suggested that Num. vii. was once divided into three sedarim.
But if this were so, Num. ix. would fall in the *second* month,
which is inconsistent with the view, so strongly emphasized by
Professor Guilding, that this chapter is an interpolation into the
existing book of Numbers in order to provide a suitable lection
for Passover. It might be possible to claim that here we have
to do with two different recensions of the Pentateuchal material,
though this is to multiply the *entia* with a vengeance and would
in any case indicate once again that the existing arrangement
of the Torah was not determined by lectionary considerations.
But, assuming the hypothetical sedarim ever existed, is not a

[5] *Op. cit.*, p. 17 and p. 27.

[6] *Op. cit.*, p. 43.

[7] It may be noted that this verse is also dated " the *second* year," although
it would fall to be read in the *third* year of a Nisan cycle. The same observation
applies to Num. ix. 1.

more likely explanation—to anticipate what will be argued more fully later—that the material in Numbers *as it now exists* was divided differently in two distinct synagogue traditions, one of which was concerned primarily to read Num. ix. in Nisan and the other to read Num. x. in Iyyar ? Further, it must again be noted that the discussion about the reading of Deut. xxxiv. on p. 27 loses much of its point unless Büchler's theory of the arrangement of the lectionary is accepted. Finally, in this connexion, a word may be said about the dates in the Flood story. Professor Guilding stresses the mentions of the second month at Gen. vii. 11 and viii. 14 and these are no doubt significant. But other months are mentioned at Gen. viii. 4, 5, 13. It could well be that the story of the Flood has a liturgical background, but this was perhaps not in the first instance the liturgy of the synagogue, and a theory of the origin of the present form of these chapters which accounts for all the dates in them, and not merely two, may appear more satisfactory.[8]

It may be concluded, then, that the Pentateuchal dates give little support to the theory under consideration. We will now examine the argument dealing with the supposed repetition of themes at the same point in the calendar. In her discussion of this question, Professor Guilding once more appears to adopt Büchler's main position, and, on this view, the end of each year of the lectionary would coincide with the end of the reading of a book of the Torah, namely Genesis, Leviticus, and Deuteronomy, a natural and obvious plan, requiring no special comment. She notes, however, that Leviticus and Deuteronomy were read during the same months though in different years and claims that this coincidence must have involved some adjustment in the Pentateuchal material : in particular, she suggests that Ex. xxxv.–xxxix. may be merely " editorial padding " inserted to make the reading of Leviticus correspond with that of Deuteronomy.[9] But such an assumption would only be necessary if the sedarim were all of approximately the same length, so that Exodus would have been used up before the desired date for its termination was reached. In fact the length of a seder varies very considerably.[10] Had the compilers of the lectionary system had before them a version of Exodus concluding with chapter xxxiv,

---

[8] For one such suggestion, cf. E. Nielsen, *Oral Tradition*, pp. 98 f.
[9] *Op. cit.*, p. 28.
[10] For the details, cf. the table at the end of this article.

the reading of which they wished to complete sometime in Elul, it would have been perfectly simple for them to shorten the sedarim, and so increase their number, in Genesis and Exodus, since many of these are much longer than the minimum twenty-one verses and the length of a seder was clearly not determined by what might be called " natural breaks." [11]   In fact, something of the sort may have happened.   In the edition of the unpointed Hebrew text of the Pentateuch published by the British and Foreign Bible Society in 1961, Genesis occupies roughly 86 pages, Exodus 73, Leviticus 51, Numbers 72, and Deuteronomy 62 : in the lectionary system, Genesis takes approximately ten months to read, Exodus seven, Leviticus five, Numbers seven, and Deuteronomy six.   The basic unit was thus the time allotted for the reading of each book as a whole, on the plan of roughly ten ' pages ' a month, except for Genesis, which was read more slowly and where the average length of the sedarim is correspondingly less than in the other four books.   The phenomenon of Genesis is to be explained either, if Büchler is correct, from a desire to make its reading extend over a single whole year, or perhaps to ensure that the reading of Exodus should not extend beyond the beginning of Elul.   In any case, there is nothing to suggest that the compilers of the lectionary had Exodus before them in other than its present form.   Again, as has already been seen, Professor Guilding regards Gen. xlix. and Deut. xxxiii. as purely liturgical additions, inserted to give the books a happy ending.   But if this was felt to be desirable on liturgical grounds, we have to ask why no similar additions were made to the other books of the Torah when they came to be read in the synagogue lectionary.   A more convincing explanation of the resemblance between the end of Genesis and the end of Deuteronomy is provided if Genesis and Exodus-Deuteronomy are viewed as originally distinct complexes, with the latter perhaps modelled on the general pattern of the former,[12] a stage in the development of the Pentateuch which would obviously precede the development of the synagogue lectionary system, though it might still have an earlier and different liturgical background.   Even if Büchler's theory is right, the fact that the chapters under consideration were read about the same time in different years

---

[11] Cf., *e.g.*, the awkwardness of ending sedarim with Gen. xxiv. 41, xxvii. 27, xliii. 13, xlix. 26, to quote only a few instances.

[12] Cf. the suggestive remarks in G. Östborn, *Cult and Canon*, p. 21 f.

is easily accounted for : Genesis, being considerably longer than the other books of the Torah, was allotted an entire year and so its final chapters would be read at the same period as those of Deuteronomy, which concluded the whole cycle.

Finally, it is necessary to review the argument which rests on the portions in the regular cycle which fell to the Festivals, and here it may readily be admitted that Professor Guilding makes out a strong case for these portions, in some cases at least, being especially appropriate for the Feasts with which they were associated in the lectionary. Perhaps not all the examples adduced are equally convincing, and we have already expressed reservations about the claims made with regard to the Day of Atonement and Hanukkah. One other dubious case may be mentioned : there is no need to call in the lectionary cycle to account for the reading of the story of Cain and Abel, for, with a lectionary beginning in Nisan, Gen. iv. would be bound to be reached somewhere about Passover, and, since Cain and Abel are the sons of Adam, the chapter is in its obvious and natural place in the Pentateuch as it stands. Once again, the Cain episode may well have an ancient ritual origin,[13] but it is questionable how far this would still have been present to the minds of the compilers of the lectionary, for the ninth century A.D. tradition referred to by Professor Guilding could at least equally as well have been derived from the lectionary, rather than the other way about. But, granting a considerable degree of correspondence between the themes of the sedarim and those of the Festivals, it still has to be asked whether this was achieved by interpolating and rearranging the Pentateuch material and not rather by varying the length of the sedarim into which the Pentateuch *as we now have it* was divided. That the latter may have been the case is suggested, first, by the fact that, unlike the special lections prescribed in the Mishnah, in many years the relation to the Festival of the regular seder would only be approximate—*i.e.*, while it would always be read near the Festival, it would not always be read on or during this. Secondly, it is noteworthy that it is precisely around several of the Festival seasons that there is evidence of some dislocation in the sedarim. Professor Guilding herself remarks on the " considerable shifting "

---

[13] Cf. S. H. Hooke, " Cain and Abel," *Folklore*, 50, pp. 58–65 (reprinted in *The Siege Perilous*, pp. 66–73).

of the sedarim of Exodus read about Passover time : [14] at the
same period in the third year of the cycle, we find the abnormally
long seder of Num. vi. 22–vii. 89. Professor Guilding, as has
been seen, conjectures that this passage may have been divided :
is the explanation of its extraordinary length perhaps that it
could *either* be read as a whole *or* divided in order to have Num. ix.
or Num. x. in the right place in different years, and that a similar
explanation accounts for the variations in the Exodus sedarim ?
The same considerations apply to two of the readings that would
fall to Pentecost in the Nisan cycle : Gen. xiv.–xvi. is divided
into three very short sedarim, one of which is only 16 verses
and another just 21, while Ex. xix.–xx. is immediately followed
by a very long seder of 60 verses and Professor Guilding's scheme
on p. 234 indicates variations in the lections at just this point.
Deut. xi. 10–xii. 20, an appropriate reading for Tishri, is immediately followed by two sedarim both under 21 verses. Even
the passages which, in Professor Guilding's view, represent
repetitions of themes sometimes display the same phenomenon.
For example, Ex. xxi. 1–xxiii. 19 is parallel to Deut. xiv. 1–
xvi. 17 : the first of these passages is divided into one abnormally
long seder (60 verses) and one rather short one (26 verses), the
second is immediately followed by two sedarim of under 21
verses. Other instances could be quoted, but we may perhaps
conclude with some remarks on Deut. xx. This passage is
assigned by Professor Guilding to Hanukkah and, once more, it
is immediately followed by a seder of only 19 verses. Professor
Guilding emphasizes the use of חנך in *v.* 5 and rightly observes
that the verb occurs in the Pentateuch only in this passage.
But the noun חֲנֻכָּה, identical with the title of the Feast, occurs
at Num. vii. 10, 11, 84, 88, so that this would be an even more
appropriate passage, especially as it refers to the dedication of
the altar, the very act which Hanukkah commemorated. If the
Numbers passage were found at a suitable point in the present
Book of Deuteronomy, it would go far to confirm Professor
Guilding's theory, but the facts as they stand seem rather to
suggest that Deut. xx. was brought into relationship with
Hanukkah by manipulation of the sedarim.

   To recapitulate : there is not a great deal of evidence for any
influence of the triennial lectionary system on the existing
pattern of the Pentateuch. Apparent instances to the contrary,

---

[14] *Op. cit.*, p. 27.

where they are not merely coincidental, were brought about not by arranging or interpolating the Pentateuchal material but by arranging the lectionary divisions, and the sedarim were devised at a time, whenever that may have been, by which the Torah had already assumed its present form. In short, the triennial cycle was superimposed on the Pentateuch, and the Pentateuch was not adapted to suit the cycle.

The following table is given to illustrate the length of the sedarim, which, in the main, are taken from the third edition of Kittel's *Biblia Hebraica*. They do not always correspond exactly, therefore, with the sedarim in Professor Guilding's table on p. 234 of her book, although I have adopted her division of the long seder Ex. vii. 8–ix. 35. Even this, consisting of 85 verses and 5 pages, is no longer than the seder Num. vi. 22–vii. 89, and the reason for the existence of both may be the same. The page lengths are calculated from the unpointed edition of the Hebrew Torah published by the British and Foreign Bible Society in 1961, and are, of course, only approximate. An asterisk indicates sedarim of less than 21 verses.

    (1) Gen. i. 1–ii. 3 : 34 verses, 2 pages.
    (2) Gen. ii. 4–iii. 21 : 43 verses, 2½ pages.
    (3) Gen. iii. 22–iv. 26 : 29 verses, 1½ pages.
    (4) Gen. v. 1–vi. 8 : 40 verses, 2 pages.
    (5) Gen. vi. 9–vii. 24 : 38 verses, over 2 pages.
  *(6) Gen. viii. 1–14 : 14 verses, ¾ of a page.
    (7) Gen. viii. 15–ix. 17 : 25 verses, 1½ pages.
    (8) Gen. ix. 18–x. 32 : 44 verses, over 1¾ pages.
    (9) Gen. xi. 1–32 : 32 verses, 1⅔ pages.
  (10) Gen. xii. 1–xiii. 18 : 38 verses, over 2 pages.
  (11) Gen. xiv. 1–24 : 24 verses, 1½ pages.
  (12) Gen. xv. 1–21 : 21 verses, 1 page.
 *(13) Gen. xvi. 1–16 : 16 verses, under 1 page.
  (14) Gen. xvii. 1–27 : 27 verses, 1½ pages.
  (15) Gen. xviii. 1–33 : 33 verses, 2 pages.
  (16) Gen. xix. 1 -38 : 38 verses, 2½ pages.
 *(17) Gen. xx. 1–18 : 18 verses, 1 page.
  (18) Gen. xxi. 1–34 : 34 verses, 1⅔ pages.
  (20) Gen. xxii. 1–xxiii. 20 : 44 verses, 2⅔ pages.
  (21) Gen. xxiv. 1–41 : 41 verses, 2⅓ pages.
  (22) Gen. xxiv. 42–67 : 26 verses, 1⅛ pages.
 *(23) Gen. xxv. 1–18 : 18 verses, under 1 page.
  (24) Gen. xxv. 19–xxvi. 35 : 51 verses, 2⅔ pages.
  (25) Gen. xxvii. 1–27 : 27 verses, 1¼ pages.
  (26) Gen. xxvii. 28–xxviii. 9 : 28 verses, 1½ pages.

(27) Gen. xxviii. 10–xxx. 21 : 69 verses, $2\frac{2}{3}$ pages.
(28) Gen. xxx. 22–xxxi. 2 : 24 verses, under 1 page.
(29) Gen. xxxi. 3–xxxii. 3 : 55 verses, 3 pages.
(30) Gen. xxxii. 4–xxxiii. 17 : 47 verses, $2\frac{2}{3}$ pages.
(31) Gen. xxxiii. 18–xxxv. 8 : 42 verses, $2\frac{1}{2}$ pages.
(32) Gen. xxxv. 9–xxxvi. 43 : 64 verses, $3\frac{1}{3}$ pages.
(33) Gen. xxxvii. 1–36 : 36 verses, 2 pages.
(34) Gen. xxxviii. 1–30 : 30 verses, $1\frac{1}{2}$ pages.
(35) Gen. xxxix. 1–23 : 23 verses, under $1\frac{1}{2}$ pages.
(36) Gen. xl. 1–23 : 23 verses, $1\frac{1}{3}$ pages.
(37) Gen. xli. 1–37 : 37 verses, over 2 pages.
(38) Gen. xli. 38–xlii. 17 : 37 verses, 2 pages.
(39) Gen. xlii. 18–xliii. 13 : 34 verses, 2 pages.
(40) Gen. xliii. 14–xliv. 17 : 38 verses, $2\frac{1}{2}$ pages.
(41) Gen. xliv. 18–xlvi. 27 : 72 verses, $3\frac{2}{3}$ pages.
(42) Gen. xlvi. 28–xlvii. 31 : 38 verses, $2\frac{1}{2}$ pages.
(43) Gen. xlviii. 1–22 : 22 verses, $1\frac{1}{3}$ pages.
(44) Gen. xlix. 1–26 : 26 verses, $1\frac{1}{3}$ pages.
(45) Gen. xlix. 27–l. 26 : 33 verses, 2 pages.
(46) Ex. i. 1–ii. 25 : 47 verses, $2\frac{1}{2}$ pages.
(47) Ex. iii. 1–iv. 17 : 39 verses, $2\frac{1}{2}$ pages.
(48) Ex. iv. 18–vi. 1 : 38 verses, over 2 pages.
(49) Ex. vi. 2–vii. 7 : 36 verses, 2 pages.
(50) Ex. vii. 8–viii. 16 : 38 verses, $2\frac{1}{2}$ pages.
(51) Ex. viii. 17–ix. 12 : 24 verses, over $1\frac{1}{2}$ pages.
(52) Ex. ix. 13–35 : 23 verses, $1\frac{1}{2}$ pages.
(53) Ex. x. 1–29 : 29 verses, 2 pages.
(54) Ex. xi. 1–xii. 28 : 38 verses, $2\frac{1}{2}$ pages.
(55) Ex. xii. 29–51 : 23 verses, under $1\frac{1}{3}$ pages.
(56) Ex. xiii. 1–xiv. 14 : 36 verses, $2\frac{1}{2}$ pages.
(57) Ex. xiv. 15–xvi. 3 : 47 verses, nearly 3 pages.
(58) Ex. xvi. 4–27 : 24 verses, $1\frac{1}{2}$ pages.
(59) Ex. xvi. 28–xvii. 16 : 25 verses, $1\frac{1}{2}$ pages.
(60) Ex. xviii. 1–xix. 5 : 32 verses, 2 pages.
(61) Ex. xix. 6–xx. 26 : 46 verses, $2\frac{1}{2}$ pages.
(62) Ex. xxi. 1–xxii. 23 : 60 verses, $3\frac{1}{3}$ pages.
(63) Ex. xxii. 24–xxiii. 19 : 26 verses, under $1\frac{1}{3}$ pages.
(64) Ex. xxiii. 20–xxiv. 18 : 32 verses, 2 pages.
(65) Ex. xxv. 1–40 : 40 verses, 3 pages.
(66) Ex. xxvi. 1–30 : 30 verses, $1\frac{2}{3}$ pages.
(67) Ex. xxvi. 31–xxvii. 19 : 26 verses, $1\frac{1}{2}$ pages.
(68) Ex. xxvii. 20–xxviii. 43 : 45 verses, nearly 3 pages.
(69) Ex. xxix. 1–46 : 46 verses, over $2\frac{1}{2}$ pages.
(70) Ex. xxx. 1–38 : 38 verses, 2 pages.
(71) Ex. xxxi. 1–xxxii. 14 : 32 verses, 2 pages.
(72) Ex. xxxii. 15–xxxiii. 23 : 44 verses, nearly 3 pages.
(73) Ex. xxxiv. 1–26 : 26 verses, $1\frac{1}{2}$ pages.
(74) Ex. xxxiv. 27–xxxv. 29 : 38 verses, $2\frac{1}{2}$ pages.
(75) Ex. xxxv. 30–xxxvi. 38 : 44 verses, $2\frac{2}{3}$ pages.
(76) Ex. xxxvii. 1–xxxviii. 20 : 49 verses, $2\frac{1}{2}$ pages.

(77) Ex. xxxviii. 21–xxxix. 32 : 43 verses, 2⅔ pages.
(78) Ex. xxxix. 33–xl. 38 : 49 verses, 2½ pages.
(79) Lev. i. 1–iii. 17 : 50 verses, 3 pages.
(80) Lev. iv. 1–35 : 35 verses, 2½ pages.
(81) Lev. v. 1–vi. 11 : 37 verses, 2½ pages.
(82) Lev. vi. 12–vii. 38 : 50 verses, 2⅔ pages.
(83) Lev. viii. 1–x. 7 : 67 verses, 4 pages.
*(84) Lev. x. 8–20 : 13 verses, ⅔ of a page.
(85) Lev. xi. 1–47 : 47 verses, 2½ pages.
(86) Lev. xii. 1–xiii. 28 : 36 verses, 2¼ pages.
(87) Lev. xiii. 29–59 : 31 verses, 2 pages.
(88) Lev. xiv. 1–32 : 32 verses, 2 pages.
(89) Lev. xiv. 33–57 : 25 verses, 1⅓ pages.
(90) Lev. xv. 1–24 : 24 verses, over 1 page.
(91) Lev. xv. 25–xvi. 34 : 43 verses, 2½ pages.
*(92) Lev. xvii. 1–16 : 16 verses, 1 page.
(93) Lev. xviii. 1–30 : 30 verses, 1½ pages.
(94) Lev. xix. 1–22 : 22 verses, 1¼ pages.
(95) Lev. xix. 23–xx. 27 : 42 verses, 2½ pages.
(96) Lev. xxi. 1–xxii. 16 : 40 verses, over 2 pages.
(97) Lev. xxii. 17–xxiii. 8 : 25 verses, 1⅓ pages.
(98) Lev. xxiii. 9–44 : 36 verses, over 2 pages.
(99) Lev. xxiv. 1–xxv. 13 : 36 verses, 2 pages.
(100) Lev. xxv. 14–34 : 21 verses, over 1 page.
(101) Lev. xxv. 35–xxvi. 2 : 23 verses, over 1 page.
(102) Lev. xxvi. 3–46 : 44 verses, 2½ pages.
(103) Lev. xxvii. 1–34 : 34 verses, 2 pages.
(104) Num. i. 1–54 : 54 verses, 3 pages.
(105) Num. ii. 1–34 : 34 verses, 1⅔ pages.
(106) Num. iii. 1–iv. 16 : 67 verses, 3⅔ pages.
(107) Num. iv. 17–v. 10 : 43 verses, 2½ pages.
(108) Num. v. 11–31 : 21 verses, 1⅓ pages.
(109) Num. vi. 1–21 : 21 verses, 1⅓ pages.
(110) Num. vi. 22–vii. 89 : 95 verses, 5 pages.
(111) Num. viii. 1–ix. 23 : 49 verses, 3 pages.
(112) Num. x. 1–xi. 22 : 58 verses, 3 pages.
(113) Num. xi. 23–xii. 16 : 29 verses, 1⅔ pages.
(114) Num. xiii. 1–xiv. 10 : 43 verses, 2⅓ pages.
(115) Num. xiv. 11–45 : 35 verses, 2⅓ pages.
(116) Num. xv. 1–41 : 41 verses, 2⅓ pages.
(117) Num. xvi. 1–xvii. 15 : 50 verses, nearly 3 pages.
(118) Num. xvii. 16–xviii. 32 : 45 verses, 3 pages.
(119) Num. xix. 1–xx. 13 : 35 verses, 2⅓ pages.
(120) Num. xx. 14–xxii. 1 : 52 verses, 3 pages.
(121) Num. xxii. 2–xxiii. 9 : 49 verses, 3 pages.
(122) Num. xxiii. 10–xxiv. 25 : 46 verses, 2⅓ pages.
*(123) Num. xxv. 1–9 : 9 verses, ½-page.
(124) Num. xxv. 10–xxvi. 51 : 61 verses, 3 pages.
(125) Num. xxvi. 52–xxvii. 14 : 28 verses, 1½ pages.
(126) Num. xxvii. 15–xxviii. 25 : 34 verses, 1⅔ pages.

(127) Num. xxviii. 26–xxx. 1 : 46 verses, 2½ pages.
*(128) Num. xxx. 2–17 : 16 verses, 1 page.
(129) Num. xxxi. 1–24 : 24 verses, 1⅓ pages.
(130) Num. xxxi. 25–54 : 30 verses, 1½ pages.
(131) Num. xxxii. 1–42 : 42 verses, 2½ pages.
(132) Num. xxxiii. 1–56 : 56 verses, 2⅓ pages.
(133) Num. xxxiv. 1–xxxv. 8 : 37 verses, 1⅔ pages.
(134) Num. xxxv. 9–xxxvi. 13 : 39 verses, 2⅓ pages.
(135) Deut. i. 1–ii. 1 : 47 verses, 3 pages.
(136) Deut. ii. 2–30 : 29 verses, 1⅔ pages.
(137) Deut. ii. 31–iii. 22 : 29 verses, 2 pages.
(138) Deut. iii. 23–iv. 24 : 31 verses, 2 pages.
*(139) Deut. iv. 25–40 : 16 verses, over 1 page.
(140) Deut. iv. 41–vi. 3 : 45 verses, 2⅔ pages.
(141) Deut. vi. 4–vii. 11 : 33 verses, 2 pages.
(142) Deut. vii. 12–viii. 20 : 35 verses, 2⅓ pages.
(145) Deut. ix. 1–29 : 29 verses, 2 pages.
(146) Deut. x. 1–xi. 9 : 31 verses, 2 pages.
(147) Deut. xi. 10–xii. 19 : 42 verses, 3 pages.
*(148) Deut. xii. 20–xiii. 1 : 13 verses, under 1 page.
*(149) Deut. xiii. 2–19 : 18 verses, 1⅓ pages.
(150) Deut. xiv. 1–xv. 6 : 35 verses, 2 pages.
(151) Deut. xv. 7–xvi. 17 : 34 verses, 2⅓ pages.
*(152) Deut. xvi. 18–xvii. 13 : 18 verses, over 1 page.
*(153) Deut. xvii. 14–xviii. 13 : 20 verses, 1⅓ pages.
(154) Deut. xviii 14–xix. 21 : 30 verses, 2 pages.
(155) Deut. xx. 1–xxi. 9 : 29 verses, 2 pages.
*(156) Deut. xxi. 10–xxii. 5 : 19 verses, 1⅓ pages.
(157) Deut. xxii. 6–xxiii. 9 : 33 verses, 2 pages.
*(158) Deut. xxiii. 10–21 : 12 verses, over ½-page.
(159) Deut. xxiii. 22–xxiv. 18 : 23 verses, 1⅓ pages.
(160) Deut. xxiv. 19–xxv. 19 : 23 verses, 1½ pages.
(161) Deut. xxvi. 1–xxvii. 26 : 45 verses, nearly 3 pages.
(162) Deut. xxviii. 1–xxix. 8 : 77 verses, 4⅔ pages.
(163) Deut. xxix. 9–xxx. 10 : 30 verses, 2 pages.
(164) Deut. xxx. 11–xxxi. 13 : 23 verses, 1½ pages.
*(165) Deut. xxxi. 14–30 : 17 verses, 1⅓ pages.
(166) Deut. xxii. 1–52 : 52 verses, 3 pages.
(167) Deut. xxxiii. 1–xxxiv. 12 : 41 verses, 2⅓ pages.

TIME IN THE OLD TESTAMENT

By NORMAN H. SNAITH

THERE are in the Old Testament three kinds of Time, three ways of thinking of Time. For want of better terms, we shall call them Circular Time, Horizontal Time, Vertical Time. We shall not deal primarily with words, whether Hebrew or Greek. There is, indeed, more to be said for the lexical approach to the understanding of the Bible than Professor James Barr is prepared to allow. Nevertheless, his two books [1] give a salutary warning that this pathway is at least as dangerous as any other, and that here especially zeal must be tempered with discretion. Barr quotes [2] three sets of passages given by G. B. Caird, and these show beyond all doubt that the difference between χρόνος and καιρός cannot be assumed to exist everywhere and in all cases. The three sets of passages are : Mk. i. 15 and Gal. iv. 4 ; Acts iii. 20–21 ; 1 Peter i. 5, 20, and Jude 18. But in spite of these three sets of passages and in spite of all that Barr has to say, it still remains true that in general χρόνος *has to do with* (this phrase is much to be preferred rather than " means ") " measured time, duration," and that, again in general, καιρός has to do with " time of opportunity and fulfilment." [3] It is just as wrong to pick out three or four instances and on the basis of these to suggest that the distinction must nowhere be assumed, as it is to cite all the other instances and then suggest that the distinction must everywhere be assumed. Nobody is Humpty-Dumpty all the time, and nobody is Humpty-Dumpty none of the time. No man should assume that any other writer is as accurate in the precise use of words as he imagines he himself is. Occasionally even Homer nods, but it is important to emphasize the " occasionally " rather than the " nods."

And so, whilst not neglecting words entirely, we would approach the subject from a different angle, topologically rather than etymologically : Circular Time, Horizontal Time, Vertical

---

[1] *The Semantics of Biblical Language* (1961), *Biblical Words for Time* (1962).

[2] *Biblical Words for Time*, pp. 21 f. Cf. Caird, *The Apostolic Age* (1955), p. 184, n. 2.

[3] J. A. T. Robinson, *In the End, God* . . . (1950), pp. 45 ff.

Time. If we are required to use Bible words to designate these three types, we would use three Hebrew verbs, *nāqaf* for Circular Time, *'ābar* for Horizontal Time, *pāqad* for Vertical Time. We insist on verbs rather than nouns, because *tempus* is always *tempus fugiens*. When Time stands still, there is no time. Our theme is that both Circular and Horizontal are proper and natural human ways of thinking about time, both inside and outside the Bible ; but Vertical Time is the essentially Biblical element, and this in the way in which it is continuously impinging upon, invading and transforming the other two types of time. The first two are of the earth, earthy ; the third is of the LORD and of heaven. The first two are " natural " (ψυχικός) ; the third is " spiritual " (πνευματικός) ; cf. 1 Cor. ii. 12 ff., xv. 46 ff.

A. CIRCULAR TIME

Writers refer to " the cyclical conception (of time) of Helenism," and say that for the Greeks " Time is circular." These statements arise presumably from Aristotle's conclusion in *Physics* IV, 14 : " for indeed time itself would appear to be a sort of circle," [4] and " so that to say that events are circular is to say that time is a sort of circle." [5] The comment of W. D. Ross is : " Aristotle here points out that the sayings which describe time as the motion of the heavenly sphere, or as a circle, are natural exaggerations due to the close relation between time and its primary measure, which is the circular motion of the heavens." [6] The sayings which Aristotle was considering are such as " human affairs form a circle," [7] and, as James Barr pointed out, " this can hardly be called a ' cyclic view of time.' " [8] He would put such a statement down as " only a rather obvious judgement from the fact that human realities come to be and pass away, exactly the same point as occupied Qohelet." Which is sound, though an equally good Hebrew illustration is Ps. xc. 3 : " Thou returnest man to dust, and sayest, Return, ye sons of man," which is a picture of the coming and passing of successive

---

[4] Καὶ γὰρ ὁ χρόνος αὐτὸς εἶναι δοκεῖ κύκλος τις.
[5] ὥστε τὸ λέγειν εἶναι τὰ γιγνόμενα τῶν πραγμάτων κύκλον τὸ λέγειν ἐστὶν τοῦ χρόνου εἶναί τινα κύκλον.
[6] Aristotle, *Physics* (1936), p. 612. Cf. also Plato, *Timaeus*, 37a–38c.
[7] κύκλον εἶναι τὰ ἀνθρώπινα πράγματα.
[8] *Biblical Words for Time*, pp. 140 f.

generations. It is therefore unlikely that Aristotle meant much more than that the primary measurement of time is the regular circular movement of the heavens, especially since (*Physics*, IV, 11) he also used the idea of a straight line. The idea of " time as a circle " is natural to man all the world over. It is the obvious way of measuring time, and is common to both Hebrew and Greek thought. It arises from the apparent circular movement of the heavens so far as the days are concerned, and the recurrence of the seasons so far as the years are concerned (Gen. viii. 22). This last involves the agricultural feasts ; cf. Isa. xxix. 1 : " let the feasts come round " (*haggîm yinqōfû*), which probably refers, not to the (say) three agricultural feasts of Canaan, but to the annual feast (*'Asiph*, Ingathering) which marked the end-beginning of the Hebrew year—Ingathering before the exile and the Tishri complex of sacred occasions (Trumpets, Day of Atonement, Tabernacles) after the exile. Other similar passages are 2 Sam. xi. 1, Ex. xxxiv. 22, 1 Sam. i. 20, etc. This type of time is pastoral time, agricultural time, since the more we become urbanized, the less we are governed by the cyclic movements of nature. This type of time is also " religious " time, " cult " time, and with the development of religious institutions it becomes " ecclesiastical " time. Among the Hebrews, time became a matter of fixing and observing correctly the sacred seasons ; cf. Gen. i. 14, where the sun and the moon are not only to separate between day and night, but also to act as signs, *'ōthōth*, " fixed (and regular) astral points for regulating cult and work." [9] The fact is that the natural circular time of man when closely dependent on the seasons and the seasonal rains becomes more and more ecclesiastical time as man becomes more urbanized. Thus a truly decisive point in Hebrew history and religion was the centralization of the worship in Jerusalem in the time of King Josiah (621 B.C.) and the sixty years, which soon followed, of submersion in the urbanized peoples inhabiting the plain of Mesopotamia. From that time onwards circular time became quite definitely ecclesiastical time : Tishri 1, the Festival of Trumpets ; Tishri 10, the Day of Atonement ; Tishri 15 (full moon of Tishri), the Feast of Tabernacles ; later, Hanukkah and

[9] G. von Rad, *Genesis* (Eng. tr. 1961), p. 54. The words within the brackets are mine. I do not think von Rad is right in his first suggestion, that " sign " here refers to abnormal happenings, such as eclipses. Cf. Skinner, *Genesis* (*ICC*), p. 25.

Purim ; Nisan 14, Passover ; Nisan 15, Unleavened Bread ; seven weeks later, the Feast of Weeks : *i.e.*, the three feasts and the festivals (*mô'adîm*, " seasons," Gen. i. 14 ; the word does not mean " seasons of the year," but those ecclesiastical set-times which were not feasts or pilgrimages).

These natural religious observances were originally all tied to the encircling seasons of the year. The Passover was originally " a seasonal apotropaic festival," which had to do with " the magical exorcism of evil spirits." It was not necessarily nomadic in origin, and it had nothing to do with firstfruits, firstlings or harvest festivals. It was essentially a spring rite, and had its Athenian counterpart in the spring festival of Anthesteria.[10] It was not particularly either Canaanite or non-Canaanite, though it seems to have been the only one of the traditional festival-feasts which the Hebrews observed before the entry into Canaan.[11]

The three feasts (*haggîm*, pilgrimages) are all Canaanite in origin, all harvest festivals, and therefore all necessarily pilgrimages because they involved the presentation of offerings at a shrine. They were thus wholly different from the Passover, which was originally apotropaic in intention, necessarily a home rite and involved no offering to the god. The Feast of Unleavened Bread (*Maṣṣôth*) was really the barley harvest festival. It involved the presentation of the barley firstfruits and the eating of unleavened cakes for the seven days of the feast. The bitter herbs belonged to the Passover rite ; the unleavened cakes to *Maṣṣôth*. The two originally distinct rites ultimately became confused and integrated, especially after the centralization of the worship caused people to go up to Jerusalem for the Passover (and fix a technical " home " there) as well as for *Maṣṣôth*. Ultimately " the Feast of the Passover " and " the Feast of Unleavened Bread " became interchangeable terms.[12] The Feast of Weeks (*Shebu'ôth*) marked the end of the cereal harvest period ; by that time the wheat had been harvested as well as the barley. This is why the Feast of Weeks was not exactly a feast " in its own right." It was an *'aṣereth*, a closing assembly. It was an occasion for the presentation of firstfruits, and indeed in course of time this is what it became *par excellence*. The fact

---

[10] N. H. Snaith, *The Jewish New Year Festival* (1947), pp. 21 ff.

[11] There was most probably a presentation of first fruits and firstlings from earliest times (Gen. iv. 3 f.), but this belongs to the cult patterns of mankind in general rather than to that of Canaan in particular.

[12] Luke xxii. 1 ; John vi. 4.

of it being a closing-feast is shown by the ceremony of Counting the Omer, that daily ceremony which began " on the morrow of the Sabbath " and continued until the fiftieth day, thus fixing the Feast of Weeks.[13] Lastly, there was the Feast of Ingathering (*'Asiph*) which, because of the change of calendar at the exile, was divided into the three sacred occasions of the month Tishri.[14] This last of the annual harvest-festivals marked the full circle of the agricultural year and was the New Year Festival. At the break up of the pre-exilic feast, the harvest-festival elements kept to the full-moon, and began on Tishri 15, the night of the Harvest Full-moon. This was the vintage feast, when they dwelt in the vineyard-huts for the seven days of the feast (not the eighth day, which was an *'aṣereth*, closing festival). All these ceremonies belong to the orginal natural rites of the circular time of the seasons. For the particular and unique Hebrew development, see below, under Vertical Time.

B. Horizontal Time

This involves the passage of the years ; not the fact that the seasons " come round " (*nāqaf*) with unfailing regularity, but that the years add up, one by one. It is χρόνος and αἰών, both. It is the ever-rolling stream of time, the straight line which goes on and on. This idea of time was necessary as soon as men found need to say " it is such and such a time since. . . ." An early attempt to fix a datum-line was the accession of the king. The complications which this ultimately involved, apart from any problem which may have been created by " regnal years," especially when the editor of Kings tried to synchronize the dates of the two sets of kings, Israel and Judah, can be seen in any study of the problem.[15] Apart from the actual difficulties of synchronization, the total of years of the reigns of the kings of Israel is 23 years too high compared with the Assyrian figures and the Judahite total to the same date is 46 years too high. Any adequate system of determining time past depends upon a satisfactory datum-line, and this is notoriously difficult to fix,

---

[13] N. H. Snaith, *ibid.*, p. 124.
[14] N. H. Snaith, *ibid.*, pp. 131–49.
[15] See especially, E. R. Thiele, *The Mysterious Numbers of the Hebrew Kings* (Chicago, 1951).

especially since in the nature of things, if the date is to be at all useful, it must be fixed at a time far back out of accurate memory. The " two years before the earthquake " of Amos i. 1 was doubtless an admirable reference for those who lived through it, but it is not satisfactory for later generations. " The four hundred and eightieth year after the children of Israel were come out of the land of Egypt," alleged (1 Kings vi. 1) to be the fourth year of Solomon, would (supposing it is right) give us a precise date, if only we knew the year of the Exodus. The only times when a date can be fixed is when a cross-reference is given to a dated event in Assyrian or Babylonian history, dates which presumably are reasonably sound because of the greater and more accurate knowledge of the Mesopotamian astrologers and star-gazers (2 Kings xvii. 5, xxv. 8, etc.).

For our purpose, the fixing of actual dates is of no importance. All we need to establish here is that the Hebrews had the notion of the duration of time, time as a horizontal movement. This idea of duration is expressed by ʿôlām, αἰών. The Hebrew word means " long duration," for a long time backwards, for a long time forwards. It can lead away into the indefinite past ; it can lead off into the indefinite future. It involves continuing, continuing, continuing. The Golden Age is to be " with no end " (Isa. ix. 6 [Eng. 7]), and this is what " from henceforth and for ever " means, lit. " from now and to ʿôlām : i.e., it begins now, when the prince is born, and it will keep on and on and on. ʿÔlām means " on and on and on," or " back and back and back." The earlier instances of the plural ʿôlāmîm are emphasizing the long continuance (Isa. xlix. 17, li. 9) ; or backwards (Ec. i. 10).

The complication starts with the contact with Persian and the ancient Zoroastrian eschatology. The existence of the world was held to last for 12,000 years, consisting of four periods of 3,000 years each. In the first period everything was invisible ; in the second, all was well and Ahura-Mazda, the good spirit, created the world and all was good. The third period marks the ascendancy of Angra-Mainyu, the evil spirit. At the end of this period there comes Zarathustra (Zoroaster), and this is the beginning of the final victory of Ahura-Mazda. Now, at the end of each 1,000 years a Saoshyant (Deliverer) appears, of the seed of Zoroaster, till at the end Angra-Mainyu is cast into the abyss and the end of the world comes. The dead will be raised, and all men will be judged. All will pass through the purifying fire and be saved. The New Age will begin, with new heavens and a new earth, and sorrow and tears, and trouble and evil will be gone for ever.[16] Each period of 3,000 years is an " age," and 'ōlām and αἰών are used. The result is that " this age " involves a period of time with a definite ending, and " the age to come " involves a time which has no necessary definite ending. Further, when the End comes after 12,000 years, there is a new world ; thus the words 'ōlām, αἰών can mean " world." Yet again, since at this stage χρόνος is thought of in terms of 'ōlām, αἰών, there is a tendency to confusion between the two words χρόνος and αἰών, and their meaning. And yet again, since καιρός (the set time, the appointed time, the crisis) is involved as the crisis of this age (hā'ōlām hazzeh), the word καιρός can infringe on the provinces of both χρόνος and αἰών. The situation may not therefore be as confused as Barr suggests. Perhaps after all they knew what they meant better than he does. The New Testament writers may not have been always as careful as we moderns try to be, but they may easily have been more accurate than we give them credit for being.

C. VERTICAL TIME

This Vertical Time is the particular Hebrew contribution. It is concerned with the direct action of the active God. It is concerned with God's involvement with the world and with men. It deals with the moment of Encounter. To the Hebrews and throughout the Bible, God is not " He who is," but rather " He who acts." It was perhaps natural for the LXX translators of Ex. iii. 14 to translate 'ehyeh 'asher 'ehyeh by the Aristotelian " I am ὁ ὤν," but it had a great deal to do with giving Christianity a classical background instead of its true Hebrew background— a static, immovable God as against an active, moving God. The LORD is certainly a High God and His home is above, away in high heaven, but He continually " visits " (pāqad) this world which He has made, and He visits men and women for good and for ill.[17] Cf. Ps. lxv. 10 (Eng. 9) : " Thou visitest (? hast visited) the earth and waterest it " ; but more often the word is used of

---

[16] Oesterley and Robinson, *Hebrew Religion* (2nd ed. 1937), pp. 388 f. ; N. H. Snaith, *The Jews from Cyrus to Herod* (1949), pp. 95 f.
[17] Cf. Georges Pidoux, *Le Dieu qui vient* (1947), G. Ernest Wright, *God Who Acts* (1952).

" visiting men and women." It is used of God " intervening " and seeing to it that Sarah conceived and bore the promised heir (Gen. xxi. 1). God visited the Israelite slaves in Egypt and took action (Gen. l. 24 f. ; Ex. iii. 16, iv. 31). He visits the iniquities of the fathers on the children (Ex. xx. 5, etc.), but He also visits men with His salvation (Ps. cvi. 4). The idea is taken over into the New Testament, where (as already in LXX) the word is ἐπισκέπτομαι. Note particularly Luke i. 68 : " He hath visited and redeemed His people." God continually " visits " the earth and " visits " men—visiting in salvation, visiting in judgement, until the last Great Day ; cf. 1 Peter ii. 12, where the reference may be to the final Day of Judgement.

The idea of God " visiting " His people with salvation is dominant throughout, and descending moment by moment, always Now, as drops of rain, each separate, but continuously descending. The Vertical downwards motion continually invades both Circular and Horizontal time.

D. The Invasion of Circular Time

The apotropaic Passover rite was changed from being a means of warding off evil spirits to warning off the Angel whose duty it was to destroy all the first-born in Egypt. More than this, the whole ceremony became a celebration of the rescue from Egypt. The first stage is Ex. xii. 27, where it is in celebration of the LORD passing over the houses of the Israelites, this being already a sign of salvation. It becomes (Deut. xvi. 1) to be observed because " in the month of Abib, the LORD thy God brought thee out of Egypt by night."

Similarly, the Feast of *Maṣṣôth* (Unleavened Bread) was changed from being a harvest feast to being a commemoration of the same rescue from Egypt. The Unleavened bread becomes " the bread of affliction " (Deut. xvi. 3), and it was all " for in this selfsame day have I brought your hosts out of the land of Egypt " (Ex. xii. 17 ; Deut. xvi. 3 ; Ex. xiii. 7 f.). The reason for the bread being unleavened becomes : " And the Egyptians were urgent upon the people to send them out of the land in haste . . . and the people took their dough before it was leavened, their kneading troughs being bound up in their clothes upon their shoulders " (Ex. xii. 33 f.). Once more the significance of the celebration has been changed because of God's " visitation " of the Israelites in Egypt.

The Feast of Weeks marked the close of the cereal harvest (Deut. xvi. 9–12) and was concerned with " the firstfruits of the wheat harvest " (Ex. xxxiv. 22). The natural association of firstfruits is of course with the harvest. The firstfruits are presented at the shrine in acknowledgment that the whole of the increase belongs to God and is therefore holy and *taboo* to men, but after the presentation God grants the people the privilege of using the rest of the crop to supply their need. But the reason for the presentation of firstfruits in Israel came to have another meaning. According to Deut. xxvi. 5–11, the Israelites recited a creed : " A Syrian ready to perish (' a wandering Aramaean ') was my father, and he went down into Egypt . . . ," and so forth, how the people were enslaved and how the LORD heard their plea, visited them and brought them into this land that flows with milk and honey. The firstfruits are the fruits of the good land into which God had brought them. Once more the visitation of God changes the significance of the Feast.

Yet again the Feast of Ingathering marked the end of the year " when thou gatherest in thy labours out of the field " (Ex. xxiii. 16, xxxiv. 22) and from the " threshing floor and winepress " (Deut. xvi. 13). The reason for dwelling in booths (cf. the Indian " *pandal* ") becomes " I made the children of Israel to dwell in booths, when I brought them out of the land of Egypt " (Lev. xxiii. 43).

Thus all four sacred occasions became changed in their significance. All the " circular " ceremonies, those which " come round " each year, have become commemorations of the rescue from Egypt. They are commemorative of the " vertical action " of the LORD, of His visitation.

E. THE INVASION OF HORIZONTAL TIME

The invasion of horizontal time is illustrated in Isa. li. 9–11. Here we get a reference to " the days of old " (*yᵉmê qedem*) and to the " generations of passing time " (*dōrôth ʿôlāmîm*), *i.e.*, generations reaching back and back and back, continuously till scarcely seen at all in the far distant past. There is a reference to the ancient creation myth with the fight against Rahab the

Sea-dragon, not, as is sometimes carelessly said, "before time began," but "before the world was made." The God who fought and overcame the Sea-monster, dried up the sea, the waters of the Great Deep (an intermingling here of the Reed Sea and the Great Deep), made the depths of the sea a path for the ransomed to cross over—this God is rescuing Israel from a second bondage and will bring His ransomed ones back once more to Zion. The interweaving of the ancient myth with the story of the Exodus had already taken place in Ex. xv. 5, and the same thing is true of the Prayer of Jonah out of the belly of the great fish (Jonah ii. ; cf. Jer. li. 34). The Jonah poem speaks of being cast into the Depth, into the heart of the seas, and the Stream (of Ocean, *nāhār*) surrounded him. The Deep (*tᵉhôm*) encompassed him. *V.* 5 (Eng. 4) is the cry of exiled Israel, looking longingly towards the Temple. We have an interweaving of the fight against the Deep, the rescue from Egypt and the rescue from the Babylonian exile. The fight of the LORD against the Sea [18] is a recurrent happening in the long course of history. Pre-history repeats itself in history, and again and again in the NOW of Israel's distress, He visits His people, and repeats His victory.[19]

The visitation of the LORD takes place not only in the great events of Israel's history and in her rescues from her distresses. He is involved in every detail of everyday life. The preface to the Ten Commandments (usually omitted [20] in Christian liturgies) concerns this same rescue from Egypt. Some of these commandments may well have had their origin in ethical and social considerations, and they may also have had from the beginning the authority of the tribal God. But this is not what came to be the case in Israel. They are the Ten Words, spoken by "the LORD thy God, which brought thee out of the land of Egypt, out of the house of bondage" (Ex. xx. 2). The "vertical action" of God, the visitation of God, applies to every deed of every day. Not only so, but why were the Israelites to use just balances, just weights, a just ephah, and a just hin ? The reason is : "I am the LORD your God, which brought you out

---

[18] Cf. the Ugarit story of the fight of Baal against the Sea, itself a variant of the old Babylonian myth.

[19] Cf. N. H. Snaith, *Studies in the Psalter* (1934), pp. 100 f.

[20] This omission is most unfortunate, since it causes the Commandments to have an ethical basis, whereas the biblical reason for obedience is that the God who speaks these Ten Words is the Saviour God, Who saved them out of Egypt.

of the land of Egypt " (Lev. xix. 36). This is why God hallows them, separates them from the peoples (Lev. xx. 26 ; xxii. 32, etc.). Thus the whole series of regulations from Lev. xviii. 1 to xxii. 33 is brought under the same governing and dominant note : " I am the LORD " ; " I am the LORD thy God " ; " I am the LORD thy God which brought you out of the land of Egypt."

F. Conclusion

Thus we see that at every Passover, at every Feast, the same action takes place. The circular time is regularly invaded by God. Each sacred occasion is an occasion for the Visitation of God, and essentially a Visitation of God who once visited those slaves in Egypt, rescued them and made them into " a peculiar treasure " (*segullāh*) unto Him from among all peoples (Ex. xix. 5). This also is true of every action and every day, as is plain, not only from Ex. xx. and Lev. xviii. 1–xxii. 33, but also in the *Shema*, as the whole of Deut. vi. makes clear. Horizontal time is continuously invaded by God, the God who saved this people out of Egypt. Round and round, year by year ; all the way backwards to the Exodus and away beyond that to the patriarchs, yet farther and farther to before the beginning of the world ; away forwards, on and on as far as thought and beyond what sight can reach—always there is the Now and NOW and *NOW* of the Visitation of God. But it is not momentarily that God " visits " the world of nature and of man, since the impetus of each Now infiltrates into the stream, both the circular stream of time and the horizontal stream of time. Καιρός merges into χρόνος and αἰών ; more accurately, *pāqad* enters into and gives life to both *nāqaf* and *'ōlām*. The action of God in His world is ever renewing, ever continuing ; always into and always in. Every point of the circle is a NOW of divine action. Every point of the horizontal line [21] is a NOW of divine action. And both the circle itself and the line itself are the sphere of divine action.

[21] I do not like Cullmann's " upward sloping line" (*Christ and Time*, p. 53). He has imported here the illusion of Herbert Spencer and the optimistic evolutionists, who assume that the " inevitability of gradualism " is necessarily from good to better and on to best of all. If we are to specify the " horizontal line of human behaviour " it must be " downward " rather than " upward." The increase of scientific knowledge and the application of this to human needs and wants do not make men better. They enable him only to do more efficiently what he has already decided on other grounds to do.

P.F.—13

To Aristotle " the Now is the link of time," [22] or again : " Time is made continuous by the Now and is divided at the Now."[23] To the Israelites this Now is the occasion of the Visitation of the living God, the Saviour of Israel. This Now is what I have called, for want of a better term, Vertical time, though properly it is not " time " at all, nor is it " space." It is different from Circular time, which belongs to the world of created things, the movement of the earth and the cycle of the seasons. It is different from Horizontal time, which is subservient to cause and effect, and always within this same horizontal scheme. It is Now, neither circular nor horizontal, but, for the Israelites, infusing, animating and *saving* both. It is NOW, the Now which is ignored by non-religious and anti-religious moderns. Aristotle saw something of the reality and the difference of this Now when he said : " The Now is certainly not a part of χρόνος, nor the cross-section of the movement, as, for instance, the point is not part of the line." [24] It divides all time ; it joins all time. It is " of God," and it is in and through this Now that He governs, directs, and saves this world of things and men.

[22] *Physics*, IV, 10 : τὸ δὲ νῦν ἐστιν συνέχεια χρόνου.

[23] *Physics*, IV, 12 : καὶ συνεχής τε δὴ ὁ χρόνος τῷ νῦν, καὶ διήρηται κατὰ τὸ νῦν.

[24] *Physics*, IV, 11 : καὶ ἔτι φανερὸν ὅτι οὐδὲν μόριον τὸ νῦν τοῦ χρόνου, οὐδ᾽ ἡ διαίρεσις τῆς κινήσεως ὥσπερ οὐδ᾽ ἡ στιγμὴ τῆς γραμμῆς.

EXPOSITION IN THE OLD TESTAMENT AND IN RABBINIC LITERATURE

By J. WEINGREEN

THE title of this article suggests that (*a*) there are literary elements in the Hebrew Old Testament which are recognized as not being original parts of the basic texts but are supplementary to them and, in consequence, are pronounced as being commentaries upon those texts and (*b*) there are distinct points of similarity between these expository notes and certain categories of exposition found in the Talmud, pointing to a continuity of pattern from the earlier to the later. The present writer has been engaged for some time in the investigation of the general question of a direct line of continuity in tradition between Old Testament and early Rabbinic times. One of the major conclusions which has emerged from this enquiry is that certain attitudes, practices, and regulations which found their mature expression in the Talmud and which, on that account, have been generally regarded as Rabbinic in character and origin are, in fact, to be detected in the literature of the Old Testament. This general thesis has been pursued in the realms of the historical, legalistic, folkloristic, and devotional writings of the Old Testament. Here we open up another avenue of enquiry into the validity of this claim. If the substance of this general proposition can be sustained also in the sphere of the authoritative exposition of Biblical texts, as stated above, then another link will have been forged in the chain of continuity from the sacred Scriptures to Rabbinic writings. The implications of this thesis for contemporary Old Testament studies will be of some importance, for they open up a new, or hitherto neglected, approach to the study of Biblical texts as we have them. There will be a revision of the view that Rabbinic literature reflects a system of post-Biblical society and religion which has no bearing upon our understanding of the civilization of ancient Israel during Biblical historical times. On the contrary, a fresh impetus will be given to the study of the Talmud to ascertain whether, by retrospective analogy, selected Rabbinic attitudes, practices, and regulations may throw light upon, and thus promote a more comprehensive understanding of, the social and religious institutions of ancient Israel.

A few years ago the present writer published an article closely related to this subject and entitled " Rabbinic-type Glosses in the Old Testament." [1] Glosses were defined as external intrusions into the text and examples were given of recognizable categories under which they could be grouped. These are, mainly, (a) explanatory, (b) extensions of application, (c) variant readings, and (d) even Massoretic-type notes. Four significant points were made. (1) These intrusive notes constituted terse, standard comments which had been written above the affected words in manuscripts which were in private hands and meant for private, that is, non-liturgical, use. Such manuscripts, it was held, were not endowed with the same degree of sacredness as those specially prepared for the public reading of the Scriptural lessons in the synagogues. [2] (2) The presence of glosses in writing above the affected words and their constant association with these words in study led, ultimately, to their being incorporated into text by lower-grade copyists. [3] (3) Since many of these glosses are to be found in the LXX translation, they must have been established in the text at least by the third century B.C. and they are, therefore, older. (4) Finally, because these glosses are the kind of notes or comments which are characteristic of certain types of Rabbinic exposition, they were designated " Rabbinic-type " glosses. The immediate inference from this phenomenon is that the Rabbinic tradition of supplying concise, authoritative comments on selected words or lines [4] goes back at least to the post-exilic period.

In this article we are not concerned with the intrusion of

---

[1] *JSS*, II, No. 2, April 1957.

[2] An instance of Biblical manuscripts meant for private use may be seen in the Qumrân Biblical scrolls, as evidenced by the numerous corrections clumsily made. Such unskilled copying and ungainly corrections would never have been tolerated, if the manuscripts had been meant for liturgical use. A modern analogy of the different degrees of sacredness ascribed to private and synagogal manuscripts in ancient times may be discerned in the attitudes towards a printed edition of the Hebrew Pentateuch and a scroll of the Torah.

[3] It was pointed out that a differentiation has to be made between the *sōpēr* (" scribe ") and the *liḇlār* (" copyist " or " amanuensis ").

[4] The Rabbinic propensity to brief commentary is indicated in the maxim recorded in *Pesāḥîm* 3b, and elsewhere, that " one should always teach one's pupil by the way of brevity " (לעולם ישנה אדם לתלמיד דרך קצרה).

external material into the texts due to the inept activity of copyists though, since glosses are standard commentary, their relevance to our present study is apparent and reference to them has been made for that reason. Our purpose here is to deal with another class of exposition, usually longer than glosses, which was placed alongside the original Hebrew text and thus represented as an integral part of it. We shall try to demonstrate that the incorporation of such additional material into the text was not the result of accidental copying, but was deliberate editorial policy. We shall show, furthermore, that when these supplementary writings are isolated from their contexts and examined separately, they will be found, like the glosses, to have the same characteristics as later Rabbinic exposition. Our aim may be stated, then, as being to establish the existence, within the Old Testament itself, of Rabbinic-type exposition. We stress the differentiation which is to be made between the kind of exposition which the Biblical editors deliberately attached to texts and such material which became incorporated into the text through faulty copying. This differentiation may be of some significance also for the history of the transmission of the text of the Hebrew Old Testament. If it is found that there are glosses on editorial elements, then it would follow that, in the glossator's day, the editorial additions had already become fixed in the text and that, consequently, they are chronologically earlier than the glosses.

It will be found useful, at this stage, to make reference to some of the main features of Rabbinic exposition, in so far as they affect our present purpose. Broadly speaking, two general categories of Rabbinic exposition have been recognized and designated by the descriptive terms *Peshat* and *Derash*.[5] The former is usually defined in terms of the objective attempt to ascertain the plain sense of a line or word in a text, in contradistinction to the latter, which permits uninhibited freedom in exposition. It should be recognized, however, that, in practice, the scope of Peshat exposition was not restricted to the objective study of a text, nor its aim confined to the determining of the plain sense. The serious study of the Old Testament invited a variety of observations which, even in our day, would be

---

[5] From the roots *pšṭ*, " to make plain," and *drš*, " to search." Since the above transliteration has become conventional, we are retaining it. In the Aramaic of the Gemara we find the terms *pešāṭā'* or, more fully, *pešāṭēy diqerā'*. The Hebrew verbal forms are also used, in the perfect *pāšaṭ* and *dāraš* and in the active participle *pōšēṭ* and *dōrēš*.

regarded as legitimate if not, indeed, indispensable to the fuller understanding of the themes, as portrayed against their backgrounds, and their implications. It was found desirable to provide the reader or listener with reasons for the occurrence of recorded events and situations and for the promulgation of laws and to extend the information given in the text. That is to say, supplementary notes, given originally orally but later fixed in written form, were provided for the fuller appreciation of the Scriptures in the light of tradition and orthodox considerations.

The Midrashic apparatus, on the other hand, was not confined in its operation to the purely homiletic sphere as a means of producing lessons for personal edification and the elaboration of themes in folklore. It was applied effectively to the legalistic sphere and it proved to be a workable method of artificially associating Rabbinic legislation with scriptural texts and thereby endowing it with Scriptural authority. A casuistic analysis of a line or a key-word in a text could be so operated as to demonstrate that the Rabbinic ruling in question was actually implicit in that line or word. In similar fashion contradictions in the statements of facts, so embarrassingly obvious in duplicated or related narratives in the Old Testament, could be harmonized. The Midrashic freedom in exposition could be so controlled as to make these contradictions appear as complementary items of information.[6]

We shall now proceed to demonstrate that editorial accretions to the original texts of the Old Testament reflect the operation of Rabbinic-type exposition, in which both Peshat and Derash, as described above, function. An examination of the Decalogue, as it appears in Ex. xx. 2–14 and Deut. v. 6–18, will serve our purpose. Though both versions exhibit discrepancies in certain details, to which reference will soon be made, they are set in the same general framework. We note that, in the second part of the Decalogue, each commandment is stated in terse language (e.g., " you shall not kill," " you shall not commit adultery," etc.) and, with the exception of the last one, there is no elaboration of the theme whatsoever. In the first group, however, the statement of each commandment is accompanied by considerable additional matter. If we accept the premiss that, in a legal code,

---

[6] An example of resolving a contradiction by the Midrashic method in the Old Testament is the statement in 1 Chron. xx. 5 that Elḥanan smote Laḥmi, the brother of Goliath, a re-writing of 2 Sam. xxi. 19.

the individual laws are framed in concise, yet adequate, language, then it follows that the extra material which accompanies the statement of the law is supplementary to it and is therefore an exposition of that law. In both versions of the Decalogue the expository elements are of three kinds : (1) official reasons or justifications for the enactment of the laws,[7] (2) authoritatively approved extensions of the scope of the application of the laws,[8] and (3) threats against the breach of prohibitions [9] and promises of reward for the fulfilment of the commandments.[10]

A comparison between the two versions of the Decalogue is instructive. The institution of the Sabbath is attributed to the cessation of the divine creative activity in the Exodus version, whereas in Deuteronomy it is associated with the deliverance from the Egyptian bondage. Though they clearly represent two variant traditions, they nevertheless agree in acknowledging the need for the provision of an authoritative explanation of the institution of the Sabbath. The prohibition of work is extended to servants in both versions, but the Deuteronomic text makes explicit the humane principle involved by adding " that your manservant and your maidservant may rest as well as you." It goes further, reinforcing the divine claim on their moral obligation to slaves by reminding them that they had once been slaves in Egypt. In the commandment to honour one's parents, both versions add a supplementary note that a prolonged life in the promised land would be the reward for its fulfilment. The text in Deuteronomy, however, has a further additional note in the phrase " and that it may go well with you." [11] This addendum may be construed as an interpretation of what is to be understood by the reward of long life ; it would be a happy one. These comparisons indicate that, in our Massoretic text, the commentary on the basic Decalogue is fuller in Deuteronomy than in Exodus.

It has already been noted that, in contrast with the first group of commandments, the prohibitions against murder, adultery, stealing, and bearing false witness have no supplementary notes

---

[7] *E.g.*, the Sabbath law.
[8] *E.g.*, in the Sabbath law, extended to include slaves and domestic animals.
[9] *E.g.*, the laws against idol worship and taking the Lord's name in vain.
[10] *E.g.*, the law to honour one's parents.
[11] It is of interest that the LXX rendering of the Exodus and Deuteronomy passages is " that it may go well with you and that your days may be prolonged . . ."

attached. It would seem that these rules were regarded as
basic and indispensable for the maintenance of any social group
and, one might perhaps add, particularly of pastoral, nomadic
tribes. Consequently, explanations or justifications for their
enactment or threats against their infringement—that is to say,
persuasion to compliance—must have appeared to be quite
unnecessary. The fact that almost half of the Decalogue commandments remained in their original, concise forms suggests
that, likewise, the original element of each of the expanded
commandments was the simple statement of the law and nothing
else. The supplying of additional information—explanatory,
extended and hortatory—implies the circulation and use of these
texts for the purposes of teaching, for teaching involves exposition.[12] The need for standard or official exposition would become
articulate, once sacred texts had become available and circulated
for instruction, even if it is conceded that the circle enjoying
this privilege might have been limited. If, then, it is reasonable
to hold that official exposition was the natural concomitant to
the study of sacred texts, can one discover how early such texts
were in circulation in Israel? This question will be the culminating point of this study.

It is noteworthy that, whereas the language of the basic,
unexpanded Decalogue is formalistic in style, the commentary is
phrased in simple and intimate terms. Furthermore, supplementary information is often introduced by key words or phrases,
such as *kî* (" because ") and *'al kēn* (" therefore "). The Exodus
editor concludes the statement of the Sabbath law and the official
reason for its institution with the final comment : " therefore
(*'al kēn*) the Lord blessed the Sabbath day and hallowed it "—
clearly, he is quoting Gen. ii. 3.[13] The Deuteronomic editor,
however, having associated the institution of the Sabbath with
the redemption from Egyptian slavery, appends the rather
irrelevant note : " therefore (*'al kēn*) the Lord, your God,
commanded you to keep the Sabbath day." Examples of the
introduction of editorial additions with the word *kî* abound in
the Hebrew Old Testament.[14] There are also many instances

---

[12] Note the Rabbinic dictum mentioned in *Qiddûšîn* 49b מאי תורה דרש תורה
(" What is (meant by) Torah ? It is the interpretation of the Torah.")
[13] " And the Lord blessed the Sabbath day and hallowed it."
[14] *E.g.*, Ex. xx. 11, " for (*kî*) in six days the Lord made the heavens and the
earth," etc. Another introductory key word is *lᵉma'an* (" in order that "), *e.g.*,
" in order that your days may be long."

of the *'al kēn* formula, but we select two examples of the latter
to reinforce the above examples. Following upon the account
of the formation of Eve from Adam's rib comes the editorial
comment : " therefore (*'al kēn*) a man leaves his father and his
mother and cleaves to his wife and they become one flesh "
(Gen. ii. 24). The story of Jacob's encounter with the angel
concludes with the statement that his thigh was put out of joint,
so that he limped. The editor added the following remarkable
item of information : " Therefore (*'al kēn*) to this day the
Israelites do not eat the sinew of the hip which is upon the
hollow of the thigh " (Gen. xxxii. 33). The former comment is
of the purely homiletic (*i.e.*, simple Midrashic) kind, while the
latter reminds one of the Rabbinic method of associating extra-
or post-Biblical laws with scriptural texts and thereby ascribing
Biblical authority to them.[15] The process by which this association was achieved may elude us, but it is sufficient for our
purpose to recognize that some Midrashic method of deduction
was employed in line with the practice of the later Talmudic
Rabbis.

What has been observed about the Deuteronomic version of
the Decalogue, as compared with that of Exodus, is equally
applicable to the law relating to the *'ebed 'ibrî* (usually rendered
a " Hebrew " slave, but it probably refers to a *Habiru* slave),[16]
as it appears in both books. The law in Ex. xxi. 2 stipulates
that, after a period of six years' service, the *'ebed 'ibrî* is to be
freed unconditionally, but no mention is made of any further
obligations on the part of the master. Deut. xv. 12–18, however,
supplements the statement of the Exodus law with much interesting detail. Firstly, the editor describes the *'ibrî* as *'ahîkâ*—
" your brother " or " your kinsman " and then he proceeds to
extend the application of the law to the female, the *'ibriyyâ*. It
was to be expected, then, that the practice of boring the ear of
the slave who preferred to remain a slave and not regain his
freedom was applied by the Deuteronomist also to the " bond-
maid." A note appended to *v.* 17 reads : " and to your bond-
woman you shall do likewise." Furthermore, the freed slave is
not to be sent away empty-handed ; the master is directed to

---

[15] A Rabbinic analogy might be the prohibition against the eating of milk
and meat, which is associated with the Biblical law " You shall not seethe a kid
in its mother's milk " (Ex. xxiii. 19 and elsewhere).

[16] See the article by Julius Levy on " Origin and significance of the Biblical
term ' Hebrew ' " in *HUCA*, XXVIII (1957), pp. 3, 4.

furnish him with specified goods. The redemption from Egyptian
bondage is again cited as the reason or justification for this
humane law, which stipulates that the free slave must be given
the means of starting an independent life—" therefore (*'al kēn*)
I command you this today." Finally, there is a further note
added urging the master not to be churlish about giving the
slave his freedom and he is reminded that " at half the cost of a
hired servant " the slave had served him for six years.

The extension of the law relating to the *'ebed 'ibrî* to include
female slaves and the humane treatment stipulated towards
emancipated slaves mark an advance on the basic Exodus law,
as it stands without any exposition. One would assume that the
extended application of this basic law was achieved by means of
established machinery which, at the same time, assured for the
extensions of the law the same authority as the basic law. Such
authority was gained by the simple method of attaching the
amendments to, and thus making them part of, the text of the
Biblical law. The Rabbis of later generations attained the same
ends by means of external interpretation only, leaving the text
unaltered and unexpanded. We feel entitled, therefore, to draw
the following conclusion. The elaborate Rabbinic system of
expounding Biblical laws in a manner which enabled them to
widen the range of their application was not a novel enterprise
inaugurated by them. It was the maturing of a traditional
practice which is older, at least, than the date assigned by the
sponsors of the Documentary theory to the final editor(s) of the
Pentateuch. Indeed, there appears no valid reason for doubting
that this practice was already normal procedure in the days
when, according to the Documentary theory, the Deuteronomist
was active. The fact that official exposition of texts was incorporated into, and thus represented as an integral part of, the
inspired writings implies that the authoritative exposition of
legal texts, with the resultant extensions of the laws to categories
and situations not mentioned in the original law, was already
firmly fixed in legal practice and goes back much further in time.
That parity with the basic text should have been accorded to the
supplementary material need not occasion any surprise, when
we reflect that a similar attitude was adopted or, shall we say,
inherited by the Talmudic Rabbis. In *Sanhedrîn*, Chapter XI,
Mishna 3, we find the following startling statement : " Greater
stringency applies to (the observance of) the words of the

Scribes than to (the observance of) the words of the (written) Law." [17]

While one cannot claim to have discovered what rules of exposition were adopted for the production of extensions, explanatory and legalistic, of the basic texts, yet it might be of some interest, if not, indeed, a pointer to likely principles employed, if we mention some of the main methods used and explicitly defined by the Talmudic Rabbis. Those which come under the broader scope of Peshat interpretation, as described earlier (p. 189) are expressed in the following formulae: (1) "Whatever is to be learned from the subject matter itself," [18] *i.e.*, by logical inference. (2) The same principle is formulated also in the maxim : "not explicitly stated, but arrived at by implication" [19] and (3) more widely, by "interpreting the Biblical law on its reason and accordingly modifying it, extending or limiting." [20] This latter rule might be more appropriately rendered "interpreting the spirit of the Biblical law." Such methods of deduction would surely be regarded as valid even today in the ordinary functioning of the law courts. They could be as old as enlightened law-making, whether the new laws were achieved by direct legislation or by the establishment of precedents in legal decisions.

Where logical inference from a text did not produce the desired result or the spirit of the law was not appropriate to their needs, the Rabbis resorted to Midrashic methods. One such method was the taking of the particle *'eṭ* appearing as the sign of the definite object as if it were the other *'eṭ*, the preposition " with," " together with." It could then be argued, in Midrashic fashion, that the presence of this particle (taken to mean " together with ") opens the way, as if by design, for extending the scope of the textual information to include the item under discussion. The terms descriptive of this method are *l^erabbôṭ* in

---

[17] חומר בדברי סופרים מבדברי תורה.   The above is the rendering by H. Danby, *The Mishnah* (Oxford University Press, London, 1954), p. 400.

[18] דבר הלמד מעיניגו —one of the thirteen principles of exposition attributed to R. Ishmel.   See Addendum to Tractate *B^erāḵôṭ*.

[19] לאו בפירוש איתמר אלא מכללא איתמר.

[20] דריש טעמא דקרא.   The above rendering is by M. Jastrow, *A Dictionary of the Targumim, the Talmud Babli and Yerushalmi and the Midrashic literature* (Verlag Choreb ;   New York, 1926), p. 543.   An example of the Rabbinic modification of a Biblical law influenced by this principle is that referring to the prohibition against taking a widow's garment in pledge (Deut. xxiv. 17).   In *Bāḇā Meṣi'a* 115a it is emended to refer only to poor widows by R. Simeon, who is described as having interpreted the spirit of the law.

Mishnaic Hebrew and *l^erabbûyē* in the Gemara Aramaic, meaning " to extend the scope," " to include." Whether or not such rules of exposition, which we designate Peshat and Derash, were adopted in pre-exilic days, it is reasonable to hold that what the Pentateuchal editors attached to the text were the results of patterns of exposition. The patterns underlying them became standard or authoritative and were transmitted to succeeding generations, of which the Rabbis were the most notable exponents. As mentioned earlier, the difference between the editors and the Rabbis lies in the means adopted for implementing the authorized extensions of the laws and for securing acceptance of official explanations. The editors integrated the results of such exposition into the text, while the Rabbis, dealing with a fixed text, restricted their activity to external exposition.

From the above analysis of the Deuteronomic version of the law of the *'ebed 'ibri* we draw the conclusion that it represents adaptations and extensions of the earlier basic Exodus law, in the same way as the Rabbis adapted and extended Biblical laws to meet the needs of their time. The Exodus law, with its crisp, concise, and formalistic language, appears to have been specially framed for the use of jurists who could, by means of juridical procedures known to them, modify and extend the range and conditions of the application of the law. By contrast, the intimate and non-technical language of the Deuteronomic version, together with the amplifications, suggests that it may have been intended, not for practising professional jurists, but rather for students. One might say that it was precisely this consideration which necessitated the introduction of additional explanatory matter, as well as the legalistic addenda. What was potentially implicit in the texts meant for professional classes was made explicit in re-written texts designed for teaching.

Before considering the general impact upon the orthodox Documentary theory of the criterion " To whom was the text addressed ? " as opposed to " By whom was it written ? " we shall try to demonstrate how this approach could lead to a fresh evaluation of duplicated records whose discrepancies have already been accounted for by conventional literary criticism. Our obvious choice is Gen. i. 1-ii. 3, and ii. 4 ff. We agree with the view that the first account was composed in a formalistic style suitable for public recital, probably at shrines on specific cultic occasions. The regular, repetitive, exalted language has the grandeur of an epic, suggesting that it was designed for officiating priests. It is likely that the recital was performed in a special chant and that the recurring phrase " and there was evening and there was morning, etc.," culminating each act of creation, was meant to be a choral response.[21] By contrast, the intimate, narrative style of the creation story in the second chapter suggests that it was specially arranged in this way for reading to or by non-professional sections of the community as an exercise in study even if, as was conceded earlier, such circles might have been restricted. The use in the second chapter of the divine term Yahweh Elohim, as against Elohim in the first section, and the reversal of the order of creation have been explained on the theory of two independent literary sources, each of which is marked by specific or characteristic features. Judged by our criterion, however, it is possible that these variations might have been due to considerations of the kind of public for which each account was intended. In the recounting of the *story* of creation, as opposed to a dramatic presentation, the story-teller would begin with a description of the state of the world before the emergence of any vegetation, animal life or human being on it. It is conceivable that professional story-telling carried with it the licence to alter the order of a factual account, in order to bring home the main theme. In this instance, man is portrayed as the central figure of creation, around whom the environmental elements of creation form his background. We are often warned against the fallacy of interpreting the mind of the Biblical narrator (and legislator) in terms of a contemporary European mind. Yet, surely, this is precisely what we are doing when we assert that the use of Yahweh Elohim and the reversal of the order of creation in the second version must necessarily postulate a different literary source. Is it not possible that, derived from a common source, a ritualistic version was designed for specific cultic purposes and a narrative version for educative ends ? That is to say, the formulation of the material in each case was determined by the use for which it was intended.

Clearly this view cannot cope with obvious contradictions in the statement of facts but, approaching certain categories of parallel texts in this way, the effect might be to modify the

---

[21] Cf. Ps. cxxxvi. 1–9, where there is a dramatic presentation of the acts of creation with regular refrains.

Documentary theory and to limit the area of its application.
Again, though this view might not invalidate the theory of
different authorships nor the broad dates accepted for the final
redaction of the texts, it would postulate, not only the use of
the same basic material, but also the interests of each writer in
terms of the audience for whom he was catering. It would also
act as a counter-measure against the tendency of some literary
critics towards the fragmentation of the Pentateuchal texts.
The issue involved here is the attempt to find an identity of
principle which would satisfactorily explain the phenomena of
(a) the dual expanded versions of the Decalogue, as against the
original, basic legal formulae, (b) the two versions of the law
relating to the ʿebed ʿibrî, and (c) the two accounts of creation.
We find that the common denominator is that, in the version
intended for non-professional readers or audiences, irrespective
of the identity or character of the author, an intimate style is
employed and supplementary, expository notes added. It would
follow, then, that the sacred texts were taught and studied in
orthodox fashion, to which end aids in the form of authoritative
exposition were provided in the same spirit as that which
animated the later schools of Rabbis.

The most explicit reference to the teaching of the Scriptures
by means of exposition is in Nehem. viii. Here we are given
an impressive account of the public assembly summoned by
Ezra, the scribe, and of the reading of the Torah to the assembled
people. The Levites were assigned a special rôle, which was to
" help the people to understand " (mᵉbînîm ʾeṭ hāʿām, v. 7), to
make the content " clear " (mᵉp̄ōrāš, v. 8) and to " give (it)
sense " (wᵉsōm śekᵉl). The Rabbinic understanding of this
passage, in Megilla 3a, that the Hebrew text was first rendered
into Aramaic and then expounded, is accepted by many scholars.[22]
One would assume that there must have been uniformity in the
exposition given by the Levites and that we are dealing, not with
individual or arbitrary items of exposition, but, rather, with an
established, authoritative pattern and with fixed details. It
would follow, then, that oral exposition, in this instance given
by the Levites, was not a novel procedure introduced by Ezra,
but that it was the traditional method of teaching the Scriptures.
The noteworthy feature of this occasion was Ezra's extending

[22] On the Hebrew mᵉp̄ōrāš the American RSV, after translating it as
" clearly," has a footnote : " or with interpretation."

the facilities of official commentary to the general public in so dramatic a fashion.[23]

That standard interpretations of strange or unexplained situations recorded in the Biblical narrative were current in later times at least is clear from certain poems of the saga kind in the Psalms and from the Book of Chronicles. The strange incident of Moses striking the rock instead of speaking to it (Num. xx. 11) is explained in Ps. cvi. 32-33, in the following words : " It went ill with Moses on their account, for they embittered [24] his spirit." Moses' disobedience to God's explicit command was out of keeping with his almost perfect character and this situation required some explanation. It was explained as being due to the intolerable strain imposed on him by the widespread spirit of revolt which embittered him. Such a deduction may be reasonably drawn from the context of the whole incident described in Num. xx. 2-11, and would come under the wider definition of Peshat, as given earlier. The point is that the text, as it stands, seems to have been regarded as deficient and that this deficiency was repaired by the official commentary which is recorded in the Psalm.

An example of how the deficiency in a narrative is filled by means of Midrashic exposition is supplied by 1 Chron. xxii. 7-10, which refers to the same situation as in 1 Kings viii. 18-19. In the latter passage God informs David that he would not build the temple in Jerusalem, but that this honour was reserved for his son. No reason is given for this disqualification, but the Chronicler attributes the ban to the fact that David was a man of bloodshed [25] while, by contrast, Solomon was a man of peace as, indeed, his name $\check{S}^e l \bar{o} m \bar{o}$ characterized him. The association of the names of personalities (and places) with events and situations is a general practice of the Biblical narrator and may be described as Midrashic. If we were to offer an objective explanation of David's failure to build the temple, we would

---

[23] An earlier occasion for the public reading of the Torah and the renewal of the covenant was at the time of Josiah (2 Kings xxiii. 1-3), but there is no reference to any exposition having been given. If we accept the view that this was the book of Deuteronomy, then official exposition was already present in the text.

[24] Taking the verb *himrû* from the root *mrr* " to be bitter " and reading, perhaps, *hēmārû*. There may be a play upon the root *mrh* (*mry*) " to rebel " and *mrr* " to be bitter," both concepts of rebelling and embittering being indicated.

[25] No stigma is cast on David's character. The writer explains that David was engaged in many battles.

say that he was continually involved in the pressing tasks of consolidating the foundations of his kingdom and of assuring the permanence of his gains and that he had not the peaceful leisure, apart from the ambition, for embarking upon any lavish building programme. On the other hand, Solomon inherited an established and stable kingdom and could indulge his luxurious tastes. Yet, to later generations it must have appeared strange that David, the ideal (or idealized) king of Israel, was not the one to build the temple. This failure must have been interpreted as having been due to a divine disqualification, the nature of which is given by the Chronicler in a fashion we are accustomed to expect from Rabbinic commentators.

It has long been recognized that the Book of Chronicles contains much expository material, in the form of modifications, additions, and even omissions, as compared with the parallel passages in Samuel and Kings. In fact, some scholars go so far as to describe this book as a Midrash on the earlier historical texts. There are others, however, who recognize in Chronicles evidence of independent sources, in addition to the selected compilations of Samuel and Kings. Yet, even from the latter point of view, the Chronicler provides commentary of the kind with which we are familiar in later Rabbinic writings. We would stress the point that the Chronicler's expository notes are not to be regarded as his own creation, but reflect orthodox established commentary. Sacred texts were taught to, or studied by, a wider circle than those professionally concerned and standard exposition was an indispensable concomitant to dealing with these texts. We find patterns of exposition incorporated into the texts by the editors of the Pentateuch, used by the Psalmist and the Chronicler and followed, in more elaborate fashion, by the Talmudic Rabbis in the spheres of Peshat and Midrash-types of explanations. Original legalistic texts served as the basis for modifying and extending the provisions of the laws by methods which produced the desired results and such developments were incorporated into later editions of these texts. A pattern of exposition was thus set and exploited by the Rabbis who, because in their day the texts of the Scriptures were fixed and immutable, restricted their activity to external exposition only.

The view has been expressed by some scholars [26] that the

---

[26] Mainly of the Scandinavian school.

reduction to writing of what was oral tradition took place after the return of the exiles and that this revolutionary step was the answer to the contemporary fear that the Scriptures would not otherwise be preserved intact. The present writer cannot find himself in accord with this view, for the presence within the texts of expository material points to exposition which, even if it were at some stage oral, nevertheless presupposes that there were texts available to expound. In the light of archaeological evidence, there appears to be every likelihood that the basic texts existed in written form and were used for the purposes of teaching and study from the period of the established monarchy. The Gezer Calendar, generally dated to the tenth century B.C., and the Samaria ostraca of the ninth-eighth century B.C., testify to the use of writing for secular purposes and indicate that, in the early days of the monarchy, writing was already a normal accomplishment among certain sections of the community. The discovery of the Ras Shamra texts proves that, as early as the fourteenth century B.C., religious texts were already to be found in written form in a neighbouring country. There seems no reason to doubt, in the present writer's view that, from the early days of the monarchy, sacred texts were available and circulated and that standard commentary, albeit originally oral, arose at that time. A pattern was set, in both narrative and legalistic texts, for authorized exposition and this pattern persisted throughout the centuries. It found its fixed written literary expression in the editorial supplements in the Pentateuch, in some Psalms, in Chronicles and, in highly developed forms, in the recorded researches of the Talmudic Rabbis.

ROYAL IDEOLOGY AND THE TESTAMENTS OF THE TWELVE PATRIARCHS

By G. WIDENGREN

THE Israelite-Jewish royal ritual is only to some extent known to us.[1] However, in later texts, dating from the Hellenistic-Roman period, passages are to be found which contain several allusions to a ritual action in the centre of which the king has his place, though this fact is somewhat veiled to us. Among these texts are the *Testaments of the Twelve Patriarchs*, and among them *Test. Levi* is the most important one. Owing to the date of these texts we must assume that the royal ritual described here belongs to Hasmonaean, not to Davidic kingship. On the other hand it stands to reason that also in the Hasmonaean kingdom many old traditions were inherited from Davidic times. If a new treatment of some relevant passages is presented here it is because these texts have been analysed by another scholar [2] much from the same point of view as my own about 15 years ago,[3] but without knowledge of my researches. Further the *Testaments*, owing to the discovery of the Dead Sea Scrolls, have been in the focus of interest since the documents of the Qumrân community were published.

In order to understand *Test. Levi* correctly we must remember the fact that in the period of the Hasmonaean rule Levi is the cryptic name for the Jewish priest-king, because Levi was considered the ancestor of the priests.[4] In the enthronement of Levi as we will meet it in *Test. Levi* we therefore have to see the pattern of the coronation of the Hasmonaean rulers, keeping in

---

[1] Cf. Widengren, *Sakrales Königtum im Alten Testament und im Judentum* (1955), esp. 34–58 ; " King and Covenant," *JSS*, II (1957), 1–32 ; Johnson, *The Sacral Kingship in Ancient Israel* (1955) ; " Hebrew Conceptions of Kingship," in Hooke, *Myth, Ritual and Kingship* (1958), 204–35, cf. my remarks, *ZDMG*, CXI (1961), 185–7.

[2] Cf. Ludin Jansen, " The Consecration in the eighth chapter of Testamentum Levi," *La regalità sacra/The sacral kingship* (1959), 356–65.

[3] Cf. *Horae Soederblomianae*, I, 3 (1947), 1–12. A summary of my views was presented in *Sakrales Königtum*, 49–53.

[4] Cf. Charles, *The Testaments of the Twelve Patriarchs* (1908), L ff.

mind that this action which—properly speaking—is played in the highest heaven constitutes the mythical background of the concrete coronation ceremonies as these took place here on earth.

Levi has a mysterious vision. He beholds the heavens opened and ascends to the third heaven. During his ascent he is initiated into the heavenly secrets, shares accordingly the wisdom of God.[5] All this is related in *Test. Levi*, chapters 3–4. He then sees " the holy temple and on the Throne of Glory the Most High." The earthly temple is only a copy of the heavenly one where God has his seat.[6] He says to Levi :

> Lo, I have given thee the blessings of the priesthood
> until I come and sojourn in the midst of Israel
> (*Test. Levi.* v. 1–2).

Levi then, shall be a priest of the Most High, Elyon.[7] But that is not sufficient The angel accompanying Levi, the *angelus interpres*, speaks to him in the following words :

> The Most High has therefore heard thy prayer
> to take thee away from unrighteousness, and that thou shouldst be
> to Him a son,
> and a servant, and a priest of His face.
> The light of knowledge thou shalt light up in Jacob,
> and as the sun shalt thou be to all the seed of Israel
> (*Test. Levi* iv. 2–3).[8]

Accordingly Levi will not only in a special way be the servant and priest of Elyon, but also His son. This is the same promise as that given in Ps. ii. and Ps. cx. (cix). Further he will be to his people a light of knowledge and as the sun—ideas to which we shall revert later.

The passages quoted are supplemented by another text which belongs organically to the same complex.[9]

---

[5] Cf. esp. *Test. Levi*, ii. 10, treated below.

[6] Cf. Widengren, " Aspetti simbolici dei templi e luoghi di culto del vicino oriente antico," *Numen*, VII (1960), 14–20 for conditions in Palestine and Syria, 1–14 for Mesopotamia.

[7] The name " The Most High," ὁ ὕψιστος, corresponds to 'Elyon, as shown by LXX. This designation is very common in Hellenistic-Jewish times. What calls for notice is the fact that the Hasmonaean rulers assumed the same title as used by Melchizedek (Gen. xiv. 18). This shows that they interpreted the oracle in Ps. cx. (cix.) 4 as referring to themselves.

[8] The ruler in Mesopotamia was a sun to his people, *e.g.*, Hammurabi was " the Sun of Babel " ; cf. Dhorme, *La religion assyro-babylonienne* (1910), 169 ; Widengren, *The Accadian and Hebrew Psalms of Lamentation* (1937), 10 f. ; Engnell, *Studies in Divine Kingship in the Ancient Near East* (1943), 183.

[9] Cf. Widengren, *Sakrales Königtum*, 105, n. 46, and Charles, in Hastings' *Dictionary of the Bible*, IV, 723.

This text reproduces certain moments of the ritual of enthronement where various attributes belonging to the ruler are handed over to Levi who receives them and puts them on. The text in translation runs as follows :

> And there again I saw a vision like the first one after we had spent seventy days there.
> And I saw seven men in white raiment saying unto me :
>> " Arise, put on the robe of priesthood,
>>   and the crown of righteousness,
>>   and the breastplate of understanding,
>>   and the garment of truth,
>>   and the plate of faith,
>>   and the turban of *justice,
>>   and the ephod of prophecy." [10]
>
> Then each of them brought forward (a thing) and put (it) on me, and said unto me :
>> " From henceforth become a priest of the Lord, thou and thy seed for ever."
>
> And the first man anointed me with holy oil, and gave me a staff of judgement.
> The second washed me with pure water, fed me with bread and wine, the holiest things,
>   and clad me with a holy and glorious robe.
> The third clothed me with a linen vestment like an ephod.
> The fourth put round me a girdle like unto purple.
> The fifth gave me a branch of rich olive.
> The sixth placed a crown on my head.
> The seventh placed on my head a priestly diadem and filled my hands with incense,
>   that I might serve as a priest to the Lord God.
> And they said to me :
>> Levi, thy seed shall be divided into three dominations,
>>   as a sign of the coming glory of the Lord
>
>   (*Test. Levi* viii. 1–12).[11]

If we look at this text somewhat closer we will find that the attributes handed over to Levi are not the same as those mentioned in the exhortation of the seven men to Levi. A comparison between them will demonstrate this fact.

[10] I use the translation of Charles, *op. cit.*, modified in a few details by Ludin Jansen, *op. cit.*, 356 f. I have accepted the convincing literary analysis given by Jansen. In viii. 2 (τὴν μίτραν τῆς κεφαλῆς) " κεφαλῆς, of course, cannot be right, since, as the parallel phrases show, we require here an abstract noun " (Charles, *The Greek Versions of the Testaments of the Twelve Patriarchs* [1908], 42). He therefore thinks that its Hebrew equivalent *rōš* is a corruption of *yōṣer* or *mišor*, and this suggestion has been hesitatingly accepted here.

[11] According to c, β, S ἄγια ἁγίων with Philonenko, *RHPhR*, XXXIX. (1959), 19.

Exhortation of the seven men.	*Handing over of the attributes.*
The robe of priesthood	The staff of judgement
The crown of righteousness	The holy and glorious robe
The breastplate of understanding	The linen vestment like the ephod
The garment of truth	The girdle like unto purple
The plate of faith	The branch of rich olive
The turban of *justice	The crown on the head
The ephod of prophecy	The diadem of priesthood

The first enumeration in all essentials corresponds to the description of the sacral garment worn by the High-Priest according to Ex. xxviii. in LXX.[12] The second enumeration on the other hand has three attributes in common with the garment of the High-Priest : [13] the ephod, the girdle, and the diadem. Here interesting agreements and deviations from the terms used in LXX are to be noted.[14]

A fact that calls for notice is that three attributes are actually handed over to Levi for which no correspondences are found in the exhortation of the seven men : the staff of judgement, the branch of rich olive, and the girdle of purple. Of them the girdle, ζώνη, is mentioned in Ex. xxviii. as belonging to the High-Priest's articles of dress, but with the significant difference that nothing is said of the purple colour.[15] This colour in the ancient Near East was a token of sovereignty and rulership.[16] The staff on the other hand, ῥάβδος, is the most appropriate attribute of a ruler. The Israelite king in the Old Testament carries a staff, and in the royal psalms ii. and cx. (cix.) this term is used in LXX.[17] Then we have the branch of rich olive. Such a branch is known from Israelite-Jewish traditions as belonging to the ruler of the people, though it is not said to be taken from

[12] The terminological correspondences are actually striking if we compare the LXX version.

[13] Not *two*, as I incorrectly said in *Sakrales Königtum*, LI, where the girdle, ἡ ζώνη, was left out of consideration.

[14] Thus in the first enumeration we have μίτρα as in LXX Ex. xxviii. 32–33, whereas the second enumeration has διάδημα. The word ζώνη is used in LXX where, however, not ἐφούδ but ἐπωμίς renders the Hebrew 'efōd. Josephus (*Antiq.* iii. 7) has the following terms : στολή (χιτών), λόγιον, ποδήρης, ζώνη, ἐφώδης, πίλος. We should observe that the crown (στέφανος) is not mentioned Ex. xxviii. Unfortunately we cannot find place here for a detailed discussion, including as it should both Philo and Jesus Sirach.

[15] On the contrary, for it is said *v.* 39 that the girdle should be made ἔργον ποικιλτοῦ.

[16] Cf. Widengren, *Horae Soederblomianae*, I, 3, 4, n. 1 with references to Xenophon, *Cyrop.*, viii. 3, 13, and Tallqvist, *Konungen med Guds nåde* (1920), 93, to which could be added Widengren, *Die Religionen Irans* (1963).

[17] Cf. Ps. ii. 9, ἐν ῥάβδῳ σιδηρᾷ, and Ps. cx. (cix.) 2, ῥάβδον δυνάμεως.

an olive tree, but from the Tree of Life. This tree, however,
may be identified with several existing trees, among them also
the olive, which would seem to explain why the olive is mentioned
in the relevant passage of our text. The background in this
case is clearly mythical, the branch associating the ruler with
paradise. The king carries a branch taken from the Tree of
Life as a sign of his possession of Life and his distribution of
Life.[18] Accordingly three royal emblems are given to the priestly
ruler Levi at the occasion of his investment. To these emblems
are to be added diadem and crown, two attributes of rulership
being part of the garb of the High-Priest, and the two expressly
priestly articles of dress, namely the holy garment and the
ephod. Thus Levi is invested with a holy garment of a character
at the same time priestly and royal.

Of great interest is the number seven of the angels who invest
Levi and undertake various ritual actions with him. We know
that the Mesopotamian ruler by various deities was given seven
attributes, and there is every reason to believe that the number
seven as the number of the planetary deities played a certain rôle
in this connexion.[19] It looks as if the seven men, dressed in a
white garment, were an Israelite-Jewish adaptation of the
Mesopotamian planetary deities. Curiously enough this idea of
the sacral king as the centre in the midst of the planets seems to
have been preserved right down into Christian times, for in the
Book of Revelation the visionary says :

> I saw seven golden lamps,
>> and in the midst of the lamps like a Son of Man,
> dressed in a long garment,
>> and girdled around his breast with a golden girdle
>>>> (Rev. i. 12–13).

According to a general opinion it is Christ who is depicted
here as the ruler of the world, the passage possessing reminiscences
even from the Testaments of the Twelve Patriarchs.[20]

Still more interesting than Levi's investment are the ritual

---

[18] Cf. Widengren, *The King and the Tree of Life* (1951), esp. 20–41, 62 f.

[19] Cf., *e.g.*, Witzel, *Keilinschriftliche Studien*, V–VII, 57 ff. ; Meissner-Rost, *Bauinschriften Asarhaddons*, CCXXXII. 52 ff. ; the group of seven deities on the great rock-relief of Maltai, cf. *RA*, XXI (1924), 187, Pl. 1–2. Every deity actually hands over to the ruler a special gift in according with its own special character.

[20] Cf. Lohmeyer, *Die Offenbarung des Johannes* (1926), 14 ff. ; Bousset, *Die Offenbarung Johannis* (1906), 193 f., where it is pointed out that in this passage Christ as the Son of Man appears in the royal and high-priestly garb.

actions in which Levi takes part. He is anointed with oil, he is purified in water, and he receives bread and wine as his food. It is quite natural that Christian interpolations were suspected in this passage.[21] Today however this hypothesis appears unfounded. Such ritual actions have been well known in Israel from of old. As to the unction we have both the royal and the priestly anointing, the latter obviously being only a copy of the former type of anointing which is attested not only in Israel but also in Mesopotamia and Egypt a long time before the priestly unction was practised. The purification in water is mentioned in Ex. xxix. 4 in connexion with the unction and investment of Aaron and his sons (cf. Ex. xl. 12). It is probable that certain water-purifications had a place in the Israelite royal consecration.[22] In the Mesopotamian ritual a central place is occupied by the anointing with oil, drinking of water, and purification in water.[23] In this connexion the expression " with pure water " (*Test. Levi* viii. 5) calls for notice, for the corresponding expression *mē ellūti* is used in a Mesopotamian ritual text as associated with the king's purification in water.[24] Behind the Israelite royal ritual there may in older times still have been an idea of imparting " life " to the king—and that in a very concrete sense too—by means of these rites of anointment and purification.

Levi receives as his food, bread and wine. As to the Old

[21] Charles, *Apocrypha and Pseudepigrapha*, II (1913), 309 asks : " Is Christian influence apparent here ? "

[22] Cf. Widengren, *Psalm* cx *och det sakrala kungadömet i Israel* (1941), 22 ff. For the question of Christian interpolations cf. Bousset, *ZNW*, I (1900), 141 ff. ; Manson, *JTS*, XLVIII (1947), 59 ff. ; Messel, *BZAW*, XXXIII (1918), 335 ff., who tried to demonstrate the Christian origin of the Testaments, but this hypothesis was generally rejected until De Jonge, *The Testaments of the Twelve Patriarchs* (1953) renewed this thesis. Soon after the discovery of the Dead Sea Scrolls it was found that many passages in them were highly reminiscent of the *Testaments*. And since fragments of an Aramaic version have appeared among the Scrolls the hypothesis of a Christian origin of course broke down completely. For the whole question as it is looked upon today cf. in general Dupont-Sommer, *Les écrits esséniens découverts près de la Mer Morte* (1959), 313–18 (rejects the idea of a Christian origin) and esp. for the problem of Christian interpolations Philonenko, *RPhHR*, XXXVIII (1958), 309–343 ; XXXIX (1959), 14–38.

[23] Cf. such passages as the Myth of Adapa, II. 31 f., 63–65 ; Maqlu, VII. 31–37 ; Surpu, IX. 13 ; Schollmeyer, *Sumerisch-babylonische Hymnen und Gebete an Samaš* (1912), No. 1, Col. III; *ZA*, XLV (1939), 192 f. From these and other texts it is possible to reconstruct a royal ritual. For the study of the *bît rimki* ritual cf. above all Laessoe, *Studies on the Assyrian Ritual and Series bît rimki* (1955), where we find the statement (p. 14, n. 14) that " typically, bathing is followed by anointing." It is interesting to note that such is the order in Ex. xxix. 4, whereas in *Test. Levi* we meet with the reverse order.

[24] Cf. Schollmeyer, *op. cit.*, xxxv. 38 ff. It is curious to note that Aa has ἁγίῳ, because *ellu* in Accadian means both " pure " and " holy."

208 PROMISE AND FULFILMENT

Testament background we are reminded of the scene when the priest-king of Jerusalem Melchizedek brings out bread and wine to Abraham (Gen. xiv. 18). This narrative in a way serves to legitimate the Davidic ruler as installed by El Elyon, for Melchizedek represents his God Elyon, and Abraham stands as a symbol for the Davidic rulers.[25] Because of this tendency the tradition in Gen. xiv. is a kind of enthronement text and for that reason it is important to find here bread and wine in a sacrifice of communion type.[26] It is essential for the background to note that in the Mesopotamian Adapa myth Bread of Life and Water of Life are supposed to be handed over to the ascending primordial king Adapa.[27] In Isa. vii. 15 cream and honey are the food of the royal child Immanuel, and this is the food mentioned in a Mesopotamian ritual text which must have had its place in the royal ritual.[28]

Of greater importance, however, is the immediate historical background. Here our thoughts go immediately to the sacral meals of the Essenes[29] where above all the description in 1 QS vi. 4–5 calls for notice.[30] The priest there pronounces the blessing of the firstfruits of bread and wine, *leḥem* and *tīrōš*. These two elements accordingly have their place in the centre of the sacral meals in Essene circles,[31] and every idea of a Christian interpolation in this passage has to be abandoned, because there is not the slightest support for such a hypothesis. On the contrary our passage would seem to be one of the connecting links between the *Testaments* and the Dead Sea Scrolls.

Of special relevance for the historical context is the fact that Levi will be the son of Elyon, a light of knowledge, φῶς γνώσεως, and like the sun to Israel (iv. 3). Here we meet with royal characteristics. Leaving aside the king's position as the Son of God in Ps. ii. and cx. (cix.), we may refer to Isa. xlix. 6 where the Servant is said to be a light to the peoples, and Hos. x. 12

[25] Cf. Nyberg, *ARW*, XXXV (1938), 363 f., 374 ff.
[26] In Mesopotamia we may refer to the enthronement of Lipit-Ištar where food, wine, and milk are mentioned as sacrificial elements, cf. Zimmern, *Lipit-Istars Vergöttlichung* (1916), xiv. 49.
[27] The Myth of Adapa, II. 63–65, but for the exact meaning of the terms used cf. Widengren, *The King and the Tree of Life*, 34 f.
[28] Cf. IV. R² 25, IV. 1–18 = *ZA*, XLV (1939), 192 f.
[29] Cf. Widengren, *Sakrales Königtum*, 105, n. 51.
[30] Cf. Philonenko, *RHPhR*, XXXIX (1959), 19.
[31] Cf. Charles, *The Testaments of the Twelve Patriarchs*, ad Test. Levi, xviii. 6.

(in LXX). Here also *Test. Levi* xviii. comes to our mind because there we find the same idea about the priestly king kindling the light of knowledge. Originally this text most probably referred to John Hyrcanus, but it is quite possible that it was interpreted in Essene circles as glorifying " the Teacher of Righteousness." [32] It cannot, however, be doubted that Levi has inherited not only the priestly but also the royal position as we have ascertained. When Levi in our text is mentioned as the priest of the Most High, Elyon, as His son, and as receiving the holy garb and the emblems of a royal ruler, we obviously come across a royal tradition, taken over from the Davidic rulers by the Hasmonaean priest-kings. It is but natural that this royal ideology then passed on to the Teacher of Righteousness.

The enthronement ritual as it is reconstructed from the *Testament of Levi* may be supplemented from the Enoch literature which belongs to the same group of writings as the *Testaments*, writings circulating among the Essenes. [33]

What is important in the Ethiopic Book of Enoch is the fact that the enthronement is associated with an initiation into divine wisdom in a much more clear way than in *Test. Levi*. So, *e.g.*, God says :

And the Elect One shall in those days sit on my throne,
and all the secrets of wisdom and counsel shall go forth from his mouth,
for the Lord of Spirits hath given to him and hath glorified him
(1 Enoch li. 3).[34]

" The Elect One " is an old term for the ruler whom God has selected to sit on His throne.[35] The pattern of enthronement here, of course, has been transferred from cultic experience to eschatological hope, a transfer characteristic of later times, the beginning of which, however, is seen already in the prophecies of Deutero-Isaiah.

[32] Cf. Dupont-Sommer, *Semitica*, IV (1951–52), 48 f.
[33] Cf. above, n. 22. I disagree to some extent with the exposition of the problem given by Larsson, *SEÅ*, XXV (1960), 109–118. He has underestimated the connexions between the Dead Sea Scrolls and the *Testaments*. It should be observed that Aramaic fragments also of the Ethiopic Book of Enoch have been found among the Scrolls (cf. Dupont-Sommer, *Les écrits*, 310–313).
[34] For the text I have followed the suggestion offered by Charles in his apparatus, reading the following text :
kʷellu ḥebū'āt ṭebab wa ḥalīnā em'afūḥū yewaḏ'e.
[35] For Mesopotamia cf. Dhorme, *op. cit.*, 150 ff. In the Old Testament we have, *e.g.*, Isa. xlii. 1 ; in the Ethiopic Book of Enoch several times, xxxix. 1, xl. 5, xlv. 3–4, xlix. 2–4. We may also mention *Test. Benjamin* xi. 4. The Israelite king is seated on God's own throne (cf. Widengren, *Psalm* cx, 4–6).

The wisdom possessed by the Elect One in the Ethiopic Book of Enoch is characteristic of Levi too. We have spoken of the light of knowledge he is to kindle in Israel. There is an explicit commission given to him when the accompanying angel in an address to him describes his task :

> Thou shalt stand near the Lord,
> and shalt be His minister,
> and shalt declare His mysteries to men,
> and shalt proclaim the redemption of Israel
> (*Test. Levi* ii. 10).

Although this proclamation is not, as the setting in life would require, spoken by God Himself, the essential trait, the sending forth with a commission, the message from God, is here preserved. As we have treated this special trait rather in detail in an earlier monograph [36] we do not enter upon a discussion of this topic here. Instead of that we refer to another passage where the association of enthronement and partaking of the Spirit is clearly expressed.

> And the Lord of Spirits *seated him on the throne of His glory,
> and the spirit of righteousness was poured out upon him
> (1 Enoch lxii. 2). [37]

The communication of the Spirit on the occasion of the king's coronation as a result of his unction is well attested in Israel.[38] The initiation into the divine secrets is described in the Second Book of Enoch, the Slavonic Enoch, xxii.–xxiii., where it is related how the heavenly books are shown to Enoch. God Himself further communicates His secrets to Enoch (2 Enoch xxiv. 1–3, and following verses). This communication follows Enoch's enthronement to the left side of God, and accordingly this moment of the ritual is split up in two parts, one before, and one after the enthronement. Here in xxiv. 1–3 Enoch is addressed by God as His " Beloved," a regular royal epithet.[39]

When Enoch has appeared before God he is divested of his earthly garment and anointed with the anointing oil of God, the appearance of which was more than a great light, shining like the rays of the sun.[40] He is then also invested with the garments

---

[36] Cf. Widengren, *The Ascension of the Apostle and the Heavenly Book* (1950).

[37] The emended text (*anbaro* instead of *nabara*) is generally accepted.

[38] Cf. Widengren, *Sakrales Königtum*, 32 with references to 1 Sam. x. 6, xi. 6, xvi. 13 ; 2 Sam. xxiii. 2.

[39] Cf. Dhorme, *op. cit.*, 163 f.

[40] This explains the attribute " light " used of the oil in *C. Celsum*, vi. 27.

of God's glory. This anointment and investment make Enoch like one of God's glorious ones (2 Enoch xxii. 4–10). There are accordingly in the ritual of the heavenly enthronement two more special moments, the anointing with God's own oil, and the investment with a robe of God's glory. Jewish religion could not possibly say that Enoch acquired a divine status, but his status is changed to that of God's angels, which seems to be as near a divine status as possible.

After the enthronement, with its investment and unction, Enoch takes no earthly food, as he tells his son (2 Enoch lvi. 2). For that reason we are able to conclude that this wonderful anointing corresponds to the " oil of Life," found in Mesopotamian texts, and fulfils the same function as the food of Life.[41]

According to our analysis the pattern of enthronement would thus seem to exhibit the following ritual :

  1. Ascent to heaven
  2. Ablution
  3. Unction
  4. Communion
  5. Investment with a priestly garment
  6. Handing over of the ruler's attributes
  7. Participating in the heavenly secrets
  8. Sitting on the throne of God.

Good reasons have been given for considering the Feast of Tabernacles, the old Israelite New Year festival, as the framework of this royal enthronement ritual.[42] Moreover, it has been pointed out that in *Test. Levi* we have before us " a scene of covenant-making " (cf. xix. 1–3).[43] This fact links *Test. Levi* with the position occupied by the king as the mediator of the covenant between God and Israel.[44] It is quite clear then that " our author formed the text of *Test. Levi* viii. on the basis of the enthronization liturgy," [45] and did not choose his material freely from literary sources.[46]

[41] For " the oil of Life " cf. Maqlu VII. 37. In the royal *bît rimki* ritual the cedar oil in a solemn invocation is called *simat bēlūti*, the adornment of rulership, Schollmeyer, *op. cit.*, No. 1, Col. III, 16.

[42] Cf. Ludin Jansen, *op. cit.*, 361.

[43] Cf. Ludin Jansen, *op. cit.*, 362.

[44] Cf. Widengren, " King and Covenant," *JSS*, II (1957), 1–32.

[45] Ludin Jansen, *op. cit.*, 361.

[46] Ludin Jansen, *op. cit.*, 362–4, shows that the cult pattern actually was stronger than the general tendency in *Test. Levi*.

Who is then the Hasmonaean ruler to whom the author alludes ? The choice can only be between Simon, John Hyrcanus, and Aristobulus, but most likely John Hyrcanus is the priestly prince who is called " Levi." [47]

The figure of " Levi," however, could be reinterpreted in the light of later experience. In xix. 1 we read :

> And now, children, ye have heard all ; choose, therefore, for your-selves either the light or the darkness, either the law of the Lord or the works of Beliar.

These words point to the special language used in the writings of the Qumrân community. It is but natural then, that this community ultimately came to interpret " Levi " as a name for their own Teacher of Righteousness, their enigmatic leader whose real historical personality is so difficult to grasp. In that way the *Testament of Levi* constitutes a link between Israelite sacral kingship and Messianic ideas.

[47] Cf. the discussion by Ludin Jansen, *op. cit.*, 364 f.

PRINCIPAL WORKS OF
PROFESSOR S. H. HOOKE

AUTHOR

Christ and the Kingdom of God (London, 1919)
Christianity in the Making (London, 1926)
New Year's Day : The Story of the Calendar (New York, 1928)
The Origins of Early Semitic Ritual (Schweich Lectures, 1935, London, 1935)
Prophets and Priests (London, 1938)
Archaeology and the Old Testament (London, 1939)
In the Beginning (Clarendon Bible : Old Testament, Volume VI, Oxford, 1947)
What is the Bible ? (London, 1948)
The Kingdom of God in the Experience of Jesus (London, 1949)
Babylonian and Assyrian Religion (1st edition in Hutchinson's University Library, London, 1953 ; 2nd edition, Oxford, 1962)
The Siege Perilous : Essays in Biblical Anthropology and Kindred Subjects (London, 1956)
Alpha and Omega : A Study in the Pattern of Revelation (London, 1961)
Middle Eastern Mythology (Harmondsworth, 1963)

EDITOR

Augustine, *De Catechizandis Rudibus*, with notes (Oxford, 1910)
Myth and Ritual : The Myth and Ritual of the Hebrews in Relation to the Culture Pattern of the Ancient East (London, 1933)
The Labyrinth : Further Studies in the Relation between Myth and Ritual in the Ancient World (London, 1935)
Myth, Ritual and Kingship : Essays on the Theory and Practice of Kingship in the Ancient Near East and in Israel (Oxford, 1958)
The Palestine Exploration Quarterly, 1933–56

TRANSLATOR

The Bible in Basic English (Cambridge, 1949)
A. Lods, *Israel from its Beginnings to the Middle of the Eighth Century* (London, 1932)
A. Lods, *The Prophets and the Rise of Judaism* (London, 1937)
C. Guignebert, *Jesus* (London, 1935)
C. Guignebert, *The Jewish World in the Time of Jesus* (London, 1939)
J. Jeremias, *The Parables of Jesus* (London, 1954)
J. Jeremias, *Jesus' Promise to the Nations* (London, 1958)
H. Metzger, *St. Paul's Journeys in the Greek Orient* (London, 1955).
A. Parrot, *Samaria : The Capital of the Kingdom of Israel* (London, 1958)

CONTRIBUTOR

" Heaven," " Immortality," " Lake of Fire," in *Dictionary of the Apostolic Church*, edited by J. Hastings, Volume I (Edinburgh, 1915) ; " Paradise," " Parousia," " Resurrection," " Sea of Glass," in Volume II (Edinburgh, 1918)
" Proverbs," in *A Commentary on the Bible*, edited by A. S. Peake (London, 1920)
" The Way of the Initiate," " Christianity and the Mystery Religions," " The Emergence of Christianity from Judaism," in *Judaism and Christianity*, Volume I : *The Age of Transition*, edited by W. O. E. Oesterley (London, 1937)
" Archaeology and the Old Testament," in *Record and Revelation*, edited by H. W. Robinson (London, 1938)
" The Early Background of Hebrew Religion," in *A Companion to the Bible*, edited by T. W. Manson (Edinburgh, 1939)
" The Religious Institutions of Israel," " Introduction to the Pentateuch," " Genesis," in *Peake's Commentary on the Bible*, edited by M. Black and H. H. Rowley (London, 1962)
Twenty-nine articles in the revised Hastings' *Dictionary of the Bible*, edited by H. H. Rowley and F. C. Grant (Edinburgh, 1963)